The Intercultural Dynamics of Multicultural Working

LANGUAGES FOR INTERCULTURAL COMMUNICATION AND EDUCATION
Series Editors: Editors: Michael Byram, *University of Durham, UK and* Alison Phipps, *University of Glasgow, UK*

The overall aim of this series is to publish books which will ultimately inform learning and teaching, but whose primary focus is on the analysis of intercultural relationships, whether in textual form or in people's experience. There will also be books which deal directly with pedagogy, with the relationships between language learning and cultural learning, between processes inside the classroom and beyond. They will all have in common a concern with the relationship between language and culture, and the development of intercultural communicative competence.

Full details of all the books in this series and of all our other publications can be found on http://www.multilingual-matters.com, or by writing to Multilingual Matters, St Nicholas House, 31-34 High Street, Bristol BS1 2AW, UK.

Project:

Coordinating institution:

Funding Institutions:

Leonardo da Vinci

FCT Fundação para a Ciência e a Tecnologia
MINISTÉRIO DA CIÊNCIA, TECNOLOGIA E ENSINO SUPERIOR

LANGUAGES FOR INTERCULTURAL COMMUNICATION AND EDUCATION
Series Editors: Michael Byram, *University of Durham, UK and* Alison Phipps, *University of Glasgow, UK*

The Intercultural Dynamics of Multicultural Working

Edited by
Manuela Guilherme, Evelyne Glaser and
María del Carmen Méndez García

MULTILINGUAL MATTERS
Bristol • Buffalo • Toronto

Library of Congress Cataloging in Publication Data
A catalog record for this book is available from the Library of Congress.
The Intercultural Dynamics of Multicultural Working/Edited by Manuela Guilherme, Evelyne Glaser and María del Carmen Mendez García.
Languages for Intercultural Communication and Education: 19
Includes bibliographical references and index.
1. Intercultural communication. 2. Interpersonal communication. 3. Discourse analysis. 4. Communication in organizations. I. Guilherme, Manuela II. Glaser, Evelyne III. Méndez García, María del Carmen.
P94.6.I5829 2010
303.48'2–dc22 2010018331

British Library Cataloguing in Publication Data
A catalogue entry for this book is available from the British Library.

ISBN-13: 978-1-84769-286-3 (hbk)
ISBN-13: 978-1-84769-285-6 (pbk)

Multilingual Matters
UK: St Nicholas House, 31-34 High Street, Bristol BS1 2AW, UK.
USA: UTP, 2250 Military Road, Tonawanda, NY 14150, USA.
Canada: UTP, 5201 Dufferin Street, North York, Ontario M3H 5T8, Canada.

Copyright © 2010 Manuela Guilherme, Evelyne Glaser, María del Carmen Méndez García and the authors of individual chapters.

All rights reserved. No part of this work may be reproduced in any form or by any means without permission in writing from the publisher.

The policy of Multilingual Matters/Channel View Publications is to use papers that are natural, renewable and recyclable products, made from wood grown in sustainable forests. In the manufacturing process of our books, and to further support our policy, preference is given to printers that have FSC and PEFC Chain of Custody certification. The FSC and/or PEFC logos will appear on those books where full certification has been granted to the printer concerned.

Typeset by Datapage International Ltd.
Printed and bound in Great Britain by MPG Books Group Ltd.

Contents

Acknowledgements vii

Contributors ix

Foreword
   Michael Byram xv

Introduction
   Manuela Guilherme 1

Part 1: Ideas and Models in Perspective
1 Intercultural Conflict Interaction Competence: From Theory to Practice
   Stella Ting-Toomey 21
2 National Occupational Standards in Intercultural Working: Models of Theory and Assessment
   Anne Davidson Lund and John P. O'Regan 41
3 Training and Intercultural Education: The Danger in 'Good Citizenship'
   Alison Phipps 59

Part 2: Intercultural Communication, Interaction, Management and Responsibility in Theory and Practice
4 Intercultural Responsibility: Power and Ethics in Intercultural Dialogue and Interaction
   Manuela Guilherme, Clara Keating and Daniel Hoppe .. 77
5 Emotional Management: Expressing, Interpreting and Making Meaning of Feelings in Multicultural Teams
   Alexandra Kaar 95
6 Intercultural Interaction: A Sense-making Approach
   Terence Mughan and Greg O'Shea 109

7 Communicative Interaction: Intercultural Verbal and
   Nonverbal Interaction
   *María Luisa Pérez Cañado and María del Carmen
   Méndez García* 121
8 Ethnography: The Use of Observation and Action
   Research for Intercultural Learning
   Katalin Illes 138
9 Biography: The Role of Experience in Intercultural Learning
   *María del Carmen Méndez García and María Luisa
   Pérez Cañado* 151
10 Diversity Management: Negotiating Representations in
   Multicultural Contexts
   Clara Keating, Manuela Guilherme and Daniel Hoppe. 168
11 Working in Multicultural Teams
   Evelyne Glaser 186

Part 3: Voices from the 'Real' World
12 Intercultural Relations at the Workplace
   Guenther Zoels and Thomas Silbermayr. 207
13 Sharing Reflections on Intercultural Learning
   Isabel Ferreira Martins. 216
14 Intercultural Education in International Management
   Anneli Kansanen and Leena Vohlonen 229

Conclusion: Intercultural Competence for Professional Mobility
   *Manuela Guilherme, Evelyne Glaser and María del
   Carmen Méndez García* 241

Acknowledgements

Firstly, we would like to acknowledge the enthusiastic commitment and hard work of all the participants and other collaborators in the ICOPROMO Project throughout the duration of the project and during the preparation of this publication. We would also like to thank all the consultants and advisors on the ICOPROMO Project, in particular those who also kindly agreed to contribute to this publication.

We are also grateful to all our interviewees, workshop participants and the host institutions that welcomed our project workshops, for enhancing our work through their information and feedback at all stages of the project.

On behalf of all the ICOPROMO project participants, we would like to thank the Leonardo da Vinci Programme for the funding it provided through its National Agency in Portugal, and the Centro de Estudos Sociais, Universidade de Coimbra, the coordinating institution, for its support, as well as all the other participating institutions, which made the implementation of this project possible (www.ces.uc.pt/icopromo).

We would also like to express our appreciation for the grants awarded by the Fundação Calouste Gulbenkian, Portugal, and the Fundação para a Ciência e Tecnologia, Portugal, which have partly supported this international publication.

Finally, we must thank the editors of the Multilingual Matters series Languages for Intercultural Communication and Education, Michael Byram and Alison Phipps, for their interest in our work, which has made this publication possible.

Manuela Guilherme
Evelyne Glaser
María del Carmen Méndez-García

Contributors

Michael Byram taught French and German in secondary school and adult education. At Durham University since 1980, he has researched the education of linguistic minorities and foreign language education. He is also an Adviser to the Council of Europe Language Policy Division. His most recent book is *From Foreign Language Education to Education for Intercultural Citizenship*.

Anne Davidson Lund is a graduate linguist who has worked in all phases of education and in business, in Western and Eastern Europe, the USA and Northern Africa. Anne has a research interest in intercultural competence for effective communication across cultural boundaries. During the last decade, Anne has held responsibilities at national level in the UK for the development of language and intercultural policy and implementation.

Evelyne Glaser is a Director of the Centre for Business Languages and Intercultural Communication at Johannes Kepler University, Linz, Austria. Her research interests include: intercultural communication, language acquisition, multicultural teams, aspects of global business and management and curriculum development. She has taught students from diverse backgrounds and cultural origins at several universities around the globe.

Manuela Guilherme is a Senior Researcher in Intercultural Communication and Education for the Centre for Social Studies, University of Coimbra, Portugal. She conceptualised and coordinated the ICOPROMO project – Intercultural Competence for Professional Mobility (Leonardo da Vinci Programme [2003–2006]) as well as the INTERACT project – Intercultural Active Citizenship Education (Sixth European Framework Programme and Fundação Calouste Gulbenkian [2004–2007]). She is the author of *Critical Citizens for an Intercultural World: Foreign Language Education as Cultural Politics* (Multilingual Matters, 2002).

Daniel da Rocha Hoppe graduated in Modern Languages and was a Junior Researcher for the ICOPROMO project from 2004 until its conclusion. His main contribution lay in the production of original training activities and their respective testing, besides giving administrative support.

Katalin Illes, PhD, BA, MA, MBA is the Director of International Partnerships at the Ashcroft International Business School, Anglia Ruskin University, Cambridge, UK. She is a passionate promoter of international business and management education, an experienced public speaker, facilitator and executive coach who incorporates lecturing, research and consultancy in her career. Katalin Illes is a leader and developer of innovative, trust-based networks and partnerships to promote practice-based, life-long growth of individuals and communities around the world.

Alexandra Kaar is a PhD student and lecturer at the Department of International Management at Johannes Kepler University Linz, Austria. Her research interests concern the internationalisation process of firms and business networks, and the associated knowledge and competence development. In her research, she has applied both qualitative and quantitative methods. Within the ICOPROMO project, she conducted qualitative interviews regarding intercultural competencies required by employees working in international organisations, and developed training materials for the project.

Anneli Kansanen is a Director of the International Management Education (IME) in Oy, Finland. She has worked in business education training, working with individuals and companies in the field of human communication for business for over 30 years. She has written several books and papers, radio and television educational programmes. She has designed and implemented numerous intercultural training programmes for both Finnish and international organisations. Her work and contacts with international companies in Finland, Russia and the Baltic countries allow her to bring real multicultural issues into her training projects.

Clara Keating is a Researcher at the Centre for Social Studies and Assistant Professor of Linguistics at the School of Arts and Humanities, University of Coimbra, Portugal. She explores links between identity, discourse, literacy and learning in Portuguese-based migrant settings, from a linguistic ethnographic perspective. Publications include 'The person in the doing: Negotiating the experience of self' in *Beyond Communities of Practice* (Cambridge University Press, 2005) and 'Changing participation in changing practice: Uses of language and literacy among Portuguese-based migrant contexts' in *Globalization and Language Contact: Spatiotemporal Scales, Migration Flows and Communicative Practices* (Continuum, in press).

Isabel Ferreira Martins is Portuguese, and graduated in Germanic Philology with a MA in Adult Education. Her experience in the field of interculturality started (1991) in the Entreculturas Board, aimed at supporting intercultural education within Portuguese schools, materialised in numerous initiatives, projects and materials, particularly within teacher training. She moved (2004) to ACIDI – High Commission for Immigration and Intercultural Dialogue, a governmental office in charge of public policies regarding immigrants' integration, including awareness-raising on the growing diversity of the Portuguese society.

María del Carmen Méndez García is a lecturer at the Department of English Philology, University of Jaén, Spain, where she teaches linguistics and ELT methodology at undergraduate and postgraduate level. She has participated in international projects on intercultural competence and is the author and co-author of publications in the intercultural field. Since 2006, she has cooperated with the Language Policy Division of the Council of Europe in the development of the project the Autobiography of Intercultural Encounters.

Terry Mughan is Professor of International Management and Director of the Centre for International Management Innovation at the Ashcroft International Business School, Anglia Ruskin University. He was the Founding President of SIETAR UK and advises numerous companies and public bodies on intercultural communication and management. His current research interests focus on the role of culture in innovation and transnational business strategies.

John P. O'Regan is a Lecturer in TESOL Education at the Institute of Education, University of London. He is the author of papers and book chapters covering a wide range of topics in applied linguistics and cultural studies. He co-edits the international journal *Language and Intercultural Communication* (Taylor & Francis) and is currently working on a book titled *Text, Theory, Practice: Critical Discourse in Education* for Multilingual Matters.

Greg O'Shea is a management consultant based in Helsinki, Finland. His clients are mainly leading Nordic organisations working with emerging and new technologies. Greg has taught on MBA programmes around leadership and HR strategy at Ashcroft International Business School in Cambridge and Multicultural Team Leadership at the Helsinki School of Economics. Greg's doctoral research lies in the field of complexity theory in organisations and global management team development.

María Luisa Pérez Cañado is a lecturer at the Department of English Philology of the University of Jaén, Spain, where she is also Vice-Dean of the Faculty of Humanities and Education. She is currently in charge of the programme for the implementation of the European Credit System in English Philology at her University and has recently been granted the Ben Massey Award for the quality of her scholarly contributions regarding issues that make a difference in higher education.

Alison Phipps is Professor of Languages and Intercultural Studies, and Director of the Centre for Studies in Faith, Culture and Education at the University of Glasgow, where she teaches modern languages, comparative literature, anthropology and intercultural education. Her most recent book is *Learning the Arts of Linguistic Survival: Tourism, Languaging, Life* (Channel View: 2007).

Leena Vohlonen is a Project Manager at International Management Education (IME) in Oy, Finland. She has about 20 years' experience of adult business training as a training manager, materials writer and trainer in business English communication, working with individual students and corporate customers. Intercultural issues and international partners are integral parts of language/communication training, and they are strongly present in international marketing as well.

Thomas Silbermayr is currently in charge of Procurement Controlling and Processes at Siemens VAI. After his master's degree in business informatics at the Johannes Kepler University in Linz, Austria, he started his professional life as project buyer at the metallurgical plant builder, VOEST-ALPINE Industrieanlagenbau GmbH & Co (VAI). During this job, he took the given opportunities for staying abroad in several countries, such as South Africa, Germany and France. In 2002, he changed to the newly created Global Procurement department to support, guide and coordinate the decentralised procurement departments of the worldwide subsidiaries. As a major task, he implemented a procurement information system and consequently built-up a controlling and reporting system for procurement. Especially after the acquisition of VAI by the Siemens group in 2005, he supported the integration and harmonisation of the procurement processes and systems as well as the implementation of rationalisation programmes.

Stella Ting-Toomey holds a Doctorate in Speech Communication and is a Professor of Human Communication Studies at California State University, Fullerton, USA. Her research interests have focused on testing and fine-tuning the conflict face-negotiation theory and the cultural/ethnic identity negotiation theory. Stella's most recent books include: *Understanding Intercultural Communication* (with Leeva C. Chung; Oxford University Press) and *The Sage Handbook of Conflict Communication* (co-edited with John G. Oetzel; Sage Publications).

Guenther Zoels is Head of the Project Procurement Department at Siemens-VAI in Linz, Austria. He has been in charge of strategic and operational procurement, project management and multidomestic development and marketing and product management of automation systems. He is also a certified life and social consultant as well as a NLP trainer and coach. He has travelled widely for business purposes and has extensive experience of working with multinational, multicultural and multilingual professional teams.

Foreword

Writing in the first days of 2010, one is tempted to join the inevitable trend to reflection on the last decade, in introducing this first publication in the LICE series of the next decade. All the more so since the first book in the series was published in 2001, with an average of two books per year since then. The context and the need for the series are captured in Manuela Guilherme's introduction to this latest book when she says that 'The world has become more cosmopolitan'. Whether the comparative 'more' is also a signal that the change is qualitative and not only quantitative, is impossible to say just yet. We may wonder whether the increase in actual and virtual mobility and exchange over this last decade is a turning point like the one half a century ago. As Eric Hobsbawm demonstrates, the world of work changed. Since the Neolithic era, people had lived off the land or the sea, but in a very few years from the 1950s, people working and living in this way dropped from 40 to 50% of the population, in almost every country of the world, to less than half that number:

> the most dramatic and far-reaching social change of the second half of this century, and the one which cuts us off for ever from the world of the past, is the death of the peasantry. (Hosbawm, 1994: 289)

Only future historians will tell us whether the changes in the world of work addressed in this book, are as epoch-making. In the meantime, at least on a personal level, they are often experienced as such by those involved. 'Multicultural working' is a major change that is taking place at an exponential rate.

This book fulfils the hopes of the editors expressed in the series description: 'to publish books ultimately informal learning and teaching, but whose primary focus is on the analysis of intercultural relationships, whether in textual form or in people's experience'. It does so, however, as the first to analyse intercultural experience in the workplace while remaining true to the aspiration to 'inform learning and teaching'. For it presents not only analyses based on theory and summarised in a theoretical model. It also includes illustrative examples of teaching materials derived directly from the theory. It carries forward the established purposes of the series, but also innovates in extending the range beyond formal education and its institutions.

The title of the book is also worth a pause beyond the attention to 'work'. The implicit contrast between 'intercultural' and 'multicultural', between a descriptive epithet for the workplace and the prescriptive intent of 'intercultural', is significant. That workplaces and the 'working' that takes place there, are in fact multicultural because there are people of many cultures present – however 'culture' is defined – is irrefutable. That this *should* lead to intercultural interaction, based on intercultural competence – as opposed to a hopeful but ultimately hopeless belief that people can work and live together merely through tolerance – is the message this book has to give us.

The reference to intercultural *dynamics* is also important. This book joins others in the LICE series in grounding its work in the notion of 'competences'. However, it also develops a definition of intercultural competence appropriate for the context, 'fit for purpose': 'a psychological readiness to be empathetic and to control one's emotions (...) and therefore, to create a different work dynamics based on a new professional culture negotiated on equal terms within the multicultural group/team'. The dynamics of the workplace are the source and the beneficiary of intercultural competence, and this is captured in the model of 'intercultural competence for professional mobility', which is fundamental to the whole project. Models abound (for a recent overview, see Spitzberg & Changnon, 2009) and each has its purpose and application, but not all embody both the competences required and the representation of their development, their dynamic, as this one does.

Finally, I would draw attention to another aspect of the link with practice, in addition to the introduction of illustrative teaching materials here and many more are available through the website: www.ces.uc.pt/icopromo. The research was based, of course, on an empirical investigation of practice, but it was also supported and guided by practitioners. It is admirable that this dimension is strongly represented in the chapters by consultants in the third part of the book. The first part written by academics is balanced by this third part written by practitioners, and the two form the 'envelope' within which the theory and practice of the ICOPROMO project is realised.

This book is an invaluable and a rather special addition to the series. I allowed myself to start with a somewhat clichéd reference to a new decade, but even if that was justified in order to contextualise this publication, it is finally more important to welcome it as a substantial and innovative contribution, whatever the year of its appearance.

Michael Byram
January 2010

References

Hobsbawm, E. (1994) *The Age of Extremes*. London: Abacus.
Spitzberg, B.H. and Changnon, G. (2009) Conceptualizing intercultural competence. In D.K. Deardorff (ed.) *The Sage Handbook of Intercultural Competence* (pp. 2–52). Los Angeles, CA: Sage.

Introduction

MANUELA GUILHERME

Mobility, Diversity and Intercultural Dialogue in the Cosmopolitan Age

Mobility, cultural (re-)creation and intercultural exchange have long been recurrent aspects of human life. However, throughout the past century, unparalleled technological progress in communication and transportation has had a dramatic impact on human ways of life and has led to a significant increase in global mobility and intercultural communication and interaction. The world has become more cosmopolitan. Although cosmopolitanism is a controversial concept, it is used here to mean 'a way of conceiving citizenship appropriate to a multicultural society, a way of being receptive to others', that is, 'it coincides with a sense that the global was not quite out there but lodged everywhere' (Mehta, 2000: 623). At the same time, political and social movements struggling for human rights, civil rights and democratic citizenship have, while supported by academic work on identity, ethnicity and multi-culturalism, argued for increasing equality in all spheres of human interaction. In sum, the work environment in the 21st century has grown even more diverse, hopefully with a tendency to equalise opportunities and rights for all. Notwithstanding such developments, here we are now, however, faced with an ethnically and culturally more diverse workforce struggling to comply with new challenges and new demands at the level of professional communication, interaction and responsibility, in the absence of any appropriate training. Nowadays, we are beginning to feel the need to equip citizens with a set of competencies, at both a personal and professional level, which will enable them to fully explore the opportunities of a world that, all of a sudden, seems to have become wide open to them.

The United Nations Secretary General's Special Representative on International Migration and Development, Peter Sutherland (2006), in his speech at the 7th meeting of the Commission on Population and

Development stated that 'the world was moving from an era of migration to one of mobility' since 'countries were no longer divided strictly into sending and receiving countries, but were increasingly sending, receiving and even transit countries'. Therefore, terms such as 'expatriate', 'emigrant' or 'immigrant' will gradually fall into disuse, for the world is becoming less divided between guests and hosts as we all have, to some extent, become guests in our own changing societies and hosts in the places to which we have moved. We are now forever in transit... in one way or another.

As Friedman (2006: 404) noted, 'human culture is a differential concept, based on the notion of difference itself'. Difference has traditionally grown and been organised within distinct communities, despite occasional contacts, or conflicts, to be more precise, between them. However, currently, due to the reasons mentioned above, cross-cultural contacts have increasingly become part of everyday routines and now often take place at the individual level, where people are brought together for the purpose of fulfilling common tasks. Moreover, and again following Friedman, we must keep in mind that 'culture is difference, of course, but the difference does not precede the practice' and, therefore, diversity generates more diversity. Difference is not static, it is generated with human action and living, that is, 'culture is a set of properties of practice, that which is the specificity of the latter'. In sum, 'social life is constituted *of culture* but not *by culture*', which means that culture does not exist in anticipation of human existence, on the contrary, it is developing with it (Friedman, 2006: 404).

Individuals are moving not only across territorially bounded cultures, but also on the edges of both host and guest communities as they attempt to construct new communities in their everyday lives, at work and in the home, as well as in-between. They have personal and professional dreams that are to some extent shared, although formulated in different ways, and, while the dynamics of social life are reflected in the workplace, new relations are created and exported back into social life. New 'communities of practice' of 'particular collectives' (Rock, 2005: 78) emerge, develop, disappear and may eventually re-emerge or evolve in different directions. As contacts between ethnic groups, now mostly through their individual members in the course of their working lives, have become more intense across national and sub-national communities, in social as well as in work contexts, intercultural relations have to be established, in public, if not in private, arenas. In addition:

any individual may have a range of experiences and competences that allow them to relate a variety of combinations of cultures so that the relationships are not just binary but plural. (Byram, 2008: 68)

Intercultural exchanges happen not only between individuals representing differentiated ethnic communities, but also between the same individuals attempting, at the same time, to find their way through their multiple identifications and life stories. This has often been viewed as a hindrance to the smooth and successful fulfilment of the tasks proposed. However, a cosmopolitan perspective can bring out the potential of diversity for enriching the goals to be set in multicultural group work. This is the position advocated in this book.

Intercultural 'mobility' therefore entails an ontological and epistemological shift, where we also look for the Other in ourselves. The term mobility here, especially if applied to professional settings, can be misleading if understood as involving mostly short-lived and superficial intercultural encounters. Following Byram, such encounters, even if brief, are only valuable to our study if they aim 'to establish and maintain relationships', which in this project are necessarily social and professional, and may or may not eventually become personal, rather than involving the mere communication of messages and exchange of information or simply direct, detached interaction (Byram, 1997). Intercultural mobility may also be perceived as a frame of mind that allows a cross-cultural encounter to evolve into an intercultural one, in that it 'transforms both parties and [which] enables both, through "languaging", to embark upon new journeys of self and social discovery', that is, 'it is a journey into intercultural being' (Phipps & Gonzalez, 2004: 22). 'Languaging' is a concept aptly developed by its authors in order to identify a 'life skill' since 'it is inextricably interwoven with social experience – living in society – and it develops and changes constantly as that experience evolves and changes' (Phipps & Gonzalez, 2004: 2). It implies a lengthy process of discovery, of travelling back and forth, of learning and unlearning, trying, struggling, appreciating and transforming. In sum, intercultural mobility eventually becomes a life journey, that is, 'a journey into intercultural being' (Phipps & Gonzalez, 2004: 22).

Intercultural mobility happens across various levels: (a) global (b) national and (c) local, and generates intercultural dialogue between different systems of beliefs, values and attitudes. Any individual can, in principle, 'travel' through these levels, unintentionally and unchanging, yet aware of the differences. That is, this individual can be physically mobile, have multicultural experiences, perhaps have a pluralistic political position by accepting and enjoying difference, yet never quite reach an intercultural stage, as defined above. It is possible for this individual to accept, enjoy and live diversity, to adapt and be personally and professionally successful in a multicultural setting. This individual may even make some progress at the ontological and epistemological level and initiate the 'engaging' and 'languaging' stages. However, to become an 'intercultural mobile being', this individual would have to go through 'a critical cycle', that is, 'a reflective, exploratory, dialogical and active stance towards cultural knowledge and life that allows for dissonance, contradiction, and conflict as well as for consensus, concurrence, and transformation' (Guilherme, 2002: 219). This process would entail the experiencing of a series of operations 'gathered in three main moments: (a) when one approaches and responds to culture(s) – experiencing, exploring, wondering, and speculating; (b) when one engages with and embarks on (inter)cultural observation, research and interpretation – appreciating, commenting, comparing, reflecting, analysing, and questioning; and (c) when one performs (inter)cultural acts and transforms cultural life – hypothesising, evaluating, negotiating, deciding, *différant*, and acting' (Guilherme, 2002: 221). Moreover, such operations require 'a cognitive and emotional endeavour that aim[ed] at individual and collective emancipation, social justice and political commitment' (Guilherme, 2002: 219). This critical intercultural endeavour, leading to an 'intercultural personhood' that, according to Kim (2008: 360), 'includes a vital component of an outlook on humanity that is not locked in a provincial interest of one's ascribed group membership', but that involves our 'becoming more and more interconnected and networked' (Beck, 2002: 25), also requires a perception of risk that goes beyond cross-cultural awareness and critical reflection. Ingeniously, Phipps (2007: 56) discerns, with regard to language learning and cultural experience, that 'perceiving the risk was in itself a mode of dynamic action'. The capacity and the way in which individuals cope with intercultural dynamics is what ultimately determines the definition of the concept of intercultural competence, which is hardly pre-determined and pre-limited because it is defined during actual communication and interaction and depends on reciprocal appraisal. The ground where it may be accomplished can, however, be laid by formal education and this is mainly what this book is arguing for.

The ICOPROMO Project Rationale

The situation outlined above was both the context and the impulse for the project on which this book is based, that is, the three-year collaborative process (2003–2006) developed under the auspices of the ICOPROMO (Intercultural Competence for Professional Mobility) project, funded by the Leonardo da Vinci Programme. The book is therefore an attempt to show how the contemporary world and the specific situations it creates can be researched with a view to developing appropriate responses. The project involved four academic teams based at the Centre for Social Studies, University of Coimbra (Portugal, coordinator), the Department of English, University of Jáen (Spain), the Language Institute, Johannes Kepler University (Austria) and the Ashcroft International Business School, Anglia Ruskin University (UK). The latter replaced the University of Göttingen during the last half of the project. The rationale behind the ICOPROMO Project was originally conceptualised and designed by Manuela Guilherme (coordinator), and further developed and implemented by the Project Management and Development Team composed of the aforementioned four teams. During an introductory stage, which lasted for the first year of the project, the four international teams attempted to define intercultural competence by analysing existing models. They then proposed their individual team models and finally agreed on a common project model as shown below. During this period, they also carried out an international needs assessment field study in which they interviewed several professionals with experience working in multicultural teams. During the following two years of the project, the teams developed, both theoretically and in practice, a common project model, shown below, which involved eight thematic axes – Biography, Ethnography, Diversity Management, Emotional Management, Intercultural Communication, Intercultural Interaction, Intercultural Responsibility and Working in Multicultural Teams. Based on these themes, the teams produced a substantial amount of material, almost 100 activities, aimed at developing intercultural competence in pre-service and in-service professionals for the purpose of work in multicultural teams/groups. These activities were to be implemented with the help of groups of pre-service and in-service professionals, ranging from unexperienced to experienced and even expert target groups (www.ces.uc.pt/icopromo). The project design aimed to step beyond individually based competencies and to focus on the communication and interaction dynamics between team-based individuals. In addition, it intended to explore the grounds between citizenship education and professional development, that is, what is more often distinguished as, respectively, education and training (Feng et al., 2009). The production of materials was closely assisted by an Advisory Group formed by various international partners, each with an established role in industry, local government or professional training: Siemens-VAI, Austria,

CEFA – Centro de Estudos e Formação Autárquica, Portugal, and IME – International Management Education, Finland. These partners provided the project with regular, timely, knowledgeable and to-the-point assessment and feedback reports drawn up by practitioners with extensive and relevant experience in the field.

The ICOPROMO Project also targeted mobility as a key concept defined, both in real and symbolic terms, as the process of entering new ethnic cultures, either abroad or at home, directly or indirectly, in person or through technology. It aimed to contribute to the process of building up a Europe of knowledge, but one whose knowledge is heterogeneous, interactive and promotes the validation of different intra- and international representations in the public arena. Societies are undergoing a transformation, moving towards new forms of politics, social life and economic organisation. Such transformations include tendencies towards increased globalisation and internationalisation, alongside the development of network structures. This process translates into a switch from a more static-functional orientation of organisations and institutions towards a more dynamic, procedural orientation (Castells, 2000, 2001). Employees must increasingly cope with inter*cultural* (not necessarily only inter*national*) encounters in their professional contexts. Therefore, they have to establish *active* communication with their colleagues, especially since virtually all organisations have gradually been promoting horizontal work structures that generate even stronger dynamics between diverse groups, which are often based in different locations.

The ICOPROMO Project brought together academics with different experiences and perspectives on this subject (vocational education, academic approach, pre- and in-teacher training, pre- and in-service professional training, etc.), who built on their more promising and fruitful ideas and concepts in order to create a comprehensive and integrated model. They drew extensively on their previous experiences – although different and not always easy to reconcile – in teaching language, culture and intercultural communication. The project also attempted to establish a dialogue between academic institutions (universities, research centres, researchers, teachers and students) and professional training organisations, as well as communities of employers and employees, at the trans- and intra-national level. This was achieved through fieldwork, the production and assessment of training materials and by presenting these materials worldwide and testing them with diverse international audiences, mainly located in the various participating countries.

As mentioned above, the project identified eight thematic axes, ranging in their level of generality, some of which drew on existing fields of research, e.g. emotional management, while others brought new aspects to the fore, e.g. intercultural responsibility. Each team was put in charge of two topics, and was therefore responsible for developing the bulk of the material for those topics. In addition, all teams contributed to all the other topics. These eight thematic areas made up the main axes that were deemed most relevant for the development of intercultural competence in the workplace (Figure 1).

This project drew on personal experience and management, such as biographical reflection and emotional mindfulness. It also involved basic ethnographic observation and a meticulous analysis of intercultural interaction. It looked at communication strategies and dared to venture into power and ethical issues. Every thematic area covered all the aspects mentioned above to a greater or lesser extent, despite their focus on one aspect in particular.

The project worked on a broader idea of competence and produced a work-in-progress concept of competence, adding to the idea that 'the evolution of competence frameworks has the potential to pose questions about the purpose of knowledge and how it contributes to the good of society and the individual' (Fleming, 2007: 54). The term 'competence' was brought into education through vocational education, where the emphasis on skills and behaviours, rather than content knowledge, was

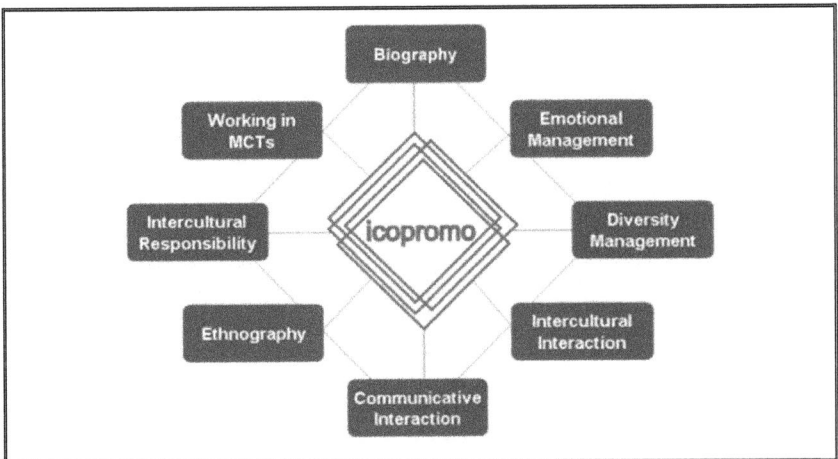

Figure 1 Intercultural competence for professional mobility (ICOPROMO)

prioritised. However, the term, which originally shifted its focus to the pragmatics of professional training, has acquired a broader scope, in particular in international guidelines for school and professional education, coming to include 'a combination of knowledge, skills, attitudes, values and behaviours' (Council of Europe, 2005; Mobility and Competency Project, 2001–2004, CoE). This has followed the trend set by other projects, e.g. the PISA – Programme for International Student Assessment (OECD) and the DeSeCo Project – Definition and Selection of Key Competences (OECD), which singles out the 'ability to interact in heterogeneous groups' as one of its three key competencies. The DeSeCo Project aimed mainly to define and select 'individually based key competences in a lifelong learning perspective' (Rychen & Salganik, 2003: 2). While identifying some 'key competences', this project aimed to provide a 'criticism of an overemphasis on knowledge in general education and specialization in vocational education' (Salganik & Stephens, 2003: 19). Furthermore, it underlines the need to respect and appreciate the 'values, beliefs, cultures, and histories of others', within a sub-category it identifies as 'the ability to relate well to others', which focuses on personal relationships, and reports that the need to acknowledge and value diversity had also been mentioned in the project's country reports (Rychen, 2003: 87). However, 'intercultural competence' is understood here as principally linked with a psychological readiness to be empathetic and to control one's emotions, that is, to be patient and tolerant towards the other without, in our understanding, necessarily implying being prepared to work in ethnically heterogeneous groups and, therefore, to create a different work dynamics based on a new professional culture negotiated on equal terms within the multicultural group/team.

In line with Fleming's (2003: 100) understanding of Wittgenstein, that 'we do not have to look inwards in order to find appropriate explanations of art, aesthetic experience and meaning but outwards into the cultural contexts in which we operate', the ICOPROMO Project mainly focused on group dynamics and, therefore, on individuals in interaction, for appropriate explanations of the intercultural experience. In other words, 'looking inwards' provided us with a backdrop for 'looking outwards' and allowed us to focus on the communicative and interactive process per se within the group, assuming that the members of the group were brought together for the purpose of completing a common, work-related task. This idea is related to the five competencies identified by Byram, which he calls *savoirs*, and which account for the development of Intercultural Communicative Competence since they are assumed to develop within the use of a foreign language: – *savoirs*, *savoir comprendre*, *savoir être*, *savoir faire* and *savoir s'engager* (Byram & Zarate, 1997; Byram 1997). Although Byram conceptualises the five *savoirs* for the purpose of formal schooling, we believe that they can also be applicable to the development of intercultural competence for professional mobility. The first competency, *savoirs*, refers to new knowledge and specific information one has to acquire, while the second, *savoir comprendre*, refers to a novel perspective of 'new' or 'old' knowledge. This, we believe, should include formal education in intercultural communication and interaction, thereby implying the possibility of a new epistemological stance. As far as the third and fourth *savoirs* are concerned, *savoir être* and *savoir faire*, they entail an ontological and a methodological change that, in our view, cannot be entirely achieved through experience alone. Finally, the fifth factor, *savoir s'engager* accounts for full civic and democratic participation. In sum, intercultural mobility is meant to contribute to the establishment and maintenance of relationships in a first stage, but ultimately it is directed towards full participation in different contexts over a period of time.

During the course of the ICOPROMO Project, a selection of four researchers representing each of the academic teams (Johannes Kepler, Coimbra, Jáen and Anglia Ruskin Universities), developed a parallel and complementary project supported by the European Centre of Modern Languages, Council of Europe. This group put forward a methodological model illustrating the work elements and procedures that had emerged from the larger team's approach to the thematic areas included in the ICOPROMO Project (Glaser *et al.*, 2007).

The methodological model (Figure 2) depicts a circular process where dispositions and challenges arise from, but also help promote, intercultural mobility, defined as 'the ability to interact effectively in intercultural professional contexts'. The 'intercultural competence development', which lies between these dispositions and challenges and intercultural mobility, across inter-spaces in language and culture and involves a whole process of learning and unlearning, is anchored on several aspects identified in the work on intercultural communication. These include awareness, cross-cultural communication, cultural knowledge acquisition, sense making, perspective taking, relationship building and social responsibility. The participants in the ICOPROMO Project attempted to bring together all these aspects and develop them coherently within a practical thematic model.

'Intercultural competence', therefore, translates into 'Intercultural mobility', generated by and feeding specific dispositions and challenges.

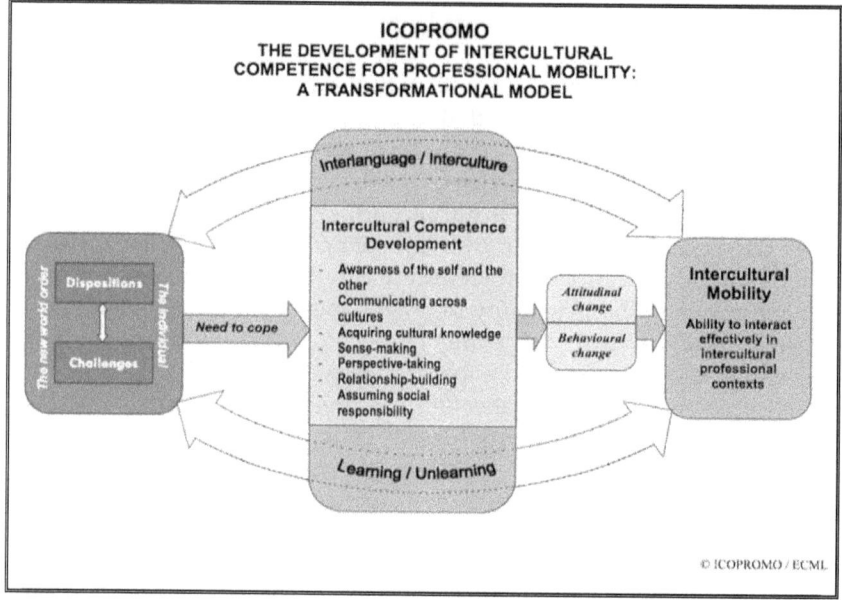

Figure 2 Intercultural competence for professional mobility (ICOPROMO)

That is, a broader understanding of intercultural competence coincides with an idea of intercultural mobility perceived as the capability to move between inter-subjective spaces of action where participants can go beyond their own epistemological and behavioural frontiers. Success in intercultural communication and interaction has been described as an interaction that is appropriate and/or effective (Smith et al., 1998; Guilherme, 2000; Ting-Toomey & Chung, 2005: 17–18). Success follows from meeting the requirements of the host culture or negotiating between one's linguistic/cultural background and the host culture with which one is engaging, both by taking from it and contributing to it. Both these alternative or complementary perspectives lie at the heart of intercultural communication and interaction and are common to the different models for the development of intercultural competence that have been put forward, which aim either at assimilation into the host culture or at a pluralist integration.

By definition, all models of intercultural communication/interaction exclude the option of rupture. In fact, effective intercultural communication and interaction has been defined, from different perspectives by different authors, as requiring: (1) 'mindfulness' (Ting-Toomey & Kurogi, 1998);

(2) 'plasticity' (Kim, 2008); (3) 'critical cultural awareness' (Byram, 1997, 2008; Guilherme, 2002); and (4) 'perception of risk' (Phipps, 2007). However, communication and interaction in the workplace, although focused on a specific task and enveloped by the organisational culture, harbour many preconceptions and biases towards gender, race, religion, language, age and socioeconomic status, all of which have been part of an individual's socialisation in the family and in other informal and formal social contexts. Even where there is a greater similarity in ethnic background, race, gender, language standards, age, social and economic status, this does not guarantee effective communication. Nor, conversely, is it inevitable that the greater the distance in terms of culture, geography or any of the other categories mentioned above, the less effective communication and interaction will be. It is in the midst of such realisations and discussions that research in intercultural communication has recently been growing within various disciplinary fields and, at the same time, developing into a recognised field of its own. Professional development in the field has also gained recognition. The aim of this book is precisely to make a timely contribution to both research and professional development in this field.

Book Synopsis

This book is divided into three parts. Part 1, titled Ideas and Models in Perspective, provides a theoretical and practical backdrop for the later chapters of the book and offers a glimpse at the theoretical and practical references that inspired and guided this project. It starts with a chapter by Stella Ting-Toomey on intercultural conflict interaction competence, where she reviews several identity-based approaches to the notion of competence before presenting her conflict face-negotiation theory. Ting-Toomey's work on a collectivistic Asian perspective of face makes a timely and valuable contribution to the individualistic Western concept of dignity, generally translated in modern times into a notion of self-esteem, which is accountable for much of the conflict behaviour that often emerges, and is ethnocentrically considered justifiable, in group and teamwork. In much of her work, and also in this chapter, Ting-Toomey articulates her notion of identity with her notion of competence, which allows her to expand the latter into broader spheres that we attempted to explore in practical terms in the ICOPROMO Project. She concludes her chapter by making some recommendations for the intercultural competent trainer, who she describes as a 'dynamic juggler and a creative code-switcher', which pave the way for the chapters that follow. This chapter is followed by the chapter authored by Anne Davidson-Lund and John O'Regan, which introduces the Project on the National Occupation Standards in Intercultural Working. It describes a UK government-funded project designed to develop 'standards which may be used as benchmarks for activities requiring a framework for work-based intercultural competence'. This Project was preceded by the INCA – Intercultural Competence Assessment Project, also described in this chapter, which developed a framework for the assessment of intercultural competence among young engineers. The INCA Project preceded and inspired the ICOPROMO Project. This chapter ends with a reflection on the cultural demography of national workforces today and the realisation that professional training needs to shift its 'focus away from differences between national cultures and the development of universalised competences within international groups, towards multiple identities and particular competences within local groups', which exist in multicultural societies. This realisation coincides with the approach adopted by the ICOPROMO Project in identifying its target groups and in developing its practical activities accordingly. Part 1 ends with Chapter 3 by Alison Phipps, who provides us with a reinvigorating reflection on professional development today. Phipps begins by reflecting on the relationship between intercultural training and 'good citizenship', then follows with a critical look at professional training sessions in academic institutions, and finally considers the response of higher education students to intercultural education and its relation to teacher evaluation in current terms.

Part 2 of the book, Intercultural Communication, Interaction, Management and Responsibility in Theory and Practice, is devoted to the main *corpus* of the ICOPROMO Project and each chapter focuses on one of the thematic axes displayed in the ICOPROMO Thematic Model. Part 2 opens with a chapter that follows the ideas displayed in the last chapter in Part 1 and introduces a new concept forged during this project, that of Intercultural Responsibility. This chapter, written by Manuela Guilherme, Clara Keating and Daniel Hoppe from the Centre for Social Studies, University of Coimbra, examines issues of power and ethics in the subtleties of intercultural communication and interaction, and explores the potential and limits of people's relationships in multicultural groups where members must pursue shared goals to accomplish a common task. The authors present as an example one of the activities designed during the project, 'Black is not White', which analyses the impact of the collective sphere on the development of individual identity and vice versa. Chapter 5, authored by Alexandra Kaar from the Johannes Kepler University Linz, looks at an issue that is also particularly sensitive in intercultural communication and interaction, that of Emotional Management. This chapter puts forward some theories and practical research findings on ways to manage emotional responses positively while expressing, interpreting and making sense of feelings in multicultural teams. The author relies on theories of emotional intelligence and considers the impact of diversity on emotional management in a multicultural micro-context. Lastly, the author considers the influence of the emotional management on the development of interpersonal trust between the participants in a multicultural group at work and explores it in a practical activity, suggestively titled Why do I Trust you? This chapter is followed by a chapter on Intercultural Interaction, in which its authors, Terence Mughan and Greg O'Shea, from the Anglia Ruskin University, develop a sense-making approach while addressing real-life situations in the workplace. Here they provide a practical example, by examining The BMW/Rover Case Study from an intercultural point of view. The authors draw on several theories supporting their sense-making approach and argue that trainers cannot lose sight of the strategies needed to make sense of real situations where different cognitive stimuli, sometimes exceeding the limits of what is normally understood as intercultural, are at stake.

Chapter 7, by María Luisa Pérez Cañado and María del Carmen Méndez García, University of Jáen, is about Communicative Interaction and focuses on intercultural verbal and non-verbal interactions. The authors draw on several theories of communication and intercultural communication in order to analyse some of the aspects of intercultural verbal and non-verbal communication and interaction, as well as to consider the relationship between language, culture and thought. To conclude, they go through excerpts of some of the activities they produced within this topic and examine in detail the activity Language, Culture and Thought. The use of observation and action research for intercultural learning is the focus of Chapter 8 on Ethnography by Katalin Illes, also from the Anglia Ruskin University, Cambridge. One of the goals successfully implemented by this project was to have participants in professional development programmes acquire basic skills of ethnographic research for the purpose of intercultural learning in action research. Therefore, this chapter includes an analysis of both of the theories that supported this undertaking, as well as of one of the practical activities that resulted from it, titled Making Decisions. This activity makes use of the Jungian personality types in order to help trainees reflect upon and understand decision processes of team partners in different kinds of organisations and situations. Chapter 9 in Part 2,

Biography, again by María del Carmen Méndez García and María Luisa Pérez Cañado, also delves into the innermost feelings of individuals in interaction and aims to provide some tools for the analysis of intercultural experience. The authors attempt to promote reflection upon our own social constructs, by developing a critical cultural awareness, and suggest ways to deal with culture-shock, as well as with reverse culture-shock, as individuals move between different cultural contexts for work purposes. In addition, the authors briefly go through excerpts of some of the activities they produced for this topic, providing one example in full, A New Institution, a New Group, a New 'Me'. The chapter concludes with the discussion of some difficulties such tasks may give rise to in training sessions, since they imply addressing private, sometimes even intimate, experiences and thoughts, which may put participants in vulnerable situations. The authors therefore also mention some strategies that may help make such meta-biographical sessions more comfortable.

Part 2 of the book ends with Chapters 10 and 11, which aim to round up some of the ideas that were developed along the thematic axes of the project. The first is about Diversity Management, written by Clara Keating, Manuela Guilherme and Daniel Hoppe, which talks about the negotiation of representations in multicultural contexts and examines the construction of spaces of intercultural intersubjectivity as permeated by issues of power. Throughout the chapter, the authors argue for the development of a 'critically creative mindset' as one that is 'aware of the conflicting historical, ideological, structural, and organisational factors that may contribute to the construction of multilayered intersubjective spaces, at personal, intra and inter group, as well as institutional dimensions'. The chapter ends with a discussion of intercultural training in general and with a practical activity, Cultural Layers, which focuses on identity issues and on creating 'the space for a critical reflection on the institutional and the historical nature of particular multicultural interactions and the management of diversity'. Finally, the chapter 'Working in Multicultural Teams', by Evelyne Glaser also from the Johannes Kepler University Linz, addresses general issues related to the underlying theme of the project by reflecting on the role of teamwork in organisations and the impact diversity has on this, namely, the role of conflict resolution strategies in professional training in the field. The sample activity provided here, Tensions in Teams, aims 'to make teams aware of the potential pitfalls faced by hybrid or semi-virtual multicultural teams' and encourages workshop participants to examine and evaluate authentic statements, collected by the authors during their fieldwork in the first

phase of the project, about original experiences in multicultural groups and the conflicts that arose in the situations described.
Part 3 of the book gives voice to some of the consultants on the project. These are experts and practitioners in the field of multicultural work and training, from different countries across Europe, namely, Finland, Austria and Portugal, and who work with international and multicultural target groups. Chapter 12 contains some practical reflections on Intercultural Relations in the Workplace by two Austrian managers of a multinational company, Guenther Zoels and Thomas Silbermayr, who give their own views on the workings of multiculturalism and plurilingualism in the business world. Chapter 13, Sharing Reflections on Intercultural Learning, is by Isabel Ferreira Martins, who is a veteran policy-maker and curriculum designer in multicultural education in Portugal, responsible for coordinating the *Entreculturas* (Education Department) at the High Commission for Immigration and Intercultural Dialogue (ACIDI), a governmental office that answers directly to the Office of the Prime Minister. The author talks about her mission in the *Entreculturas* project – a project whose main objective is also to design intercultural education materials – and establishes the relationship between this and her experience as an evaluator of the ICOPROMO Project products. Furthermore, she offers some practical and relevant advice for anyone involved in training in the field. Part 3 ends with Chapter 14 authored by Anneli Kansanen and Leena Vohlonen from IME – Intercultural Management Education in Finland, who put forward their own ideas about Intercultural Education in International Management, based on their experience as international management trainers in Northern Europe and as consultants and evaluators on the ICOPROMO Project.

References

Beck, U. (2002) The cosmopolitan society and its enemies. *Theory, Culture & Society* 19 (1–2), 17–44.
Byram, M. (1997) *Teaching and Assessing Intercultural Communicative Competence*. Clevedon: Multilingual Matters.
Byram, M. (2008) *From Foreign Language Education for Intercultural Citizenship: Essays and Reflections*. Clevedon: Multilingual Matters.
Byram, M. and Zarate, G. (eds) (1997) *The Sociocultural and Intercultural Dimension of Language Learning and Teaching*. Strasbourg: Council of Europe.
Castells, M. (2001) *The Internet Galaxy: Reflections on the Internet, Business and Society*. Oxford: Oxford University Press.
Castells, M. (2000) Toward a sociology of the network society. *Contemporary Sociology* 29 (5), 670–693.

Council of Europe (2005) *The Competency Workbook.* Mobility and Competence Project (2001–2004). On WWW at https://wcd.coe.int/com.instranet.Instra Servlet?Command = com.instranet.CmdBlobGet&DocId = 1155136&SecMode = 1&Admin = 0&Usage = 2&InstranetImage = 124228.

Feng, A., Byram, M.S. and Fleming, M. (eds) (2009) *Becoming Interculturally Competent through Education and Training.* Bristol: Multilingual Matters.

Fleming, M. (2007) The Use and Misuse of Competence Statements with Particular Reference to the Teaching of Literature, *Towards a common European framework of reference for language(s) of school education.* Proceedings of an international conference organised by the Council of Europe and the Jagiellonian University in Kraków, Poland, 27–29 April, 2006.

Fleming, M. (2003) Intercultural experience and drama. In G. Alred, M. Byram and M. Fleming (eds) *Intercultural Experience and Education* (pp. 87–100). Clevedon: Multilingual Matters.

Friedman, J. (2006) Culture and global systems. *Theory, Culture & Society* 23 (2–3), 404–406.

Glaser, E., Guilherme, M., Mendez-Garcia, M.C. and Mughan, T. (2008) *ICOPROMO: Intercultural Competence for Professional Mobility.* Graz: European Centre for Modern Languages.

Guilherme, M. (2002) *Critical Citizens for an Intercultural World.* Clevedon: Multilingual Matters.

Guilherme, M. (2000) Intercultural competence. In M. Byram (ed.) *Routledge Encyclopaedia of Language Teaching and Learning* (pp. 297–300). London: Routledge.

Kim, Y.Y. (2008) Intercultural personhood: Globalization and a way of being. *International Journal of Intercultural Relations* 32, 359–368.

Mehta, P.B. (2000) Cosmopolitanism and the circle of reason. *Political Theory* 28 (5), 619–639.

Phipps, A. (2007) *Learning the Arts of Linguistic Survival: Languaging, Tourism, Life.* Clevedon: Multilingual Matters.

Phipps, A. and Gonzalez, M. (2004) *Modern Languages: Learning and Teaching in an Intercultural Field.* London: Sage.

Rock, F. (2005) 'I've picked some up from a colleague': Language, sharing and communities of practice in an institutional setting. In D. Barton and K. Tusting (eds) *Beyond Communities of Practice: Language, Power, and Social Context* (pp. 77–104). Cambridge: Cambridge University Press.

Rychen, D.S. (2003) Key competencies. In D.S. Rychen and L.H. Salganik (eds) *Key Competencies for a Successful Life and Well-Functioning Society* (pp. 63–107). Toronto: Hogrefe & Huber.

Rychen, D.S. and Salganik, L.H. (2003) Introduction. In D.S. Rychen and L.H. Salganik (eds) *Key Competencies for a Successful Life and Well-Functioning Society* (pp. 1–12). Toronto: Hogrefe & Huber.

Salganik, L.H. and Stephens, M. (2003) Competence priorities in policy and practice. In D.S. Rychen and L.H. Salganik (eds) *Key Competencies for a Successful Life and Well-Functioning Society* (pp. 13–40). Toronto: Hogrefe & Huber.

Smith, S.L., Paige, R.M. and Steglitz, I. (1998) Theoretical foundations of intercultural training and applications to the teaching of culture. In D.L. Lange, C.A. Klee, R.M. Paige and Y.A. Yershova (eds.), *Culture as the Core: Interdisciplinary Perspectives on Culture Teaching and Learning in the Language*

Curriculum. Center for Advanced Research on Language Acquisition (CARLA), Working Paper Series: University of Minnesota, (pp. 53–91).
Sutherland, P. (2006) *International Migration One of the Great Challenges of the 21st Century*. On WWW at http://www.un.org/News/Press/docs//2006/pop946.doc.htm. Accessed 2.6.06.
Ting-Toomey, S. and Kurogi, A. (1998) Facework competence in intercultural conflict: An updated face-negotiation theory. *International Journal of Intercultural Relations* 22 (2), 187–225.
Ting-Toomey, S. and Chung, L.C. (2005) *Understanding Intercultural Communication*. Los Angeles, CA: Roxbury.

Part 1
Ideas and Models in Perspective

Chapter 1
Intercultural Conflict Interaction Competence: From Theory to Practice

STELLA TING-TOOMEY

In this chapter, intercultural communication training is defined as a skillful facilitation process in which trainees are given ample opportunities to acquire culturally relevant knowledge, increase self-awareness and other-awareness, confront emotional and communication challenges and practice context-pertinent communication skills (Bennett, 2003; Brislin & Yoshida, 1994a; Ting-Toomey, 2004). The 'big picture' goal of intercultural (IC) communication training is to prepare individuals to communicate appropriately and effectively across a diverse range of cultures or in a particular culture and to achieve a comfortable degree of 'goodness of fit' between the new culture and the homeland culture.

More specifically, IC conflict competence training refers to competence-based training of individuals to manage emotional frustrations and interaction struggles mindfully due primarily to cultural group membership differences. Such differences can stem from perceived or actual incompatibility of cultural values, norms, face orientations, goals, scarce resources, processes and/or outcomes in a face-to-face (or mediated) context (Ting-Toomey & Oetzel, 2001). The greater the cultural distance between the two conflict parties, the more likely the assessment or judgment of the conflict negotiation process would be polarized and misconstrued. The cultural membership distances can include deep-level differences, such as historical grievances, cultural worldviews and beliefs. Concurrently, they can also include the mismatch of applying different expectations in a particular conflict scene.

Through competence-based IC training, trainers can mindfully transform the mindsets, affective habits and behavioral routines of the trainees and help them to communicate adaptively across cultures. For a thorough overview of the history of the IC communication training domain, readers can consult Pusch (2004) on the historical trends of the IC training field. This chapter is organized in three sections. The first section reviews major theory-practice approaches related to IC identity-based interactions. The second section draws out the applied implications of the identity-based conflict competence lenses. The chapter concludes with some suggestions for becoming a competent IC communication trainer. In this chapter, an identity-based competence perspective is emphasized because identity issues – whether they surround cultural or ethnic group membership issues or personal identity issues – are viewed as the anchoring concepts that sojourners, immigrants and local hosts have to deal with on an everyday interaction basis. Furthermore, when it involves IC conflict process work, most entangled conflict situations between polarized groups or individuals have a strong identity locus.

Intercultural Identity-based Conflict: Three Lenses

Some very useful identity-based theories exist in the IC conflict competence and IC adjustment training literature. I have used the following criteria to guide my selection of three identity-based competence approaches for a synoptic review: (a) the approach covers either a strong conceptual-research angle or an applied angle to explain culture-based identity competence issues; (b) the framework has either been systematically tested in a wide range of international cross-cultural settings or has been utilized functionally with a wide range of diverse cultural/ethnic groups; (c) the theory or model has a heuristic function for bridging conflict interaction issues with applied competence practices; and (d) the IC or intergroup concepts are readily accessible in published chapter or paper format for further readings by curious IC researchers or practitioners.

Identity is conceptualized in this chapter as reflective self-images constructed, experienced and communicated by individuals within a culture and in a particular interaction situation (Ting-Toomey, 2005a). I have selected the following three frameworks for discussion in this section: the integrated threat (IT) theory (Stephan & Stephan, 2003), the conflict face-negotiation theory (Ting-Toomey, 1988, 2004) and the cross-cultural code-switching model (Molinsky, 2007).

Integrated Threat Theory

Throughout the years, Stephan *et al.* (1999) have collaborated closely and influenced each others' ideas in their respective development of the

IT theory and the anxiety/uncertainty management theory (Gudykunst, 2005a, 2005b). The IT theory (Stephan, 1999; Stephan & Stephan, 2003) is a theory that fuses various affective theories in the social identity and intergroup prejudice literature and emphasizes one key causal factor on prejudice, namely, feelings of fear or threat. Feelings of fear or identity threat prompt intergroup animosities and conflicts. Feelings of fear or threat are closely aligned with Gudykunst's (2005a) notions on anxiety management issues and ineffective communication concepts.

The IT theory can serve as a macro-level conflict theory that explains intergroup or IC antagonism. Macro-level theory factors refer to the 'big picture' socio-economic, institutional and/or historical factors that frame intergroup relations in a society. According to the IT theory, there are four antecedent conditions that prime the various perceived threat types. These conditions are: prior conflict history, ignorance or knowledge gap, contact and status. According to Stephan (1999: 32), *intergroup conflict history* is 'the single most important seedbed of prejudice'. More importantly, past intergroup conflict history serves as a backdrop to current intergroup contact relations. The more damaging and protracted the past conflict, the more perceived threats and prejudiced attitudes exist in the intergroup relations. Second, *intergroup knowledge gap or ignorance* of the outgroup refers to the fact that when intergroup members know very little of each other or they think they know too much (i.e. based on their overgeneralized, stereotypic lens), they are likely to perceive the other group as threatening in the context of an intergroup hostility situation. Third, the *type* (positive versus negative) *and frequency of intergroup contact* also affect feelings of security or insecurity, familiarity or unfamiliarity, trust or mistrust between members of different identity groups (Ting-Toomey, 2005a). The more positive and personalized the contact, the more likely members of both groups can see the 'human face' beyond the broad-based identity group categories. The more negative and surface-level the contact, the greater the perceived negative stereotypes and prejudice justifications.

Fourth, *societal/group membership power status* refers to both institutional power dominance/resistance issues and individual power perception issues. On the institutional power level, dominant group members in a society can be perceived as controlling the key political, economic and media functioning of a society. On the individual power level, it can refer to how high-status group members view low-status group members in a society or in a particular institutional setting, and vice versa. Frequently, 'high-status' or dominant group members may want to reinforce their own power positions and not want to give up their power resources.

They might also worry about hostility or competition from the 'low-status' (i.e. in the pecking order of the societal or institutional power scheme) minority group members in snatching away their precious resources in the community. Minority group members might, indeed, resent the power resources or positions amassed by the dominant group members. They might already experience the historical legacy of inequality, injustice, prejudice and unfair treatment weighted on them. Thus, some minority group members are often emotionally frustrated because of the uneven playing field. The wider the cultural relation schism and the wider the perceived power schism, the more anxiety or fear generated in the escalatory conflict cycles. These antecedent conditions can either escalate or de-escalate the perceived threat level in intergroup conflict.

The four basic identity threat types that lead to escalatory prejudice and conflict cycles are: intergroup anxiety, negative or rigid stereotypes, tangible/realistic threats and perceived value/symbolic threats. The theory also emphasizes *subjectively* perceived threats posed by the other 'enemy' group (Stephan, 1999). The first type of threat, *intergroup anxiety/ anticipated consequences*, often arises in unfamiliar intergroup encounter processes (Gudykunst, 1995, 2005b). In intergroup encounters, people can be especially anxious about anticipated negative consequences, such as negative psychological consequences (e.g. confusion, frustration, feeling incompetent), negative behavioral consequences (e.g. being exploited, harmed) and negative evaluations by outgroup members (e.g. rejection, or being identified with marginalized outgroup members). Individuals have anticipated intergroup anxiety because they are concerned about potential face threats or their identities being stigmatized, embarrassed, rejected or even excluded in intergroup contact situations (Jackson, 1999, 2002). Emotional fear or anxiety is usually heightened and intensified when there exist intergroup historical grievances, low or little prior intergroup contact or that the contact is consistently antagonistic or reinforcing existing negative stereotypes.

The second type of threats, *rigid stereotypes or negative stereotypes*, pose as threats to the ingroup (especially dominant ingroup) because ingroup members typically learn negative images and traits of outgroups through the mass media and second-hand sources. These negative images can generate negative self-fulfilling prophecies and expectations, thereby arousing negative intergroup encountering processes and outcomes. Rigid positive stereotypes can also be considered a potential intergroup threat because of the fear that this particular group is taking over the educational system, the technological field or the medical health care profession. Overly positive and negative stereotypes can activate both dominant-minority and minority-minority intergroup conflicts in a multicultural society. This rigid or inflexible stereotypic mentality leads to a third type of identity threat.

The third type of threats, *tangible/realistic threats*, refer to perceived content threats from the outgroups, such as the battle for territory, wealth, scarce resources and natural resources, and also the perceived threats and competitions of economic, housing, education placements and/or political clout. The fourth type of threats, *perceived values/symbolic threats*, are founded in cultural/ethnic membership differences in morals, beliefs, values, norms, standards and attitudes. These are threats to the 'standard way of living' and the 'standard way of behaving' of the dominant ingroup. Outgroups who hold worldviews and values that are different from the ingroup threaten the core value systems of the ingroup, which may then lead to fossilized ingroup ethnocentrism and outgroup avoidance or rejection. Values or symbolic threats can be experienced by minorities, disadvantaged groups and subordinate groups, as well as by majority groups. Research studies testing the four threat types demonstrated that three (i.e. intergroup anxiety, tangible threats and values/symbolic threats) out of the four threat types consistently predicted prejudice and attitudinal animosity from mainstream dominant groups (e.g. European Americans) toward minority groups (e.g. African American, Asian American and Mexican American groups; Plant & Devine, 2003; Stephan *et al.*, 2000) and immigrant groups (e.g. Cuban American immigrants; Spencer-Rodgers & McGovern, 2002; Stephan *et al.*, 1999) in a multicultural society.

In sum, intergroup anxiety and fear can color our expectations and intensify our perceived identity threat levels in dealing with culturally dissimilar strangers or what we consider as our 'enemies'. On the macro-level of analysis, if the backdrop of the intergroup relations evokes continuous, acrimonious hostilities, it is difficult for identity group members to come together with a clean slate. With historically tainted glasses and competition for scarce resources, members from dominant and minority groups might view each other with certain mistrust, suspicions, disrespect and face destruction outlook.

The Conflict Face-Negotiation Theory

On the meso level, IC conflict often involves different face-losing and face-saving behaviors. Face refers to a claimed sense of desired social self-image in a relational or international setting (Ting-Toomey, 2004, 2005b).

Face loss occurs when we are being treated in such a way that our identity claims are either being directly or indirectly challenged or ignored. Face loss can occur either on the individual level or the identity group level, or both. Repeated face loss and face threat often lead to escalatory conflict spirals or an impasse in the conflict negotiation process.

In response to the heavy reliance on the individualistic Western perspective in framing various conflict approaches, Ting-Toomey (1988) and Ting-Toomey and Kurogi (1998) developed an IC conflict theory, namely, the conflict face-negotiation theory, to include a collectivistic Asian perspective in order to broaden the theorizing process of various conflict orientations. In a nutshell, Ting-Toomey's (1988, 2005b) conflict face-negotiation theory assumes that: (1) people in all cultures try to maintain and negotiate face in all communication situations; (2) the concept of face is especially problematic in emotionally threatening or identity-vulnerable situations when the situated identities of the communicators are called into question; (3) the cultural value spectrums of individualism-collectivism (Triandis, 1995, 2002) and small/large power distance (Hofstede, 2001; House *et al.*, 2004) shape facework concerns and styles; (4) individualism and collectivism value patterns shape members' preferences for self-oriented facework versus other-oriented facework; (5) small/large power distance value patterns shape members' preferences for horizontal-based facework versus vertical-based facework; (6) the value dimensions, in conjunction with individual, relational and situational factors, influence the use of particular facework behaviors in particular cultural scenes; and (7) IC facework competence refers to the optimal integration of knowledge, mindfulness and communication skills in managing vulnerable identity-based conflict situations appropriately, effectively and adaptively. For a recent review of research findings in testing the conflict face-negotiation theory, readers can consult Ting-Toomey (2005b) and Ting-Toomey and Takai (2006).

More specifically, for example, in a direct empirical test of the theory (Oetzel & Ting-Toomey, 2003; Oetzel *et al.*, 2001), the research program tested the underlying assumption of the face-negotiation theory that face is an explanatory mechanism for cultural membership's influence on conflict behavior. A questionnaire was administered to 768 participants of four national cultures (China, Germany, Japan, and the USA) in their respective languages, asking them to recall and describe a recent interpersonal conflict. The major findings of the study are as follows: first, cultural individualism-collectivism had direct effects on conflict styles, as well as mediated effects through self-construal and face concerns. Second, *self-face concern* was associated positively with a dominating style and *other-face concern* was associated positively with avoiding and integrating styles. Third, German respondents reported the frequent use of direct confrontive facework strategies and did not care much for avoidance facework tactics; Japanese respondents reported the use of different pretending strategies to act as if the conflict situation did not exist; Chinese participants engaged in a variety of avoiding, obliging and also passive aggressive facework tactics; and US Americans reported the use of upfront expression of feelings and remaining calm as facework strategies to handle problematic conflict situations. Within the pluralistic US sample, multiethnic research (Ting-Toomey *et al.*, 2000) has also uncovered distinctive conflict interaction styles in relation to particular ethnic identity salience issues.

While previous research studies have focused on testing the relationship between the value orientations of culture-based individualism-collectivism to conflict styles and facework strategies, recent research effort has focused more on unpacking the value spectrums of small/large power distance value dimensions and relating these value dimensions to facework expectancies and actual social practices. For example, Merkin (2006) has integrated small/large power distance value dimensions to the individualism-collectivism value dimension in explaining face-threatening response messages and conflict styles in multiple cultures. She found that high-status individuals from large power distance cultures tend to use both direct and indirect facework strategies to deal with face-threatening situations – depending on whether they were delivering positive or negative messages. Furthermore, Kaushal and Kwantes (2006) uncovered that the dominating conflict style of 'high concern for self/low concern for others' was positively associated with both vertical individualism and vertical collectivism. However, the interpretation of 'positive or negative messages' or the interpretation of the 'dominating' conflict style as 'high concern for self/low concern for others' carries strong cultural shadings – depending on whether the dominating style is viewed as a constructive motivational strategy or an oppressive de-motivational tactic. Likewise, from the Western models of interpreting the avoidance conflict style, avoidance has been consistently viewed as an indifferent or passive 'flee the scene' conflict strategy that reflects the 'low concern for self and low concern for others' phenomenon (Thomas, 1976; Thomas & Kilmann, 1974). The individualistic-oriented conceptualization of 'avoidance' has been continuously challenged by cross-cultural conflict style researchers (Cai & Fink, 2002; Kim & Leung, 2000; Ting-Toomey, 1988, 2005b) and their cross-national research findings. From the Asian collectivistic lens, the conflict style of avoidance can be regarded as a 'high concern for self and high concern for others' tactic pending on situational and relational factors. The notion of 'face' or 'claimed communication identity' is considered one key domain out of the several domains of the larger identity negotiation process.

The Cross-Cultural Code-Switching Framework

Drawing heavily from the identity negotiation theory (Ting-Toomey, 1993, 1999), international management and the social psychology literature, Molinsky (2007) developed a new IC adjustment training model. According to Ting-Toomey (1999, 2005a), as individuals cross cultural boundaries from a familiar turf to an unfamiliar environment, five identity change dialectics await them: identity security-vulnerability, identity inclusion-differentiation, identity predictability-unpredictability, identity connection-autonomy and identity continuity-change. These five themes form the basic building blocks of the identity negotiation adjustment process. There are maximum and minimum thresholds for identity dialectics' enactments. For example, too much security can bring tight ethnocentrism and complacency, and too much emotional vulnerability can bring intergroup fear and isolation. Thus, individuals often need to swing between the various dialectical poles depending on relative and summative circumstances. Keeping the thresholds as backdrops, Molinsky (2007) fused some of these identity ideas with the social psychology literature (e.g. Adair *et al.*, 2001; Frederickson & Branigan, 2005; Ward, 2004) and the cultural intelligence literature (Earley & Ang, 2003; Earley & Peterson, 2004), and developed what he labeled the 'Cross-cultural Code-switching Model'.

This model emphasizes the identity and behavioral change challenges of the IC adjustment process, with its focus on communication code-switching within single interaction episodes. These ongoing, day-to-day interaction episodes form the basis of the long-term IC adjustment process. Molinsky (2007: 624) defines cross-cultural code-switching as 'the act of purposefully modifying one's behavior in an interaction in a foreign setting in order to accommodate different cultural norms for appropriate behavior'. In order to qualify as a 'cross-cultural' code-switching situation, a situation must have 'norms that are either unfamiliar to the switcher or in conflict with values central to the switcher's identity' (Molinsky, 2007: 625). Central to his theory are two psychological challenges that need to be met: code-switchers need to execute the new behavior in such a manner that insiders of the culture judge the 'task performance' dimension as appropriate to the context;

and, secondly, the code-switchers are eventually able to form a coherent sense of 'identity dimension' via seeing the meaningful relevance of the behavior-in-context.

In sum, cross-cultural code-switching refers to the intentional learning and moving between culturally ingrained systems of behavior. For example, when Japanese managers interact with US managers in US business settings, they might slowly realize that maintaining direct eye contact is a dominant norm of the mainstream US culture. However, it might take them a while before they are able to connect the foreign behavior of 'direct eye contact' as reflecting the values of 'honesty and sincerity and personal respect'. They might still continue to use the deeply ingrained values and behaviors (e.g. averting direct eye gaze) from the roots of the Japanese culture to evaluate (e.g. 'Americans are so aggressive – they're constantly staring you down') the various communication contact points. In cumulative interaction episodes on a daily basis, psychological tolls start to superimpose on one another. Molinsky (2007) developed this idea further, resulting in a second model, known as the 'Psychological Toll Model'. Psychological toll is defined as 'the depleting and burdensome feeling a person experiences when the act of switching elicits high levels of negative emotion' (Molinsky, 2007: 624).

Under the model, there are three explanatory components: contextual and personal variables, mediating psychological states and experienced emotions. The first component has three *contextual and personal value variables*. The first variable is 'psychological safety norms', which refers to an atmosphere that is safe for interpersonal risk taking. The second variable is 'norm complexity'. Norm complexity refers to the complexity or intersection of embedded interaction norms due to cultural differences. The third variable concerns 'norm discrepancy', for example, how US workplace motivational norms differ from Japanese motivational norms and that those norms are in actual conflict with one another.

The second component of the Psychological Toll Model refers to *mediating psychological states*. There are three psychological conditions under this component. The first psychological state condition is 'experienced face threat or validation' (Ting-Toomey, 1988). Face threat occurs when the cross-cultural code-switching episode encounters norm complexity, discrepancy, safety/risk and cultural knowledge ignorance factors. These factors happen in conjunction with the second psychological state condition, the 'experienced performance difficulty or performance efficacy'. When individuals experience performance difficulty, they encounter their own inadequacy or communication impotence. With communication impotence, cultural sojourners are flooded with emotional anxiety and interaction uncertainty. On the other hand, individuals who experience performance efficacy often report renewed face pride and enhanced self-worth. With increased interaction confidence, they reach out further in establishing social network contacts and forming friendships with local hosts or other expatriates. The third psychological state condition refers to 'experienced identity conflict or identity fit'. Identity conflict or crisis refers to the experienced negative emotions involving the feelings of distress, anxiety, shame and even guilt. An identity conflict occurs when the particular new norm makes it impossible to behave in a culturally appropriate manner and, at the same time, also honoring an individual's core values and beliefs (Molinsky, 2007). These individuals now have to come up with more creative-adaptive strategies to either reject, conform, replace/substitute, compensate, delay or use some hybrid adaptive method to navigate the challenging customs or practices. With time, institutional and network support, and a constructive psychological mindset, some sojourners or immigrants might eventually experience 'identity fit' when they feel accepted by the local hosts and they are comfortable communicating in a manner congruent with their evolving cultural or personal self (Kim, 2001, 2004).

The last component of the Psychological Toll Model is *experienced emotions*. Individuals who encounter an embarrassing communication situation often experience face threat if they do not know how to handle the situation with dynamic code-switching competence. If they experience further performance anxiety, they would suffer a heavy psychological toll with increased negative emotions. However, they can also learn to manage their anxious emotions via the systematic mastery of some new and context-appropriate behavioral competence skills. From managing all these intersecting components, individuals would eventually feel sustained pleasant or unpleasant emotions based on their successful or unsuccessful mastery of the new and adaptive code-switching behaviors. Institutional, workplace, family and social network support, personality and motivational orientation factors coupled with competent adjustment skills will move many of the sojourners from identity insecurity to security, and identity interaction awkwardness to identity interaction poise.

Intercultural Identity-based Competence Training: Application Ideas

Managing identity threat issues

The focal ideas on intergroup conflict competence concentrate on the reduction of emotional or identity threat and the promotion of accurate knowledge between the two polarized identity groups. Stephan and Stephan (2003) recommended some possible remedies to lighten the perceived emotional anxiety and intergroup threat loads: (a) gaining accurate knowledge of major cultural value difference dimensions to enhance mutual understanding and decrease ignorance; (b) promoting information about overriding human values (such as family security, respect and compassion) common to all cultures, in order to decrease prejudice about outgroup members; (c) pursuing accurate data concerning the exaggerated nature of people's beliefs concerning the scarcity of resources in a conflict situation; (d) creating or developing superordinate identities so that both cultural groups can realize the connected humanistic souls that exist between them; and (e) reminding people of the multiple social categories or overlapping circles to which they belong.

Additionally, setting up opportunities for two or more identity groups to engage in cooperative learning techniques (e.g. team-building activities and working on positive interdependent tasks) would help both groups to see the 'human face' beyond the broad-based stereotypic group membership labels. Cooperative learning techniques include face-to-face active communication engagements between the dominant group and minority groups in solving an interdependent problem and that the outcome holds a positive reward incentive. More importantly, both groups should be able to experience some concrete interdependent contributions to the problem-solving task. Cooperative learning techniques also have built-in semi-structured time to promote friendships and a mutual personalized sharing process. Thus, the contact condition should allow individuals to get to know each other on a personalized, culture-sensitive sharing level versus a superficial, stereotypic level. Lastly, the intergroup contact process should be strongly supported by key authority figures or change agents in the organization or the community and, hopefully, with adequate resource funding. In these cooperative settings, the *positive goal interdependence* between cultural/ethnic groups has been identified as the key causal factor in accomplishing positive interpersonal relationship and achievement outcome (Stephan & Stephan, 2001).

Thus, from the identity threat theoretical lens, the appropriate conflict management approach emphasizes creating a culture-sensitive 'third-space' setting in which members from different identity groups could come together and really get to know each other beyond superficial acquaintanceships. Another appropriate factor is to watch for the 'balanced timing' factor in which to implement this intergroup contact process. Balanced timing connotes that the meeting should take place at such a time when cultural members are still impacted by the conflict incident but, at the same time, their intergroup animosities are somewhat defused. In addition, the endorsement or strong support of an appropriate leader or team leaders (from both cultural groups) will greatly enhance the eventual effectiveness of the accomplishment of the positive interdependent goal. Ideally, the team leaders should promote both relational and task development effectiveness throughout the series of face-to-face intergroup meetings. They should mark the incremental accomplishment of the task goals with recognition and celebrations. They should intentionally create dialogue sessions so that group members can get to know each other on both the cultural and personalized identity levels. In authentic dialogue sessions, intergroup members can make a mindful effort to move beyond their rigid stereotypic lens (Barge, 2006; Broome & Jacobsson Hatay, 2006).

Managing culture-based facework issues

According to Assumption 7 of the conflict face-negotiation theory, IC facework competence refers to the optimal integration of knowledge, mindfulness and communication skills in managing vulnerable identity-based interaction scenes appropriately, effectively and adaptively (Canary & Lakey, 2006). Knowledge is considered the most important component, underscoring the other components of facework competence. Without culture-sensitive *knowledge*, conflict parties cannot learn to uncover the implicit 'ethnocentric lenses' they use to evaluate behaviors in an IC interaction situation. Without knowledge, negotiators cannot have an accurate perspective or reframe their interpretation of an interaction situation from the other's culture standpoint and lens. Knowledge here refers to developing in-depth understanding of important culture-based worldview systems and communication concepts that can help to manage IC or intergroup conflict constructively.

To be a mindful decoder of IC conflict, one must develop a holistic view of the critical factors that frame the interactive nature of an IC conflict negotiation process. She/he also needs a 'big picture' outlook in understanding the social ecological factors and embedded contexts (Oetzel *et al.*, 2006) that frame and shape the particular IC conflict episode. To be a mindful communicator across cultural boundaries, she/he needs to have both the macro-level and micro-level viewpoints within her/his imaginative field. Mindfulness can be practiced and reflected through a deep state of listening and watching without judgment (Thich, 1991, 1998). It is a process of 'noticing' without reactivity. *Mindfulness* means attending to one's internal assumptions, cognitions and emotions and, at the same time, becoming attuned to the other's interaction assumptions, cognitions and emotions (Ting-Toomey, 1999). To be mindful means to 'notice' the use of words, gestures, sounds, silence, space, breath and the arising emotions within and between the two human faces, above and beyond the cultural faces and masks.

In training individuals to develop a set of mindful attributes, an IC interaction competence trainer can emphasize the following characteristics of 'mindfulness': (a) learning to see behavior or information presented in the conflict situation as novel or fresh; (b) learning to view a conflict situation from several vantage points or perspectives; (c) learning to attend to the conflict context and the person in whom we are perceiving the behavior; (d) learning to create new categories through which this new behavior may be understood; and (e) learning to cultivate options in face of emotional ambiguity and interaction uncertainty (Langer, 1989, 1997; Ting-Toomey, 1999). Through mindfulness training, hopefully, trainees can learn to shift perspective and be able to understand a conflict episode from the other's cultural frame of reference and resonate affectively from an ethnorelative lens (Bennett & Bennett, 2004).

While understanding cultural differences is paramount in analyzing IC interaction clashes, Coleman and Raider (2006) believe that mastering collaborative negotiation skills is one of the most important conflict resolution tasks in navigating any IC interaction collusions. They note that many cultural or identity group differences become exacerbated in a competitive negotiation interaction climate. Thus, it is the 'culture' of collaboration that is, ultimately, the premium factor in promoting constructive IC conflict resolution. In their IC conflict resolution training (CRT) program, Coleman and Raider (2006) emphasize the following three objectives: (1) knowledge objectives: for example, to become more aware of key ways in which worldviews differ and how that can manifest into conflict, and also to develop awareness that competition and collaboration are two main strategies for negotiation and resolving conflict; (2) attitude objectives: for example, to shift trainees' attitude in ways that they will commit to the larger goal of increasing the use of collaborative conflict negotiation skills at all levels to create a more just society, and also to develop an appreciation of cultural difference as a source of richness rather than a liability; and (3) skills objectives: for example, to learn to listen when one's own identity group is under attack and be able to avoid ethnocentric or rigid identity-based responses, and also to create a collaborative climate through the use of *informing, opening* and *uniting* behaviors. In fact, their collaborative conflict negotiation model – AEIOU – stands for 'attack, evade, inform, open, unite and with an added "y" to symbolize yes'.

The IC conflict trainers also emphasize the important difference between the *intent* and the *impact* of any verbal and nonverbal message and follow up by introducing how cultural differences (such as individualism-collectivism, small/large power distance, monochronic versus polychronic time schedule, low-context versus high-context patterns; Hall, 1959, 1976) might affect the conflict resolution process. They then offer their trainees a 'big picture' view of a four-stage conflict resolution model – ritual sharing (i.e. setting the climate and rapport building), identifying positions and clarifying needs, reframing particular issues and prioritizing the issues (i.e. aiming to incorporate the common interests of both parties), exploring concrete alternatives, evaluating the alternatives and arriving at a creative problem-solving outcome (i.e. via the informing, opening and uniting communication skills).

Managing cross-cultural code-switching interaction issues

One of the goals of competent IC adjustment training is to break down the seemingly complex cultural norms in the new culture to understandable cultural values and beliefs' terms. The IC trainers need to focus on training the trainees to accept the cultural differences without a biased, ethnocentric mindset. In order to get to the identity fit or identity meshing stage, the sojourners or immigrants have to learn to stretch, practice and internalize some of the new cultural norms and rules. While they do not have to accept or adapt to all the customs or practices in a wholesale fashion, some interaction adaptations and changes are needed in order to achieve a balanced psychological state and fit. This spiraling change phenomenon has been labeled the 'stress-adaptation-growth' trajectory (Kim, 2001, 2004). Concurrently, the host culture's institutional and organizational support, available transitional resources and rewards, recurring positive versus negative interaction experiences would critically help the sojourners or immigrants to move toward the 'identity fit' stage.

In translating the first component (the 'contextual and personal value variables' component) of the Psychological Toll Model into practice, the trainers need to work hard to motivate the trainees to reframe their outlook in viewing the unfamiliar, complex norms or behaviors as 'doable'. For example, in addressing the 'norm discrepancy' variable (e.g. encouraging some of the trainees to switch from a verbal self-effacing mode to a verbal self-enhancement mode in a performance appraisal session), the IC competence trainers need to reinforce the logic (or deeper values' explanation) that frames the behavioral differences in the two contrastive organizational/cultural systems. Concurrently, the IC trainers should actively solicit from the trainees or probe for the different situations (or under particular relationships) in which the seemingly unfamiliar verbal or nonverbal mode might be used in their own cultural context system. They should then encourage the trainees to transfer this behavioral repertoire into the new cultural context and with a deeper mastery of the nuanced 'how's' and 'why's' of the appropriate interaction rules. Alternatively, the unfamiliar behavior might not have any cross-cultural equivalence in the trainees' cultural frame of reference. The trainers then need to create and design a diverse range of interaction activities (e.g. real-life case studies' analysis, critical incidents' analysis, video clips' discussions) in which the trainees can deeply understand the meaning relevance and context pertinence of the unfamiliar interaction script.

In dealing with the second component (the 'mediating psychological states' component), the trainees need to engage in positive introspective dialogue to realize that some of these perceived face-threat pressures are often self-imposed. Relaxation exercises, mindful meditation exercises, journaling or other creative IC training techniques (e.g. storytelling or artifacts' sharing or sculpting) may help to enhance some of the cognitive-oriented training methods and pave the way to more affective, experiential training activities (LeBaron, 2003; Ting-Toomey & Chung, 2005c). For short-term sojourners, achieving 'identity fit' may not be as critical as for long-term sojourners in which the psychological tolls or continuous identity dislocations can exacerbate sojourners' mental health or physical health issues.

Lastly, in addressing the third component (the 'experienced emotions') and helping trainees to move from stressful emotions to more responsive emotions to the various communication challenges is an important IC competence training step. IC training techniques on affective self-acceptance, awareness of deep similarities and common grounds, and cultivating internal spiritual practices can help trainees to accept identity conflict, ambiguity and borderland status. Providing trainees with abundant help-seeking resources, conducting enjoyable field trips to historical local sites, and bringing successful role models or mentors to facilitate the stressful transitional period of the sojourners would help to ease their stressful emotions. According to Pedersen *et al.* (2007: 54), affective acceptance refers to 'the development and emotional acknowledgment of culturally learned assumptions and a network of co-memberships across cultural boundaries that include both patterns of similarity and difference'. Affective acceptance, in conjunction with cognitive knowledge and appropriate interaction, can bring about constructive change and a heightened sense of IC empathy (Pedersen et al., 2007).

Becoming a Competent Intercultural Trainer: Conclusions

Drawing from the various identity-based competence approaches, a competent IC trainer is one who mindfully attends to the audience's interests, needs and priorities. From the integrative threat theory lens, a competent IC trainer needs to be honest with her/his mental files and biased assumptions concerning her/his trainees, training contents, designs and methods. She/he needs to work hard to facilitate a level playing field in the training room in such a manner that both dominant and nondominant group members have equal voices and access to the training process and training outcome. From the conflict face-negotiation theory lens, how to save face and honor face in the training room might help greatly to facilitate trust and discussion openness among diverse group members. Culture-sensitive facilitation skills such as mindful listening and inclusive dialogue skills, acknowledgment of visible and invisible identity issues in the training room and a willingness to share part of the vulnerable self with responsive timing would help to foster a safe, learning climate between the facilitators and the audience.

From the cross-cultural code-switching lens, a competent IC trainer is a dynamic juggler and a creative code-switcher all at once. She/he needs to possess bicultural or multicultural interaction code-switching skills – smoothly switching from low-context to high-context communication mode, and vice versa. She/he also needs to be fluent in multiple learning style modalities and be 'in-the-moment' in switching from auditory, visual, to kinesthetic facilitation. She/he also needs to have a good grasp of the learning rhythms of diverse learners, such as the assimilating learners (e.g. learning by observing experts and attending to theory and model development) versus the accommodating learners (e.g. learning by doing the work in the field and influencing others through actions), or the divergent learners (e.g. learning by reflecting on diverse viewpoints and via close engagement with others) versus the convergent learners (learning by experimenting with new ideas and setting goals and solving problems) (Kolb, 1984, 2005).

Skillful IC trainers are ones who mindfully balance safety and risk issues in the training room. They will share the necessary culturally relevant knowledge patterns to help their trainees to function adaptively and dynamically in a multitude of cross-cultural contexts. They will push their trainees to probe deeper into their self-identity, other-identity and identity change-consistency dialectical issues. As Guilherme (2002: 209) astutely notes: 'The negotiation between antithetical modes such as equality/difference, consensus/dissent, progress/relativism [...] makes for a multiple perspective that enriches the comprehension of cultural complexities and allows for some flexibility in understanding intra- and intercultural interactions'. The mindful IC trainers will help their trainees to confront emotional and interaction challenges and be prepared to stay grounded and not be unraveled during a communication crisis. They will help the audience to practice context-pertinent interaction skills, at the same time realizing that such skills need to be conducted with flexibility and imagination. Competent IC trainers train their learners to cultivate multiple options to respond to different IC situations, realizing that with each choice there are also multiple ethical consequences and implications – to self, others and the vibrant living community.

References

Adair, W.L., Okumura, T. and Brett, J.M. (2001) Negotiation behavior when cultures collide: The United States and Japan. *Journal of Applied Psychology* 86, 371–385.

Barge, J.K. (2006) Dialogue, conflict, and community. In J. Oetzel and S. Ting-Toomey (eds) *The Sage Handbook of Conflict Communication: Integrating Theory, Research, and Practice* (pp. 517–548). Thousand Oaks, CA: Sage.

Bennett, J.M. (2003) Turning frogs into interculturalists: A student-centered development approach to teaching intercultural communication. In R. Goodman, M. Phillips and N. Boyacigiller (eds) *Crossing Cultures: Insights from Master Teachers* (pp. 157–170). London: Routledge.

Bennett, J.M. and Bennett, M.J. (2004) Developing intercultural sensitivity: An integrative approach to global and domestic diversity. In D. Landis, J. Bennett and M. Bennett (eds) *Handbook of Intercultural Training* (3rd edn) (pp. 147–165). Thousand Oaks, CA: Sage.

Brislin, R. and Yoshida, T. (1994) *Intercultural Communication Training: An Introduction*. Thousand Oaks, CA: Sage.

Broome, B. and Jacobsson Hatay, A-S. (2006) Building peace in divided societies: The role of intergroup dialogue. In J. Oetzel and S. Ting-Toomey (eds) *The Sage Handbook of Conflict Communication* (pp. 627–662). Thousand Oaks, CA: Sage.

Cai, D.A. and Fink, E.L. (2002) Conflict style differences between individualists and collectivists. *Communication Monographs* 69, 67–87.

Canary, D. and Lakey, S.G. (2006) Managing conflict in a competent manner: A mindful look at events that matter. In J. Oetzel and S. Ting-Toomey (eds) *The Sage Handbook of Conflict Communication* (pp. 185–210). Thousand Oaks, CA: Sage.

Coleman, S. and Raider, E. (2006) International/intercultural conflict resolution training. In J. Oetzel and S. Ting-Toomey (eds) *The Sage Handbook of Conflict Communication* (pp. 663–690). Thousand Oaks, CA: Sage.
Earley, P.C. and Ang, S. (2003) *Cultural Intelligence: Individual Interactions Across Cultures*. Palo Alto, CA: Stanford University Press.
Earley, P.C. and Peterson, R.S. (2004) The elusive cultural chameleon: Cultural intelligence as a new approach to intercultural training for the global manager. *Academy of Management Learning & Education* 3, 100–115.
Fredrickson, B.L. and Barnigan, C. (2005) Positive emotions broaden the scope of attention and thought-action repertories. *Cognition and Emotion* 19, 313–319.
Gudykunst, W.B. (1995) Anxiety/uncertainty management (AUM) theory: Current status. In R. Wiseman (ed.) *Intercultural Communication Theory* (pp. 8–58). Thousand Oaks, CA: Sage.
Gudykunst, W.B. (2005a) An anxiety/uncertainty management (AUM) theory of effective communication: Making the mesh of the net finer. In W.B. Gudykunst (ed.) *Theorizing about Intercultural Communication* (pp. 281–322). Thousand Oaks, CA: Sage.
Gudykunst, W.B. (2005b) An anxiety/uncertainty management (AUM) theory of strangers' intercultural adjustment. In W.B. Gudykunst (ed.) *Theorizing about Intercultural Communication* (pp. 419–458). Thousand Oaks, CA: Sage.
Guilherme, M. (2002) *Critical Citizens for an Intercultural World: Foreign Language Education as Cultural Politics*. Clevedon: Multilingual Matters.
Hall, E.T. (1959) *The Silent Language*. New York: Doubleday.
Hall, E.T. (1976) *Beyond Culture*. New York: Doubleday.
Hofstede, G. (2001) *Culture's Consequences: Comparing Values, Behaviors, Institutions, and Organizations Across Cultures* (2nd edn). Thousand Oaks, CA: Sage.
House, R., Hanges, P., Javidan, M., Dorfman, P. and Gupta, V. (eds) (2004) *Culture, Leadership, and Organizations: The GLOBE Study of 62 Societies*. Thousand Oaks, CA: Sage.
Jackson, R. (1999) *The Negotiation of Cultural Identity*. Westport, CT: Praeger.
Jackson, R.L. (2002) Cultural contracts theory: Toward an understanding of identity negotiation. *Communication Quarterly* 50, 359–367.
Kaushal, R. and Kwantes, C. (2006) The role of culture and personality in choice of conflict management strategy. *International Journal of Intercultural Relations* 30, 579–603.
Kim, M.S. and Leung, T. (2000) A multicultural view of conflict management styles: Review and critical synthesis. In M. Roloff (ed.) *Communication Yearbook 23* (pp. 227–269). Thousand Oaks, CA: Sage.
Kim, Y.Y. (2001) *Becoming Intercultural: An Integrative Theory of Communication and Cross-Cultural Adaptation*. Thousand Oaks, CA: Sage.
Kim, Y.Y. (2004) Long-term cross-cultural adaptation. In D. Landis, J. Bennett and M. Bennett (eds) *Handbook of Intercultural Training* (3rd edn) (pp. 337–362). Thousand Oaks, CA: Sage.
Kolb, D.A. (1984) *Experiential Learning: Experience as the Source of Learning and Development*. Englewood Cliffs, NJ: Prentice Hall.
Kolb, D.A. (2005) *The Kolb Leaning Style Inventory Booklet: Version 3.1*. Boston, MA: Hay Resources Direct.
Langer, E. (1989) *Mindfulness*. Reading, MA: Addison-Wesley.
Langer, E. (1997) *The Power of Mindful Learning*. Reading, MA: Addison-Wesley.

LeBaron, M. (2003) *Bridging Cultural Conflicts: A New Approach for a Changing World*. San Francisco, CA: Jossey Bass/John Wiley.

Merkin, R. (2006) Power distance and facework strategies. *Journal of Intercultural Communication Research* 35, 139–160.

Molinsky, A. (2007) Cross-cultural code-switching: The psychological challenges of adapting behavior in foreign cultural interactions. *Academy of Management Review* 32 (2), 622–640.

Oetzel, J.G. and Ting-Toomey, S. (2003) Face concerns in interpersonal conflict: A cross-cultural empirical test of the face-negotiation theory. *Communication Research* 30, 599–624.

Oetzel, J.G., Ting-Toomey, S., Masumoto, T., Yokochi, Y., Pan, X, Takai, J. and Wilcox, R. (2001) Face behaviors in interpersonal conflicts: A cross-cultural comparison of Germany, Japan, China, and the United States. *Communication Monographs* 68, 235–258.

Oetzel, J.G., Ting-Toomey, S. and Rinderle, S. (2006) Conflict communication in contexts: A social ecological perspective. In J.G. Oetzel and S. Ting-Toomey (eds) *The Sage Handbook of Conflict Communication* (pp. 727–739). Thousand Oaks, CA: Sage.

Oetzel, J., Ting-Toomey, S., Yokochi, Y., Masumoto, T. and Takai, J. (2000) A typology of facework behaviors in conflicts with best friends and relative strangers. *Communication Quarterly* 48, 397–419.

Pedersen, P., Crethar, H. and Carlson, J. (2007) *Inclusive Cultural Empathy: Making Relationships Central in Counseling and Psychotherapy*. Washington, DC: American Psychological Association.

Plant, E. and Devine, P. (2003) The antecedents and implications of interracial anxiety. *Personality and Psychology Bulletin* 29, 790–801.

Pusch, M. (2004) Intercultural training in historical perspective. In D. Landis, J. Bennett and M. Bennett (eds) *Handbook of Intercultural Training* (3rd edn) (pp. 13–36). Thousand Oaks, CA: Sage.

Stephan, C. and Stephan, W. (2003) Cognition and affect in cross-cultural relations. In W.B. Gudykunst (ed.) *Cross-Cultural and Intercultural Communication* (pp. 111–126). Thousand Oaks, CA: Sage.

Stephan, W. (1999) *Reducing Prejudice and Stereotyping in Schools*. New York: Teachers College Press/Columbia University.

Stephan, W., Diaz-Loving, R. and Duran, A. (2000) Integrated threat theory and intercultural attitudes: Mexico and the United States. *Journal of Cross-Cultural Psychology* 31, 240–249.

Stephan, W. and Stephan, C. (2001) *Improving Intergroup Relations*. Thousand Oaks, CA: Sage.

Stephan, W., Stephan, C. and Gudykunst, W.B. (1999) Anxiety in intergroup relations: A comparison of anxiety/uncertainty management theory and integrated threat theory. *International Journal of Intercultural Relations* 23, 613–628.

Stephan, W., Ybarra, O. and Bachman, G. (1999) Prejudice toward immigrants. *Journal of Applied Social Psychology* 29, 2221–2237.

Thich, N.H. (1991) *Peace is Every Step: The Path of Mindfulness in Everyday Life*. New York: Bantam.

Thich, N.H. (1998) *The Heart of the Buddha's Teaching*. Berkeley, CA: Parallex Press.

Thomas, K.W. (1976) Conflict and conflict management. In M. Dunnette (ed.) *Handbook of Industrial and Social Psychology* (pp. 889–935). Chicago, IL: Rand McNally.
Thomas, K.W. and Kilmann, R.H. (1974) *Thomas-Kilmann Conflict MODE Instrument*. New York: Xicom.
Ting-Toomey, S. (1988) Intercultural conflicts: A face-negotiation theory. In Y.Y. Kim and W. Gudykunst (eds) *Theories in Intercultural Communication* (pp. 213–235). Newbury Park, CA: Sage.
Ting-Toomey, S. (1993) Communicative resourcefulness: An identity negotiation perspective. In R.L. Wiseman and J. Koester (eds) *Intercultural Communication Competence* (pp. 72–111). Newbury Park, CA: Sage.
Ting-Toomey, S. (1999) *Communicating Across Cultures*. New York: Guilford Press.
Ting-Toomey, S. (2004) Translating conflict face-negotiation theory into practice. In D. Landis, J. Bennett and M. Bennett (eds) *Handbook of Intercultural Training* (3rd edn) (pp. 217–248). Thousand Oaks, CA: Sage.
Ting-Toomey, S. (2005a) Identity negotiation theory: Crossing cultural boundaries. In W.B. Gudykunst (ed.) *Theorizing about Intercultural Communication* (pp. 211–234). Thousand Oaks, CA: Sage.
Ting-Toomey, S. (2005b) The matrix of face: An updated face-negotiation theory. In W.B. Gudykunst (ed.) *Theorizing about Intercultural Communication* (pp. 71–92). Thousand Oaks, CA: Sage.
Ting-Toomey, S. and Chung, L.C. (2005c) *Understanding Intercultural Communication*. Los Angeles, CA: Roxbury Publications/Oxford University Press.
Ting-Toomey, S. and Kurogi, A. (1998) Facework competence in intercultural conflict: An updated face-negotiation theory. *International Journal of Intercultural Relations* 22, 187–225.
Ting-Toomey, S. and Oetzel, J.G. (2001) *Managing Intercultural Conflict Effectively*. Thousand Oaks, CA: Sage.
Ting-Toomey, S. and Takai, J. (2006) Explaining intercultural conflict: Promising approaches and directions. In J. Oetzel and S. Ting-Toomey (eds) *The Sage Handbook of Conflict Communication* (pp. 691–723). Thousand Oaks, CA: Sage.
Ting-Toomey, S., Yee-Jung, K., Shapiro, R., Garcia, W., Wright, T. and Oetzel, J.G. (2000) Ethnic/cultural identity salience and conflict styles in four U.S. ethnic groups. *International Journal of Intercultural Relations* 24, 47–81.
Triandis, H. (1995) *Individualism and Collectivism*. Boulder, CO: Westview Press.
Triandis, H. (2002) Individualism and collectivism. In M. Gannon and K. Newman (eds) *Handbook of Cross-Cultural Management* (pp. 16–45). New York: Lawrence Erlbaum.
Ward, C. (2004) Psychological theories of culture contact and their implications for intercultural training and interventions. In D. Landis, J.M. Bennett and M.J. Bennett (eds) *Handbook of Intercultural Training* (3rd edn) (pp. 185–216). Thousand Oaks, CA: Sage.

Chapter 2
National Occupational Standards in Intercultural Working: Models of Theory and Assessment

ANNE DAVIDSON LUND and JOHN P. O'REGAN

Introduction

Our aim in addressing the theme of this chapter is to report on a UK government-funded project to develop National Occupational Standards in Intercultural Working (NOS IW). These are standards that may be used as benchmarks for activities requiring a framework for work-based intercultural competence: activities including recruitment, team working, leadership, business development, marketing and service delivery, training and assessment. The standards may also be used as a reference framework for the monitoring of diversity and equality policies and procedures in the workplace. As participants in this project, we, the authors, came to it from slightly different angles, one as the chair of the project steering group (Lund), and the other as an academic consultant (O'Regan). The NOS project, which was led by the National Centre for Languages (CILT), took place over a period of two years (2006–2008), and was grounded on formative work that had begun in 2001 (see below). At the outset of the project a steering group was established, which met on a regular basis to guide and advise the project team. In addition to the discussions of the steering group and the project team, and informing them, several rounds of consultation took place with relevant stakeholders in business and in the intercultural skills training sector as consecutive drafts of the standards were produced. The stakeholder consultations occurred through focus group meetings UK-wide and via online surveys and questionnaires. Forming a backdrop to these activities, an extensive review of theoretical approaches in intercultural communication and of the tools that have been used for its assessment was undertaken, and from this desk-study, two reports were produced. (Humphrey, 2007; O'Regan & MacDonald, 2007a) It is therefore in the context of the development of the NOS project and its review of models of intercultural communication theory and assessment that this chapter is presented. We begin by outlining the background to the NOS project and then move to a summary and discussion of the models themselves.

Background to the National Occupational Standards

In 2001, the then Languages National Training Organisation (LNTO) led a four-country partnership project to develop a means of assessment for intercultural competence.

At the time, the LNTO was funded to help build the UK's capacity in all languages other than English in and for the workforce. The LNTO was also the UK's national occupational standards-setting body for languages, translation and interpreting.

The LNTO merged in 2003 with CILT, the Centre for Information on Language Teaching and Research, to form CILT, the National Centre for Languages (CILT). One team at CILT continues the work of the former LNTO. It is concerned with the creation and promotion of tools that help raise awareness and understanding about languages and intercultural skills among employers, employees, employer representatives and social partners, and providers of education and training, whether state-subsidised or commercial, to improve workforce effectiveness and profitability in a competitive international and multicultural trading and recruitment environment.

The LNTO had identified a need among employers for intercultural skills. Many major UK employers were investing in training to address the need, and there was a requirement for a form of underpinning, a benchmark to support the review of the quality of such training and any related materials, modules and assessment.

The need was recognised very clearly by the Engineering sector across Europe and the Intercultural Assessment Project (INCA) was developed and piloted in that sector.

The Intercultural Assessment Project

The three-year project involved partners from business, industry and universities in Austria, the Czech Republic, Germany and the UK. The main products are archived on the website www.incaproject.org.

Objectives

Young trainees in the engineering professions need to develop intercultural competence in order to be employable and work effectively in an international industry, and to give their employer a competitive advantage. Engineering companies need engineers and managers capable of working in international teams, capable of being aware of, appreciating and working productively with cultural assumptions, environments and attitudes different from their own. The INCA project was funded to develop a framework against which training programmes and training materials might be evaluated. The associated diagnostic tool would be designed to assess the young engineers' skills in intercultural competence, producing results for use in recruitment and benchmarking, and to evaluate the effectiveness of a training intervention. The record of competence would offer a means for the individual to record experiences, learning, achievements and reflection.

In the Council of Europe Common European Framework[1] it was acknowledged that

> all aspects of sociocultural competence are, however, very difficult to scale for a number of reasons. ...This is not to say that a scale for sociocultural competence cannot be produced, but that its production is likely to be most successful if it is undertaken in a separate project set up for that purpose.

INCA was set up for that purpose.

Process

The INCA project brought together engineering professionals and trainers with academic experts in intercultural competence and diagnostic testing and assessment from a range of disciplines.

Taking as a starting point the Common European Framework and existing lists of competences (e.g. Byram, 1997; Kühlmann & Stahl, 2000), the project team created a draft framework for the assessment of intercultural competence. Engineering professionals were consulted on the framework and its integration into existing assessment processes in each project partner country and setting. Using the model developed by Kühlmann & Stahl, the experts drew together a bank of tests and linked them to the framework to create a part-computerised diagnostic tool. The diagnostic tool was piloted and evaluated for the effectiveness of both its process and its content. The portfolio-style record of competence was developed for use with the framework and tool and was also tested with pilot groups. While designed for the engineering sector, the INCA products had the potential to be adapted for wider use.

Products

The INCA project developed

- a framework for the assessment of intercultural competence;
- a part-computerised suite of assessment tools;
- an Assessor Manual and an Assessee Manual and guidelines for their use;
- an Assessor training programme;
- a record of competence for use with the framework, similar in style to the European Language Portfolio (ELP).

A theory paper was also produced, setting out the underpinning theoretical model developed by three of the project's team members, Professors Byram, Kühlmann and Müller-Jacquier.

A definition of intercultural competence

The partnership developed a definition of intercultural competence for the INCA project:

> *Intercultural competence is the range of knowledge and skills an individual needs to interact with colleagues from other countries, cultures, language backgrounds and social identities.*
>
> - the aims of Intercultural Competence are effectiveness and mutually accepted practices
> - we only deal with situations of cultural overlap where people with specific sets of values, beliefs and behaviours interact and thereby try to create an Interculture
> - a definition of Culture (whether corporate, national, gender/job-role related or other) is therefore: a specific set of values, beliefs and behaviours
> - Intercultural competences are skills, knowledge *and* attitudes
> - Intercultural Competence comprises four main activities: to perceive-to interpret-to act-knowledge (to know). Knowledge includes both knowledge about culture and knowledge about intercultural situations

The INCA framework

It was accepted that while theory was essential, for intercultural competence to be accepted as a skill alongside other skills of use to employers, to be developed through education, training and work-based learning, it would need to be assessed, and a transparent framework would be needed against which training materials, programmes, even qualifications, might be calibrated. The framework drew on the model of the Common European Framework and the UK NOS in Languages.[2] The intention of the INCA team was to produce something similar: to define a limited number of component skills within the overall definition of intercultural competence, then define, through an iterative process, levels of competence in each skill.

Six component skills were identified (see left-hand column in the following table). It was agreed that competence in each component would comprise an individual's motivation, skill and knowledge, and behaviour.

	(A) *Motivation*	*(B)* *Skill/knowledge*	*(C)* *Behaviour*
(i) Tolerance for ambiguity	Readiness to embrace and work with ambiguity	Ability to handle stress consequent on ambiguity	Managing ambiguous situations
(ii) Behavioural flexibility	Readiness to apply and augment the full range of one's existing repertoire of behaviour	Having a broad repertoire and the knowledge of one's repertoire	Adapting one's behaviour to the specific situation
(iii) Communicative awareness	Willingness to modify existing communicative conventions	Ability to identify different communicative conventions, levels of foreign language competences and their impact on intercultural communication	Negotiating appropriate communicative conventions for intercultural communication and coping with different foreign language skills

	(A) Motivation	(B) Skill/knowledge	(C) Behaviour
(iv) Knowledge discovery	Curiosity about other cultures in themselves and in order to be able to interact better with people	Skills of ethnographic discovery of situation-relevant cultural knowledge (including technical knowledge) before, during and after intercultural encounters	Seeking information to discover culture-related knowledge
(v) Respect for otherness	Willingness to respect the diversity and coherence of behaviour, value and belief systems	Critical knowledge of such systems (including one's own when making judgements)	Treating equally different behaviour, value and convention systems experienced in intercultural encounters
(vi) Empathy	Willingness to take the other's perspectives	Skills of role-taking de-centring; awareness of different perspectives	Making explicit and relating culture-specific perspectives to each other

(Extract from INCA Theory, An Overview, July 2004 paper included with final report to LdVII)

Three 'levels' of competence were agreed: Basic, Intermediate and Full, and descriptors for each level of each component were created, tested and refined. The Assessor framework begins thus:

INCA Framework (Assessor version)

Level ⇨ Competence ⇩	1 'Basic'	2 'Intermediate'	3 'Full'
General profile	The candidate at this level is on the ladder of progression. They will be disposed to deal positively with the situation. Their responses to it will be piecemeal and improvised rather than principled, even though mostly successful in avoiding short-term difficulties. These will be based on fragmentary information.	The candidate at this level has begun to induce simple principles to apply to the situation, rather than improvise reactively in response to isolated features of it. There will be evidence of a basic strategy and some coherent knowledge for dealing with situations.	The candidate at this level will combine a strategic and principled approach to a situation to take the role of a mediator seeking to bring about the most favourable outcome. Knowledge of their own culture and that of others, including work parameters, will be both coherent and sophisticated.
(i) Tolerance of ambiguity	1T Deals with ambiguity on a one-off basis, responding to items as they arise. May be overwhelmed by ambiguous situations which imply high involvement.	2T Has begun to acquire a repertoire of approaches to cope with ambiguities in low-involvement situations. Begins to accept ambiguity as a challenge.	3T Is constantly aware of the possibility of ambiguity. When it occurs, he/she tolerates and manages it.

Level ⇨ Competence ⇩	1 'Basic'	2 'Intermediate'	3 'Full'
(ii) Behavioural flexibility	1B Adopts a reactive/defensive approach to situations. Learns from isolated experiences in a rather unsystematic way.	2B Previous experience of required behaviour begins to influence behaviour in everyday parallel situations. Sometimes takes the initiative in adopting/conforming to other cultures' behaviour patterns.	3B Is ready and able to adopt appropriate behaviour in job-specific situations from a broad and well-understood repertoire.
(iii) …	…	…	…

(Extract from INCA Assessor Manual, 2004)

While it was possible to posit a theoretical framework, there was a need to verify its reliability through testing in the field. A series of assessment tasks was designed.

A part-computerised suite of assessment tasks, handbooks and guidelines
The assessment tasks comprised a number of different exercises. Each was designed to assess an individual's competence in one or two components of the INCA framework, and guidelines were provided for assessors. A number of the exercises were computerised. An Assessor Handbook and an Assessee Handbook were developed and trialled, also an Assessor Training Programme.

The INCA Portfolio
The final product of the project was the Portfolio. Based on the model of the ELP, as developed by the LNTO in the UK for use by adults and in work-related education and training, the INCA Portfolio is a means for an individual to record his/her developing intercultural competence.

Since the project finished in 2004, CILT has continued to pursue the goal of an assessment benchmark. The principal reason for this has been the requirement to respond to developing British government and European Union policy in respect of education and training.

The Context

In 2002, the government in England published its Skills Strategy.[3] It seeks to develop the UK's capacity to respond to global economic trends. It underpins radical measures to restructure the publicly supported education and training system, and is premised on the belief that employers know what skills needs they have and will have in future, and can articulate those for providers of education and training to respond accordingly. It is therefore essential to engage with employers to achieve changes and improvements in the UK system and/or provision.

Employers are articulating a need to deal with diversity, and there is an urgent need to align this with work on intercultural competence, to set standards for intercultural competence and to ensure their inclusion in all the skills- and standards-related developments that will colour much of the UK's education and training for the future.

National Occupational Standards in Intercultural Working

Feasibility study

UK NOS provide a quality framework against which performance in the workplace can be measured. They can be used for a variety of purposes, such as designing qualifications, devising training materials, recruitment, assessment and benchmarking skills. Although there is growing awareness of the need for intercultural skills, and training programmes are on the increase, there have to date been no NOS, nor is there a nationally recognised definition of what it is to be interculturally competent.

In 2004–2005, CILT researched the feasibility of developing NOS in intercultural competence and reviewed the INCA framework as a potentially appropriate basis for the development of such NOS. The research recommendations were adopted and work began in 2006.

The National Occupational Standards in Intercultural Working

The NOS project had the following objectives:

(1) to raise awareness and consult on the development of NOS in intercultural skills with employers and key providers;
(2) to research the latest approaches and thinking in intercultural skills;
(3) to re-evaluate the draft NOS framework developed in the feasibility study in light of new research;
(4) to develop detailed full occupational standards in the requisite format to meet the needs of employers and providers.

Early on, the term 'intercultural skills' was replaced by the term 'intercultural working' in order to reflect better the principal orientation of the NOS and to capture the fluidity as well as the dynamic nature of the concept to which the standards were to be applied. An important concern of the project has been whether INCA ought to continue to be the main point of reference for developing the NOS. Of significance here were the initial responses of employers to the INCA framework. Consultation revealed that the definitions and descriptors that the INCA framework used were considered to be 'too academic' to be understood and easily applied. Since a primary purpose of NOS is to assist employers in developing and embedding intercultural awareness competences within their own workforces, this finding seemed to call into question INCA's usefulness for this purpose. Therefore, it was considered essential that the NOS should seek to meet the expectations and requirements of this constituency in particular. Consequently, in the research that followed, the perspectives of employers towards INCA formed a point of reference in examining and evaluating them, in addition to the INCA model itself.

Paradigms in intercultural communication theory and research
The desk research undertaken for the NOS (Humphrey, 2007; O'Regan & MacDonald, 2007a) identified three theoretical paradigms as being current to intercultural communication theory and research:

(1) The social science approach

This type of approach is most often associated with authors such as Edward T. Hall, Geert Hofstede, William Gudykunst and others, who have applied social-psychological understandings to the study of culture and cultural difference. In this perspective, culture is viewed as a complex phenomenon that is not easily generalisable, and where cultural variation is not simply confined to differences *between* national groups, but is an *intra*-national and *intra*-cultural phenomenon as well. Despite this recognition, the social science approach has for the most part been applied to cross-cultural rather than multicultural encounters; that is, intercultural communication as it occurs across borders when a person or persons from one country come into contact with those in another. Aspects of the social science approach have been criticised, however, for being over-generalised and too focused on the nation, leading to problems of cultural stereotyping as well as ethnocentrism. The undifferentiated view of culture, which the focus on cross-cultural difference has encouraged, is still to be found in a wide range of intercultural communication training programmes, coursebooks and materials.

(2) The critical approach

The critical approach takes a more politicised view of culture, concerning itself with the socio-historical contexts of cultural identity formation and the ideological perspectives that are brought to bear on social communities in making them cohere. Issues of power and exclusion are salient to this approach, particularly in respect of questions concerning race, gender and social inequality. The approach is associated with an interdisciplinary range of authors within intercultural, applied linguistic and critical pedagogical traditions, such as Paulo Freire, Henry Giroux, Norman Fairclough and Catherine Wallace. The critical approach may be described as having a modernist/enlightenment view of intercultural communication due to its strong ethical character and the emancipatory vision that underlies much of its thinking.

(3) The interpretative approach

The interpretative approach is closely linked to the critical approach by adopting a similarly politicised perspective of intercultural communication, particularly on questions of power and ideology in the construction of identities. That said, it can be much more radical and individualist, viewing culture as multidimensional and always in flux. As its name suggests, this approach is openly interpretational, with the consequence that it questions modernist critical perspectives, particularly regarding the nature of knowledge and truth (O'Regan & MacDonald, 2007b). Relevant authors in this tradition include Flavia Monceri, Bruno Latour, Alistair Pennycook and Fred Casrnir.

The three paradigms are usefully understood as being located on a continuum (see graph). At the one extreme there is 'essentialism'. It is towards this end that traditionalist, nation-based perspectives on intercultural communication are to be found. At the other extreme is 'non-essentialism', and it is more towards this end that the social science, critical and interpretative approaches are located, and approximately in that order. While principally heuristic, this illustration also presents assessment and critique as existing on the same continuum. The more mechanistic and epistemologically static the approach, the more readily it is able and willing to orient itself to determining measureable outcomes. On the other hand, the more fluid and epistemologically differentiated the approach, the less it is able or willing to do this, and the more it critiques fixed and generalisable views.

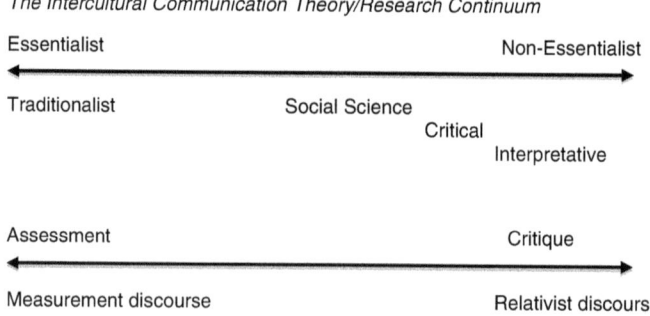

The two extremes of the continuum articulate contrasting discourses – one of measurement and another of relativism – in which measurement assumes the possibility of certainty and precision, and relativism assumes the reverse. This divergence between discourses thus highlights the issue that lies at the heart of the intercultural assessment debate, whether intercultural competence can in fact be assessed.

Models of intercultural communicative competence and assessment
Assessment tools in intercultural communication are for the most part referenced to a range of conceptual competence models in the social science and critical research traditions. They include:

- Ruben's Seven Dimensions of Intercultural Communicative Competence (1976).
- Spitzberg and Cupach's Component Model (1984).
- Bennett's Developmental Model of Intercultural Sensitivity (1993).
- Fantini's Awareness Attitudes Skills Knowledge (A-ASK) framework (1995).
- Byram's *'Savoirs'* for the Council of Europe (1997).
- Van den Boom's Model of Individual Intercultural Communicative Competence (2003).

To these can be added the theoretical competence model of INCA (2004). What these models all have in common is that they each identify a set of knowledge attributes and behavioural competences as being significant to the development of intercultural competence and which persons who wish to be considered interculturally competent would to some extent be expected to have. For example, Spitzberg and Cupach place emphasis on effectiveness and appropriacy in communication, such that interculturally competent persons are expected to be able to identify goals, assess resources, predict responses, choose workable strategies, and recognise and understand cultural expectations and constraints; Ruben, Bennett and van den Boom point to qualities such as respect for others, the ability to be non-judgemental, empathy, the acceptance of the non-universality of cultural values, motivation and the ability to deal with uncertainty; and Fantini and Byram draw attention to attributes of curiosity, openness, flexibility, patience, interest, humour and awareness, while also echoing at several points the competences identified by the others. There seems to be considerable agreement across the conceptual models as to what the significant competences are.

There are over 100 assessment tools available for measuring intercultural competence and most of these are attached to commercial providers of intercultural training. For the desk research, 16 models of assessment were compared and their predominant themes identified.

Within the time constraints of the project, a more thorough comparative study was not practicable. Thus, the selection that was made is only indicative of the range of tools employed.

The first observation was that in broad terms assessment tools are either 'behavioural psychometric' or 'behavioural performative', although the two approaches are also occasionally combined. Behavioural psychometric tools tend to be based on questionnaires, with discrete items to check off and scenarios to respond to. Performative tools, by comparison, are more qualitative by being based on the observation of individuals' behaviour in the context of real-time tasks or interviews. Examples of psychometric tools include the Intercultural Development Inventory (Bennett and Hammer), the International Profiler (WorldWork Ltd.), the Language On-Line Portfolio Project (LOLIPOP), the Intercultural Readiness Check (Trompenaars, Hampden-Turner) and the Discovery Personal Profile (Insights Group). Performative tools include the INCA Framework (also partly psychometric), the Pro-Group Tolerance Scale (Pro-Group Inc.) and the International Management Assessment (LTS Training & Consultancy – also partly psychometric).

In psychometric models, questionnaire responses may be used for self-reflection and evaluation purposes or to produce a profile for an assessor to score. The self-reflection tools are more common to educational settings, and the profiling tools are more common to business settings. Psychometric tools seem to find favour with employers because of their capacity to produce clearly defined and targeted outcomes.

> In working with WDG [Workforce Development Group], I came to respect the science of cultural assessment work. They create surveys that are highly usable and pinpoint root causes. The analysis is simple and straight forward and the recommendations are actionable. WDG really helps you focus your energy on the areas that will have the biggest impact on the business. (Kristi McFarland, Senior Manager, Global Diversity, Gap. Inc.; WDG website)

In performative models on the other hand, where precise measures and causes are less of an issue, assessment can involve role playing, individual and team activities, problem solving, and in some cases interactions with specially-trained actors. In educational and commercial training, both types of tool are used, with the main difference being that in the commercial sector much greater emphasis is placed on intercultural communication for business, and on using psychometric tests for employee profiling and evaluation.

The second theme that the desk research highlighted is that most of the available assessment models seem to be predicated on the assumption that intercultural communication is principally a cross-cultural and corporate concern. That is to say, intercultural communication is assumed to occur in international contexts in which employees from one culture have been required to cross into another for work-placement or other business purposes, and that where this is not the case, intercultural communication is then a function of a company's existence as a multi-national concern. Either way, where intercultural communication is assumed to occur, it is business communication for professionals that the assessment tools and their users typically consider to be at issue. The following statement from a commercial website is representative of this type of assumption:

> We help our clients to think and operate on an international scale, and we provide intercultural skills and competencies for leaders, managers, global teams, expats and employees. We support clients in managing international and domestic diversity and help safeguard valuable ideas by promoting multinational synergy in cross-border innovation. We adapt our training and coaching programs to the local context for branches in domestic and foreign markets. We make sure that our clients feel confident that their employees are appropriately prepared to manage their global business. (Intercultural Communication b.v. website)

Since the great majority of assessment tools have their origins in commercial training environments like this one, such attitudes and assumptions are to be expected. Nevertheless, a constriction of approach inevitably ensues. In addition to the ideological narrowness of the platform of operation, concomitant with this is a universalisation of the competences that are viewed as relevant to assess, and of approaches to their assessment. By this we mean that intercultural competence assessment has become over-generalised and too narrowly defined. That is, there has been a 'backwash' effect on assessment tools so that what they assess is over-determined by the contexts in which it is presumed they will be used. In the process, local non-corporate contexts of intercultural communication and the particular skills and tools these call for — e.g. in mediation, negotiation, tolerance, empathy, team-working, openness, pragmatics and flux — have been neglected or even ignored.

In the last 20 years in the UK for example, in sectors such as retail, transport, leisure, building, manufacturing, services, agriculture, hospitality, healthcare, aviation and elsewhere — that is, in local sectors and contexts rather than international ones – intercultural communication between workers has become an everyday reality. These are sectors that are familiar for having increasingly heterogeneous, multiply-identified and culturally-diverse workforces. Within these sectors in towns and cities across the UK, it is increasingly the norm that workers such as shop assistants, bus drivers, beauticians, builders, heating engineers, farmhands, waiters, nurses and cleaners lead intercultural working lives. These are not peripatetic border-crossers or corporate professionals engaged in global business, but ordinary people in extraordinary circumstances. They might be migrant workers or indigenes, but they are not working to the internationalist format that most intercultural assessment models generally assume, although they are working together. For this reason, not only do assessment tools have little to say about the intercultural working relations of such groups, it is debatable whether they are relevant to them at all.

Conclusion

More research is required into the cultural demography of national workforces and how these are changing, but it does seem that intercultural assessment tools have yet to take these developments into account. New tools are required for local intercultural contexts as much as they are for global ones, and this is why the NOS IW are important. They attempt to move the focus away from differences between national cultures and the development of universalised competences within international groups, towards multiple identities and particular competences within local groups. It is perhaps their unique contribution that they seek to redress the balance by making the local and the everyday central to their purpose. In this way, the NOS highlight a significant reality among the advanced nations of the world today – that where intercultural competence and its assessment is concerned we need to look within national borders as much as we look outside them.

Notes
1. Education Committee, Council for Cultural Cooperation (1996) *Modern Languages: Learning, Teaching, Assessment. A Common European Framework of reference (Draft 2)* (pp. 140–141). Strasbourg: Council of Europe.
2. CILT (2005) *National Language Standards* (revised). London: CILT.
3. Treasury/DTI/DfES/DWP (2003) *21st Century Skills: Realising our Potential: Individuals, Employers, Nation.* London: HMSO.

References

Behavioural Assessment Scale for Intercultural Competence. On WWW at http://www.ala.org/ala/aasl/aaslpubsandjournals/kqweb/kqarchives/volume31/315Abilock.cfm.
Bennett, M.J. (1993) Towards ethnorelativism: A developmental model of intercultural sensitivity. In R.M. Paige (ed.) *Education for the Intercultural Experience* (2nd edn) (pp. 21–71). Yarmouth, ME: Intercultural Press.
BF/M Institute Assessment Centers. On WWW at http://www.bfm@uni-bayreuth.de.
Byram, M. (1997) *Teaching and Assessing Intercultural Communicative Competence.* Clevedon: Multilingual Matters.
Byram, M. and Zarate, G. (1994) *Definitions, Objectives, and Evaluation of Cultural Competence.* Strasbourg: Council of Europe.
Davidson Lund, A. (2006) Intercultural Competence Assessment: Using the INCA framework to underpin creation of study modules for employers and national occupational standards in intercultural competence. ICOPROMO Dissemination Conference, Lisbon, 9 October 2006.
Developmental Model of Intercultural Sensitivity and the Intercultural Development Inventory. On WWW at http://www.mdbgroupinc.com/idi_background.htm.
Fantini, A.E. (2000) A central concern: Developing intercultural competence. *Occasional Papers Series* (pp. 25–33). Brattleboro, VT: SIT Publications.
Global Intelligence Model. On WWW at http://www.yinyangamerica.com/.
Gourvès-Hayward, A., Kennedy, F. and Sudhershan, A. (2007) *The Intercultural Dimension in LOLIPOP*. SIETAR.
Holliday, A., Hyde, M. and Kullman, J. (2004) *Intercultural Communication*. London: Routledge.
Humphrey, D. (2007) *Intercultural Communication Competence: The State of Knowledge*. (CILT) The National Centre for Languages.
ICOPROMO. On WWW at http://www.ces.uc.pt/icopromo/index.php.
INCA Project. On WWW at http://www.incaproject.org/.
Insights Discovery Personal Profile. On WWW at http://www.insights.com/LearningSolutions/Tools/PersonalProfile.aspx.
Intercultural Communication B.V. On WWW at http://www.intercultural.nl/index.html.
Intercultural Readiness Check. On WWW at http://www.ibinet.nl/cat.htm.
International Management Assessment. On WWW at http://www.synergy-associates.com/synergy/ima.htm.
International Profiler (TIP). On WWW at http://www.worldwork.biz/legacy/www/docs2/tip.phtml.
Lolipop. On WWW at http://lolipop-portfolio.eu/.
Mendenhall, M., Kühlmann, T.M. and Stahl, G.K. (eds) (2000) *Developing Global Leaders*. Westport, NH: Quorum Books.
National Occupational Standards in Intercultural Working. On WWW at http://www.cilt.org.uk/standards/intercultural.htm.
O'Regan, J.P. and MacDonald, M.N. (2007a) Consultation Report on the Development of National Occupational Standards in Intercultural Working: Phase I. (CILT) The National Centre for Languages.

O'Regan, J.P. and MacDonald, M.N. (2007b) Cultural relativism and the discourse of intercultural communication: Aporias of praxis in the intercultural public sphere. *Language and Intercultural Communication* 7 (4), 267–277.

Process Communication Model. On WWW at http://www.taibikahlerassociates.com/index.phtml.

Progroup Tolerance Scale. On WWW at http://www.progroupinc.com/site/page/pg4527-pn_Diversity_Terms_Definitions.html.

Ruben, B.D. (1976) Assessing communication competency for intercultural adaptation. *Group & Organization Studies* 1, 334–354.

Ruben's Intercultural Behavioral Assessment Indices. On WWW at http://cart.rmcdenver.com/instruments/intercultural_behavior.pdf.

Spitzberg, B.H. (2000) A model of intercultural communication competence. In L. Samovar and R. Porter (eds) *Intercultural Communication: A Reader* (9th edn) (pp. 375–387). Belmont, CA: Wadsworth.

Spitzberg, B.H. and Cupach, W.R (1984) *Interpersonal Communication Competence*. Beverly Hills, CA: Sage.

TELOS Language Partner. On WWW at http://wwwsprachlernmedien.de.

The Cross-Cultural Capability Inventory. On WWW at http://www.jmu.edu/assessment/wm_library/ccai.pdf.

Trompenaars - Hampden-Turner Model. On WWW at http://changingminds.org/explanations/culture/trompenaars_culture.htm#ind.

Chapter 3
Training and Intercultural Education: The Danger in 'Good Citizenship'

ALISON PHIPPS

Purity and Danger

In her seminal work on anthropology, Douglas (1966: 3) makes the stunning claim that 'The whole of the universe is harnessed to men's [sic] attempts to force one another into good citizenship'. Perhaps even more remarkably, far from making this claim in a book on law, or ethics or even education, she makes this claim in *Purity and Danger: An Analysis of the Concepts of Pollution and Taboo* (Douglas, 1966). Good citizenship is found at the heart of discussion of pollution and taboo.

Research that is undertaken in order to enable the development of intercultural competence for professional mobility is research that aims at producing 'good citizenship'. What does pollution and taboo have to do with intercultural training? Well, quite a lot, as I shall show. In the context of intercultural training for professional mobility, we find Douglas's claim centre stage albeit rendered in a different tone and style. In their preface to *Intercultural Competence for Professional Mobility* (2007), Byram and Silva maintain that:

> There are major demands on someone who has to metaphorically and literally "find their way" in a new cultural environment, and they may equally become "lost" both literally and metaphorically. As a consequence, a practical interest has arisen in cross-cultural training for those who are professionally mobile, which has flourished in recent decades. Much of this is based on common-sense and intuition but there has also been a realisation that there is a need for sound theoretical understanding. Otherwise it is possible to do more harm than good, to reinforce prejudice and overgeneralisation, for

example, to advocate stereotypical response to new experience. (Byram & Silva in Glaser *et al.*, 2007: 7)

The danger, in intercultural competence for professional mobility, as stated in this preface, is doing harm, reinforcing prejudice, overgeneralising, advocating stereotypes. Training – 'harnessing' is Douglas's actual word – is something that can enable 'good citizenship' in the professional contexts of global mobility and intercultural encounter.

Because of the potential negative effects as well as the enrichment mobility can bring, people need preparation, need guidance, need time for reflection and the intellectual tools of analysis. (Byram and Silva in Glaser *et al.*, 2007: 8)

In this chapter, I suggest that in this harnessing of the whole universe to good citizenship there are some questions to be asked of assumptions made in the intercultural training and education paradigms. It does not, however, seek to take this paradigm at face value and merely restate a now well-worn argument that would suggest education is a long-term endeavour and that training is about quick fixes to evident problems.

This is a divide that holds to itself a good deal of history and animosity and can be found in many fields of endeavour: the divide between theory and practice; between 'those who think' and those who 'actually teach', between those who 'get their hands dirty' and those in the 'ivory towers' or 'groves of the academy'. And here we have it, pollution, dirt, disorder attached, powerfully, to the fields of endeavour of others, to those who might have a common purpose – attempts at working towards 'good citizenship' – but who begin this endeavour by defining themselves, hastily, against others doing similar things. Instead, it is the argument of this chapter, that the work of being intercultural – within training or educational contexts – requires us to reach beyond the paradigms that are sustained by intercultural discourse, to reach into dirt, mess and disorder and to re-fashion our pruning hooks.

In the volume *Becoming Interculturally Competent through Education and Training* (Feng *et al.*, 2009), Fleming suggests that this divide may be understood as the difference between deep and surface approaches, as well as between vocational and non-vocational approaches to education in general. Following Winch (1995), Fleming traces the differences between them back to the Enlightenment and Rousseau:

The pedagogic emphasis on discovery and the creation of a genuine desire to learn can be found in *Emile* and is also reflected in later progressive theorists. Education was thus traditionally distinguished from training both on the basis of ends (independent, thinking human beings) and means (student-centred, discovery methods). (Fleming in Feng et al., 2009: 4)

Of course, the divisions as presented here between training and education are constructed. The visceral language of pollution that is often used by differing parties when interpolated into discursive subject positions that require this kind of diremption, this kind of violent discursive othering, betrays questions of power and territory, money and prestige, which are masked as 'discovery' or 'engagement', as 'independent thinking' or the 'good honest hard work' where you 'roll your sleeves up and get stuck in'. How many of us have not been party to such conversations or initiators of them ourselves? There is something more at work here in the 'harnessing of the whole universe to these attempts to force others to good citizenship' (Douglas, 1966: 3), and our vested interests in the means of so doing, than theory or method, surface or depth. Ideology is in play, shaping the values, attitudes and beliefs of trainers and educators, and the reception in training contexts.

Why I've come to hate training

It's with a considerable sense of foreboding that I turn up to the 'risk assessment training' which is 'compulsory' for all members of the senior Faculty management in the university. It's August. August used to be the time when either I took a holiday in the hills or when I could get down to some writing but now it is the time for compulsory management training. The institution has brought in a well-known and very expensive financial consultancy to run the training. Obviously, because we are being trained by 'professionals from business' it will be far better training than could be offered in-house. The experience, pedagogically, is dreadful, socially, fascinating. One sure way of ensuring solidarity of purpose among teams – cultural or intercultural – is to put them all through a gruelling ritual of pointless boredom, the point of which not one of them can see, upon whose facile nature all are agreed and whose conclusions are ideologically opposed to those held by the majority of the group. So it was, that we were trained in risk assessment. Fed a language which was not our own, nor did we have any desire to take it into ourselves. And of this in the strong knowledge that we are here to have our behaviour modified in line with powers whose desire is nothing to do with minimising any risk except to the bottom line of profit.

According to Ulrich Beck (1986): the production of wealth and the production of risks go hand in hand. Much of the training I have experienced is like this. Much of the education I experienced was not. Education has, though, at times been equally facile, and today operates, as we shall see, according to similar principles. The whole history of education demonstrates that as an endeavour it is not immune from ideological manipulation of the powerful by those seeking to maintain their positions; a point well captured in Paulo Freire's description:

> Daí que, o que poderia parecer um diálogo destas com as massas, uma comunicaçao com elas, sejam meros "communicados", meros "depósitos" de conteúdos domesticadores. [Consequently, any apparent dialogue or communication between the elites and the masses is really the depositing of "communiqués," whose contents are intended to exercise a domesticating influence.] (Freire, 1970: 92)

In training contexts such as those I describe – and experience tells me these are widespread – much of what passes for managerial attempts at improving 'communication' is nothing to do with 'communication' and everything to do with 'the depositing of communiqués intended to exercise a domesticating influence' (Freire, 1970: 92). In contexts such as these, we may find ourselves not just culturally but also politically opposed to the prevailing view of 'good citizenship', where, in the example above, the whole universe involves our writing and holiday time as it is harnessed to force us into these dominant and uncontestable models of good citizenship.

There are other examples I could bring to bear where the fear of legal measures brought as a result of 'a lack of intercultural awareness' (for which I read inappropriate comment apropos race, gender or class in interview situations) requires 'all staff serving on recruitment or selection panels' to attempt a full day's training course on equality and diversity. The training course contains nothing but what Freire denounced as 'banking' education, based entirely on transmission models of knowledge, which will of course be accepted entirely unproblematically by all women and men, young and old, ethnic background and cultural perspective, and in exactly the same way (or in fact, not!). When workers are managed as if they are machines, and cultures as if they are homogeneous and static, then the models of training created by those imaging human beings – individually and culturally – in this way, are bound to be models that permit no deviation, no place for critique, no space for divergence or difference. There is nothing in this training course that will prevent people from behaving in racist, sexist, ageist or classist manners.

It has become the domain of communication professionals who define it in terms of problem-solving, participation, and collaboration around predetermined tasks, the outcome of which can be subjected to quality assessment and quality improvement. (Kramsch, 2006: 250)

And as a way of forcing others into good citizenship, the definition of 'good' is defined most precisely, under such technicist models of training and education.

Technical devices [...] follow a principle, and it is the principle of optimal performance: maximizing output (the information or modifications obtained) and minimizing input (the energy expended in the process). Technology is therefore a game pertaining not to the true, the just, or the beautiful, etc., but to efficiency: a technical "move" is "good" when it does better and/or expends less energy than another. (Lyotard, 1984: 44)

Why intercultural education is also a bit of a problem

In 'A Critical Perspective on Teaching Intercultural Competence in a Management Department' (Feng et al., 2009), Jack offers a searchingly honest retrospective assessment of his own attempt to bring intercultural and critical education approaches into mainstream management degree courses.

For me, this course was always about more than academic achievement. It was an attempt to get management students to think beyond the confines of management discourse, and in particular the dimensionalising impulse that characterises work in CCMM [cross-cultural management and marketing]. It was an attempt to make culture intertwine with politics and ethics, as much as, probably even more than, capital accumulation. It was an attempt to bring different stories and different voices into the milieu of a management classroom in a British university. That the outcomes of the course in terms of students' cognitive and affective learning were highly differentiated is testament to the fact that teaching is never an unequivocal success. Perhaps teaching for any kind of learning (critical intercultural or otherwise) is always, perhaps necessarily, ambiguous and imperfect. (Jack, 2009: 110–111)

What Jack describes, through careful discussion of transcripts and evaluations, is a course that fails to raise critical intercultural awareness among all his students, where the outcomes were in some instances diametrically opposed to those he had intended, and where those who did meet the intended learning outcomes (ILOS), demonstrating welcome degrees of criticality, were doing so without their own intercultural privilege being brought into question as a subject position.

Perhaps the problem here is that the course is harnessed by an educational discourse of ILOS, which, however resistant or engaged the praxis of the lecturer, will always mean that the instant product, not the process, is the ultimate arbiter. It will mean that the 'good citizenship' aimed at through the framework thus imposed is one at odds with that of the resistant, critical lecturer.

There is also a wider problem with expecting any organised educational or training framework to remove the danger of intercultural encounter, to provide the smooth and pure experience desired by students, academics, managers and staff. Intercultural encounter is a volatile, tricky and messy process that, like the learning of other languages to which it is inherently allied, changes the bedrock of the self and of self-understanding. In such a context there is no room for an immediately 'satisfying' critical outcome, other than a performance of critical transformation in stated understandings about difference and culture and 'the way things are always going to be'.

> To my mind, the students most highly resistant to this course seemed to adopt a cosmopolitan attitude to cross-cultural learning. By cosmopolitan I do not mean that these students were open to different ways of being with the Other; instead, I think they resisted these possibilities through the deployment of triumphalist capitalist discourse. By cosmopolitan what I have in mind is a negative sense of cosmopolitanism expressed, for instance, in the work [of] Zizek (1997) for whom cosmopolitanism is capital's latest cynical way of incorporating and thus appropriating (ethnic) differences into the structural organisation of production and consumption. (Jack, 2009: 111)

Intercultural training and intercultural education sit uncomfortably with these kinds of conclusions and this is no bad thing. Trainers and educators are both now judged by their outcomes, by the satisfaction expressed in the evaluations, by the 'usefulness' of the courses or workshops in fulfilling a specific set of customer- or client-based expectations. These expectations are (1) therapeutic – they expect to 'feel good' about what they experience and to have fun; (2) consumerist – offered as part of a menu of choice as part of staff development of degree course options; (3) technocratic – aiming at solving problems that they were part of creating in the first place; and (4) imperialist (to modify slightly Brueggemann's (2007) taxonomy) in that they aim to ensure the health of wealth, and the health of symbolic capital, as attained through education.

It is easy to see how such training comes about. Senior managers sit around worrying about the possibility of their organisation being sued for breach of 'purity' in the guise of the new 'good citizenship' tests – i.e. prejudice against people – and therefore, fundamentally, worrying about 'danger' to their financial health. The question 'How can we prevent this?' comes up and this is answered in the default way all questions relating to quick, cheap solutions to what are believed to be 'skills shortages' are answered, 'with a training course on intercultural mobility', 'with a training course on recruitment and selection', 'with a training course on risk assessment!'. So staff training or development (a euphemism for training, forcing) divisions are tasked with the job of ensuring that all 'staff are trained'. The model is based entirely on a deficit model where danger is imminent. 'No one in this room knows anything about this subject; all are going to cost us lots of money if we don't train them. If we train them then it's not our responsibility if they do anything for which we are sued, because we trained them, so we are not going to be culpable corporately. It therefore doesn't matter at all how bad the training is'.

And so it is that all staff are trained. The whole universe is harnessed. 'Purity' is achieved, under the terms of the implicit framework. Belief in otherness and difference is reinforced and in this context stereotypes provide the necessary base material for the critical approaches of courses. But the result is not people who are any more able to deal with the mess and struggle of dialogue, human trust, subtlety of context-based understanding, a disposition that is enabled, through careful sensory perception to be attuned to a new habitat, a new place, a different context. The result is often a reinforcing of a simplistic belief that 'stereotypes are wrong' (I happen to believe they can actually be subtle and important aspects of our dialogue, vital points in the way we approach one another, and certainly in no way damaging unless used violently when they are revealing, rather than concealing of structural and historical injustice).

But it is equally easy to see how critical educational courses come into being, too. Through critical engagement with literature in cultural studies, anthropology, sociology, politics, literature and language, experiences which are part of an academic education form the basis for the countering and questioning of the status quo. Added to this is a different purpose; not necessarily (though I would contest this) the pursuit of capital or avoidance of legal redress, but a pursuit of Kantian purity in the form of learning for learning's sake; learning to participate in the field of academic endeavour and to compete for its (increasingly dubious and expensive) prizes. Evans puts this even more crudely: 'Increasingly, students are being asked to pay for the costs of the regulations of higher education rather than education itself' (Evans, 2004: x). The former – training – is part of the wealth protection enterprises of global capitalism; the latter – education – requires release from material necessity to pursue its reflections on the world (Bourdieu, 2000).

Hence, the struggle, the critical challenge. The quick fix solution to the hard work of intercultural dialogue and what Guilherme (this volume) has called 'intercultural responsibility' does not lie in a model of education for intercultural competence any more than it lies in a training model. This isn't because those designing the models are intentionally subversive or just bad trainers or educators, but because coercive frameworks/models of training or education may produce outward signs of success (very differently defined as damage limitation financially (training), or damage limitation socially (education)), but do not transform people. Arguments suggesting this is to do with 'deep or surface learning' are not sufficient for the levels of complexity in play and are simply re-enacting the pollution hierarchies described earlier, ignoring the place of ideology and politics in the learning process.

How transformation happens is not understood by philosophers, poets, artists, educators, anthropologists or even psychologists. That it happens is widely acknowledged. I too have seen students transforming themselves and their understandings in intercultural classrooms where I have been teaching. I have watched adults change their lives and leave behind addictive or destructive behaviours through holidays with holistic or healing purpose. I have marvelled as young people have come together and [enfleshed] the words of a drama script with an exciting performance after six weeks of intensive rehearsal and training for the stage. I can point to a whole palette of models, methods and training/educational approaches that have been applied in these contexts, but I cannot say for certain that this model will always work in this context every time. In fact, I fear I can only say with any certainty that it will depend on the relationships and quality of dialogue and trust that is present in any given situation. This is not to say that there are not essentials or universals of behaviour – I fundamentally believe that there are – but it is to say that no moment in time, no training or class is ever repeatable. It is always live and like any live performance, never to be repeated, and always infinitely diverse. We can only access the fundamental danger of these universals through one-off local happenings. That the big questions are still unanswered after millennia of thought is intellectually and emotionally exciting. That the big questions – 'how might we learn to live together so as to prosper one another?' 'how do we communicate?' 'what is learning?' – are still intact is perhaps fundamentally the whole point and be it in the quick fix intercultural training context or the long-term intercultural education discovery modes, the elusive, tantalising nature of these questions will mean we have to continually try to do other, to do again, to do differently, to work and walk on through.

Paulo Freire: Críticos seremos, verdadeiramente, se vivermos a plenitude da práxis (We will only truly be critical, if we live out the fullness of praxis)

This is where the genius of Guilherme's conceptualisation of the ICOPROMO project proposal rests. Here we have an open weave of dialogue, critique and activism between academics, educators and trainers, all aware that 'there is more to this' than coercion or prescription or even ILOS:

> Intercultural mobility in the workplace, as we define it and if we are to consider its ontological, epistemological, methodological and civic dimensions, certainly depends on individual vision and commitment, on work group dynamics as well as on organisational structure and culture. However, it is also shaped by a national legal and political framework that is multicultural and stimulates the individual to act as an intercultural citizen and is inspired by counter-hegemonic globalisation which "is animated by a redistributive ethos in its broadest sense, involving redistribution of material, social, political, cultural and symbolic resources" (Santos, 2005: 29; Glaser et al., 2007: 46)

Intercultural mobility means that questions of purity and danger are now writ large across the global educational context, not just confined to relatively stable communities. Under the conditions of intercultural mobility, good citizenship is of necessity critical citizenship (Guilherme, 2002). Now as in previous ages the biggest issue facing us, interculturally, is how we share our bread, to paraphrase George Macleod. Both are present in the discourses we bring to bear in the contexts of intercultural training and intercultural education. It is easier to remain within the discursive space of what Freire terms either 'verbalism' where we critique others or 'activism' where we launch new, ill-considered projects and programmes. If we wish to walk on through, to stick with the tough, enduring questions, to be more than people with a gut reaction against stereotypes, but to be open to more than predetermined scripts of therapeutic, technocractic, consumer militarism (Brueggemann, 2007), then critique and action need to be worked out as what Freire terms 'praxis'. For this to occur, the intercultural dialogue, intercultural responsibility and a sixth savoir, to add to Byram's (1997) five, is necessary – that of knowing to change oneself, savoir se transformer (Phipps, 2006). This sounds rather easy, but, like Byram's other *savoirs*, it is a competence that is processual, difficult and messy. It requires learned and practiced degrees of self-awareness, and self-reflexivity, yes, but also melded with these self-critical aptitudes it requires that practical and perceptual changes be made, over and over again, to the ways in which we behave, one to another. Such transformational work is always locally oriented, often first and foremost domestic, it occurs in the places where we encounter pollution, dirt and disorder most viscerally. It happens when suddenly we are out of routine and in another environment, when what is temperate is hot and sticky, when our patterns of sleep and digestion are disturbed, when our bodies move and bring and make mess, when the ways of inhabiting the world and our well-practiced, comfortable values, attitudes and beliefs (about when to go to bed, what to drink, where the rubbish goes) are thrown into disarray. For there to be harmony – social and bodily –there will need to be changes and we will need to learn to discern what these might be.

Who is served by transformation?

I'd like to venture, in conclusion, that intercultural training and intercultural education, at their best, offer a praxis in discernment. When discernment rather than solution is at the core, the questions, open ended and not unproblematic, begin by considering what interests are being served by these divisions of purity and danger, gender, race and class and their rather stark polarities. Discernment requires the self to be the subject *and* object of the learning: who is served when I – and I do this – am dismissive of intercultural training approaches? What kinds of investments do I have in intercultural education and what do I gain from these?

Furthermore, and perhaps more importantly, discernment praxis needs the question to be asked: who is served by understanding these things better? Who is served by democratic and critical paradigms if these merely get soaked up by the dominantly powerful to serve their own needs? Famously, Freirean techniques and educational models have been found to be extremely successful in the training of people for work with the FBI/CIA. The hunger of capitalism, happily taking on equality and diversity, cultural difference, social class, environmental care into consumption hoovers up everything to serve its voracious appetite for anything new. We see this in Jack's reflections:

> The cultural difference they came to class to learn about is the cultural difference of an imagined cosmopolitanism, of world cities, airport lounges, exotic foods and comfortable communicative possibility. It seemed to me that courses in CCMM [cross-cultural management and marketing] like mine that did not provide this "shopping-cart" for knowledge, its embodiment and future performance was at best suspect, at worst wasted. (Jack, 2009: 112)

But perhaps, just perhaps, there is a way through – the walking on through way, the continual discernment way – which does not need us to reach such despairing conclusions, though as an educator in this field I know well the delights of watching students learn how to transform themselves through their thinking and engagements and the disappointments of those who use their experiences for purposes with which I fundamentally disagree. As an educator, I know that this has to be the deal. If I move from a position where I will not brook such disappointment then I am no longer educating. If I believe that this is 'at worst, wasted' then I am back with dirt, disorder, purity and danger.

> ideas about separating, purifying, demarcating and punishing transgressions [such as bad or potentially damaging intercultural behaviour] have as their main function to impose system on an inherently untidy experience. It is only by exaggerating the difference between within and without, about and below, male and female, with and against, that a semblance of order is created [we are all trained now, phew!]. (Douglas, 1966: 4)

Santos (2004), in a suggestively titled paper, reaches back into the disappointments, the failed critical dreams, into the longevity of education, training and action and rails 'against the waste of experience'. Such an approach offers a way of countering the imperialist purities in the intercultural present not by creating ever better models or ways of training, educating or understanding, but with dialogic, interhuman ways of discerning and being intercultural. If we follow Douglas in her argument, we learn that dirt is simply 'matter out of place'. What we define as dirt, or difference or disorder tells us a great deal about the cosmologies we inhabit, and the universes we harness to force others into 'good citizenship'.

> In my home is a destitute young man from North Africa. He is with us because he is denied a place to stay by the state and it is illegal for him to earn any money. He doesn't wish to disturb us, moving around the house with respect, quietly. He cooks for himself in our kitchen in the late evenings. One night, I wake to the smell of burning. I doze a while and then am woken again, rudely, by a loud explosion in the kitchen below. I run downstairs to find that the eggs he was boiling have boiled dry and exploded leaving charred remains all over the walls, floor, ceiling. Everywhere there is matter out of place and it's 3am, and our house guest has just woken up terrified by what he's inadvertently done and we are beginning to clean up the mess.

This was a real intercultural encounter; you will have had many similar ones yourself. It was messy, dangerous and my instant reactions were not particularly those of a 'good citizen'. They rarely are at 3 am. I have some strong principles, creedally shaped and for which I am determinedly accountable, in my life, when it comes to shaping my life, with as much discernment as I am capable of, as a 'good citizen'. I believe, for example, that the use or threatened use of weapons of mass destruction is morally indefensible. This means I campaign against their existence. I believe, for example, that this beautiful world of ours contains enough for our need, but not for our greed. This means I continually try and adapt my life to live simply and it means that intercultural education has to be about more than the boundaries of the classroom if I am ever to discern ways of living that might have any degree of intercultural integrity. Yet in this experience and in the heart of a small attempt at good citizenship, according to my own ethical, creedal principles there is, at times also, mess, and a strong desire to vomit, such is my disgust at the smell.

CODA: Grafting

At the close of the 20th century, Robert Young (1996) wrote a profound critical account of intercultural communication. He was concerned in this work to find ways of articulating the profound violence and disintegration he saw as emanating from the end of the imperial and colonial ages and the possibilities for hope for the future. His sense of good citizenship, like Douglas's work, is palpably aware of the difficulties human beings have always faced when trying to live together peaceably. Importantly, his 'wager on hope' insists that there is no technology and no externally designed model that can offer the means to intercultural communication. Action, he sees as creative and as carried out by participants in any give situation. His conclusion is one written for professionals and mandating critical action and reflecting on our general capacity for intercultural critique:

> Specific professionals are not at the margin of society, they are at the centre. They are the people who make postmodern society work. ... the task of critical professionals is to make that centre a multicultural, democratic centre. (Young, 1996: 212)

Young's mandate, like the vision of the ICOPROMO project, is one that attempts to place intercultural professionals, those entrusted with the critical and creative stewardship of democratic institutions, in a dialectic of hope and critique. Like the ICOPROMO team, he attempts to show that power and professionalism come with responsibility to question, reflect, consider and also to demonstrate, *in situ*, what intercultural hope might be imagined to be, and how it might be enacted.

This will always require hard work, and periods of rest for reflection – times of doing the work and times out of routine, in training sessions or classrooms as professionals, when a different kind of work can be done. The results will rarely be perfect or anything other than ambiguous. Professionals will want to try new things out, change the structures or patterns, find other ways of relating, will be discerning and critical, accepting and considerate, at their best.

At the level of culture, as well as at the level of the individual, Young suggests that it is possible and desirable for all cultures to change, but not to change by blending with one another or being submerged by a single culture:

> Each culture must change to the extent necessary for it to recognize differences, to acknowledge the *prima facie* validity of other cultures, to incorporate some degree of tolerance of cultural diversity, and to discover some common ground in the new intercultural space thus created, ground upon which a conversation about intercultural understanding and cooperation can be built. (Young, 1996: 3)

'Common ground and discernment': back to dirt, culture as cultivation, raking over the living with the dead to make good earth for growing. Throughout this chapter, I have wrestled with notions and experiences of training and education. Both words, for me as a gardener, have strong roots through their etymology, with gardening. Training is what I do in my garden. Carefully, usually in the spring when the runner beans have actually survived the last danger of late frost and the merciless onslaught of slugs; when the green stems are strong with rising sap and growth is flourishing, then and only then is it time to 'train' the runners up the bean poles. Nurseries are places where young plants are raised, as with young children, and this links back to the notion of education as nurture and not, as often erroneously stated, as leadership.

But here, neither concept satisfied. In their place I'm settling on the metaphor of 'grafting'. Grafting, in colloquial English means work, hard work, embodied work – not some kind of mental abstraction, but engaged with the messiness of life and its patterns at a given time and place. 'Grafting' has a further sense, however, for it is how new apple trees are created on old root stock, how a purple and white lilac might come to live together as the same tree. Grafting is what comes when we don't waste intercultural experience, and when we take into ourselves what we would otherwise cast as different, dangerous, unconscionable.

References

Beck, U. (1986) *Risikogesellschaft. Auf dem Weg in eine andere Moderne.* Frankfurt am Main: Suhrkamp.
Bourdieu, P. (2000) *Pascalian Meditations.* Cambridge: Polity.
Brueggemann, W. (2007) *Mandate to Difference: An Invitation to the Contemporary Church.* Louisville, KY: Westminster John Knox Press.
Byram, M. (1997) *Teaching and Assessing Intercultural Communicative Competence.* Clevedon: Multilingual Matters.
Douglas, M. (1966) *Purity and Danger: An Analysis of the Concepts of Pollution and Taboo.* London and New York: Routledge.
Evans, M. (2004) *Killing Thinking: The Death of the University.* London: Continuum.
Feng, A., Byram, M. and Fleming, M. (eds) (2009) *Becoming Interculturally Competent through Education and Training.* Bristol: Multilingual Matters.
Freire, P. (1970) *Pedagogia do Oprimido.* São Paulo: Paz e Terra.
Glaser, E., Guilherme, M., Méndez García, M. and Mughan, T. (2007) *ICOPROMO – Intercultural Competence for Professional Mobility.* Graz and Strasbourg: Council of Europe Publishing.
Guilherme, M. (2002) *Critical Citizens for an Intercultural World.* Clevedon: Multilingual Matters.
Jack, G. (2009) A critical perspective on teaching intercultural competence in a management department. In A. Feng, M. Byram and M. Fleming (eds) *Becoming Interculturally Competent through Education and Training* (pp. 95–114). Bristol: Multilingual Matters.
Kramsch, C. (2006) From communicative competence to symbolic competence. *Modern Language Journal* 90 (2), 249–252.

Lyotard, J. (1984) *The Postmodern Condition*. Manchester: Manchester University Press.
Phipps, A. (2006) Whose chances? People, place and praxis in languages for intercultural communication. In A. Hahn and F. Klippel (eds) *Sprachen schaffen Chancen* (pp. 27–43). München: Oldenbourg.
Santos, B.d.S. (2004) A critique of lazy reason: Against the waste of experience. In I.M. Wallerstein (ed.) *The Modern World-System in the Longue Durée* (pp. 157–197). Boulder, CO: Paradigm.
Santos, B.d.S. (2005) *Democratizing Democracy: Beyond the Liberal Democratic Canon*. London: Verso.
Winch, C. (1995) Education needs training. *Oxford Review of Education* 21 (3), 315–325.
Young, R. (1996) *Intercultural Communication: Pragmatics, Genealogy, Deconstruction*. Clevedon: Multilingual Matters.

Part 2
Intercultural Communication, Interaction, Management and Responsibility in Theory and Practice

Chapter 4
Intercultural Responsibility: Power and Ethics in Intercultural Dialogue and Interaction

MANUELA GUILHERME, CLARA KEATING and DANIEL HOPPE

Introduction: 'Intercultural Responsibility' in the Workplace

The information-based society, economic globalisation, networking and mobility have changed both professional and personal relationships in the workplace. Not only have organisational demands had to keep up with new societal and market requirements, but also different cultural, taken-for-granted, responsive actions have been brought face to face in such a way that individual workers have been forced to conform and correspond to the expectations of and pressures imposed by the various interests, including their own. Furthermore, the differences between individual workers, both in terms of power within the organisation and in personal character, as related to their cultural and ethical norms, have given rise to diverging attitudes in relation to contextual beliefs and values.

The public space has been changing, gradually but steadily, to become more multicultural, although this has happened more reluctantly in the workplace because organisational structures have managed to hold back the societal changes within their own spheres and, to some extent, to keep discrimination more subtle. Furthermore, there has been an increasing and more pervasive awareness that 'the recognition that a society had become multiethnic or multicultural was not simply about demographics or economics' and that it went beyond that into 'an understanding that a new set of challenges were being posed for which a new political agenda was necessary (or alternatively, had to be resisted: the view of certain conservatives...)' (Modood, 2007: 5). However, a change in the political rhetoric alone is insufficient. As the information and knowledge-based society was constructing a new paradigm, leaving the goal of cultural hegemony behind and moving into an intercultural construct of society, this intercultural ideal also began to impregnate organisational spaces and, therefore, to modify prevailing paradigms of interaction.

Issues such as corporate citizenship, defined as 'the extent to which business strategically meet the economic, legal, ethical and philanthropic responsibilities' (Ferrell et al., 2005: 48), and corporate social responsibility, defined as the 'organization's obligation to maximize its positive impact and minimize its negative impact on society' (Ferrell et al., 2005: 67), have been viewed almost exclusively from a macro and top-down perspective, that is, only the organisation as a whole and its CEOs were made responsible and their actions generally assessed quantitatively (Resick et al., 2006). However, the duty of workers-in-interaction to be responsibly intercultural deserves to be given more attention in the literature, since 'TNCs [transnational corporations] are no longer the monolithic, vertically organized entities they were in most of the twentieth-century' and, in fact, 'they have undergone fundamental changes in the last decades, facilitating the horizontalization of their corporate structures' (Palacios, 2004: 390). Moreover, it is a given fact that 'the workplace as a venue of communication simply changes the location of the interaction, not the predispositions and stereotypes that human beings bring to the situation' (Asante & Davis, 1989: 376) and, as mentioned above, the organisational structures have, to a great extent, kept these challenges hidden beneath other more pressing constraints related to corporate profit and political and individual interests. In the meantime, the social responsibility of both governmental and non-governmental organisations is perceived as untouchable, in the case of the former due to their legal status and in the latter due to their soundly established goals. Therefore, in none of them is the intercultural responsibility of their workers opened for discussion and their responsibility to be interculturally committed is not always a seriously taken commitment. Their intercultural competence is, as one might expect, perceived to be innate, intuitively achieved and to grow according to their length of experience. Workers in governmental and non-governmental organisations have less access to education/training on intercultural development as they are expected to act according to hierarchically established norms and to safe purposes, while companies invest in the intercultural education/training of their workers, but only when they recognise any power in their interlocutors and always in direct relation to their profit goals. Intercultural responsibility is, however, a dimension that aims to go beyond a straightforward notion of intercultural competence, that is, in order to not only be able to communicate appropriately and effectively across cultures, but also to dig deeper into the relationships established between people in professional contexts, despite the fact that the relationships themselves are often not profound.

Putting Intercultural Responsibility in Perspective

The notion of intercultural responsibility in a multicultural work group/team was originally introduced by the ICOPROMO – Intercultural Competence for Professional Mobility project, funded by the Leonardo da Vinci Programme, in September 2003, and was then developed into practical activities mainly by the team at the *Centro de Estudos Sociais* also with the contribution of other teams. Intercultural responsibility is understood here as a conscious and reciprocally respectful, both professional and personal, relationship among the team/group members, assuming that they have different ethnic backgrounds, whether national or sub-national. This means that members-in-interaction demonstrate that they are aware of the particularities of collaborating with their co-workers, either in an inter- or intra-national context, recognising that their identities have been socially and culturally constructed based on different ethnic elements and influences that have brought to bear, at different stages, more or less weight, and whether this is more or less visible. Intercultural responsibility also implies that every member is responsible not only for identifying and recognising the cultural idiosyncrasies of every other member-in-interaction, but also for developing full and reciprocally demanding professional relationships with them. Such relationships entail that every member-in-interaction should collaborate in a sound and committed manner, expects no more and no less than what, in their view, can be expected of oneself, and demands of oneself no less and no more than what, in their opinion, should be demanded of their co-workers. Coherence is, therefore, an important factor for the development of intercultural responsibility in that it provides the glue that holds together the various fragmentary and relativistic standpoints. If some flexibility is required while adapting ethical principles to a particular interactional context, it is fundamental that there is also some coherence among responses and between the latter and underlying moral principles. Coherence represents here the *leitmotif* that supports and promotes intercultural responsibility. However, empathy and solidarity are also essential building blocks for the development of intercultural responsibility, whether communication and interaction involve shorter or longer distances.

Communication in ethnically diverse organisations is usually considered difficult and believed to hinder effective interaction. There appears to be a consensus in the literature in the field that unequal treatment, in general, and inadequate linguistic performance in the working language, in particular, may be detrimental to participants who display such impediments, and that both are more prone to happen in multicultural teams. Some studies have shed further light on such issues by focusing on the relationship between communication at work and employees' job attitudes, and their results have not always confirmed their initial hypotheses. For example, in their study on 'the role of communication in an ethnically diverse organization', Dinsbach et al. (2007) concluded that their 'hypothesis that ethnic minority employees, due to their disadvantageous position would communicate less and would have less positive attitudes than ethnic majority employees was not supported by [their] study', although they do 'seem to encounter difficulties in maintaining personal relations at work' (Dinsbach et al., 2007: 740). However, further clarification is needed here about who or what motivates such difficulties. Other studies have emphasised the need for the development of an 'intercultural group climate' that induces group members to appreciate and promote diversity no less than similarity in values, and have argued, for example, that 'when employees value the diversity in their workgroup, lack of perceived similarity in values does not necessarily lead to lower identification levels' (Luitjers et al., 2008: 156).

The notion of 'global ethics', that 'requires precisely the calling into question both of one's embedded particular ethical practices and also of the very claim of their universality' (Odysseos, 2003: 188, emphasis by the author), is also of relevance to the definition of the concept of intercultural responsibility within the scope of multicultural groups in work contexts. Multiethnic group members, while in interaction with the aim of performing a joint task, need to put their own ethical standards into perspective and realise that coming to a consensus does not have to entail the universalisation of standards that are particular to one specific, but dominant, cultural framework. On the other hand, 'ethical judgements can only be taken on the basis of the factual situation and its specification' (Odysseos, 2003: 197), that is, they have to be suitable to the particular situation, although this does not imply the ruling out of general principles. Closely related to this idea is that of a 'meta-ethics or layered contextual position', suggested by Ting-Toomey and Chung

(2005), which involves a 'more analytical perspective' where 'the application of ethics can be understood only through peeling away the different layers of the ethical dilemma' (Ting-Toomey & Chung, 2005: 339). The discussion about 'global ethics' has essentially put into question the understanding of universality as the abstraction, neutrality or transculturalisation of ethical principles and raised awareness of the fact that the process of universalisation involves the imposition of a particularity. However, the same authors cannot help but suggest a 'derived ethical-universalism position', which they put forward as an ideal model to be sought and in which they emphasise an 'integrative culture-universal and culture-specific interpretive framework' (Ting-Toomey & Chung, 2005: 339). None of the approaches shown above replace a universalistic with a relativistic perspective, but rather they try to reconcile and balance one with the other by re-framing them into a new approach.

The notion of intercultural responsibility adds a moral, although cosmopolitan, element to global ethics. Cosmopolitanism is understood here as an idea for the post-Westphalian age 'marked by the promise of perpetual peace, human rights and global governance', celebrating 'the collective endeavour to *humanize*, by holding responsible' (Fine & Boon, 2007: 7–8, emphasis by the author). We may also consider the idea of an 'empowering ethics' that 'involves re-imagining and re-inventing the different ways in which people are self-constituted in relation to the institutions and procedures within which they operate' (Ibarra-Colado *et al.*, 2006: 46) as complementary to the notion of responsibility, if we perceive the latter as comprehending an emancipating dimension in the implementation of intercultural ethics. This understanding of ethics responds to the challenges of intercultural responsibility in that it appeals to the exercise of emancipatory citizenship and the corresponding re-framing of institutions and organisations.

However, 'reframing is a conversational practice that helps characterise the interplay of incompatible frames in moral conflict', moreover, it 'means developing a new way of interpreting a situation' (Agne, 2007: 550, 552), that is, in intercultural interactions it is fundamental that ethical standards remain flexible and open to discussion. When it comes to an intercultural conflict, 'mindful reframing' is put forward as a helpful strategy, described as 'the mindful process of using language to change the way each person or party defines or thinks about experiences' (Ting-Toomey & Chung, 2005: 282–283). Furthermore, it is essential to keep the assumption of reciprocal intercultural responsibility at hand to prevent intercultural communication and interaction turning into fragmented, splintering multicultural performances, or even an 'anything goes' approach. It is nevertheless important not to forget that workgroup interaction is never symmetric, which means that participants do not always act or respond in a uniformly balanced manner. Workgroup interaction is ultimately communicative, dialogical, dynamic and dialectical. According to some authors, 'coordination rather than cooperation is the basic strategic interaction that underlies group action' (Buskens et al., 2008: 207).

Language resources also play an important role in the development of intercultural responsibility among the members of multicultural groups/teams. In this setting, participants usually share a common language that is, at least for some of them, second or foreign, and speak first languages that are to a lesser or greater extent – but necessarily – different from each other. The simple fact of communicating through a medium that is perhaps not deeply-rooted in all of them may generate some sense of partnership, companionship, or even complicity and solidarity, and therefore also, to some extent, a sense of intercultural responsibility for one another. The issue here is then whether this sense of intercultural responsibility is a mindful, knowledgeable and determined commitment. According to Byram (2008: 11), 'by sharing a language, an individual shares a reality within a social group and is a member of that group', be it a small community group or the larger national group. However, this idea can be expanded beyond any, smaller or larger, already established native community into the temporary linguistic groups built up for work or other purposes. This process, which Phipps (2007: 12) calls 'languaging' and describes as an 'act of dwelling', perfectly serves the act of communicating and growing interculturally responsible. Moreover, because the act of dwelling in another language is expressed here as 'to take that language as the point of departure, and in such a way as to live out the full knowledge and reality of the disconnection and unbreachability (sic) of the linguistic wounds between speakers' (Phipps, 2007: 147). The relation between language and intercultural responsibility is therefore not one of charity and harmony, but one of struggle and stamina, honour and honesty. Phipps (2007: 19) goes on to define intercultural communication as 'the process of embodied learning with languages'.

Intercultural responsibility illustrates and incorporates this process since it intensifies and deepens the notion of intercultural communication by embodying learning with 'languaculture(s)' with an ethical perspective. This term was borrowed from Friedrich and modified by Agar, who puts it forward as a coherent frame within the scope of one hegemonic linguistic entity. Although he already hints at some problems with this understanding by pointing out that 'we naively generalize, usually to a language or a national/state identity' and recognises that 'the disappearance of the traditional community on which *culture* was based predicts the problem at any rate' (Agar, 1994: 233, emphasis by the author), he still bases his Intercultural Practitioner (ICP) model on the coexistence of two 'languacultures' as if they were separate coherent entities. This understanding has also been questioned by other authors, such as Risager who 'prefer[s] to say that language users spread in social networks *across* cultural contexts and discourse communities, but they carry languaculture with them' (Risager, 2007: 170, emphasis by the author). The notion of intercultural responsibility epitomises the discussion about languaculture(s) in intercultural communication because it raises issues concerning the negotiation between the similar and the contrasting aspects of different ethical frameworks, in particular how this negotiation is verbalised and performed. This is one other sensitive issue that makes professional training difficult as far as intercultural communication and interaction in group/team work are concerned.

Challenges in Material Design and Professional Development

Preparing professionals to deal with the issues of intercultural responsibility while carrying out a professional task in a team/group involves risks and challenges for both trainers and trainees. Firstly, developing a workshop consisting of either theoretical input or hands-on-activities only, whether interesting and helpful or not, is certainly easier than attempting to build a bridge between *theory and practice (a)* and trying to find a balance between them. However, the latter was established as our goal in the materials we produced, since nowhere is this balance more important than in the development of intercultural responsibility, where theory informs practice and vice versa. To have one without the other makes this undertaking weak and the results will not be as clear, sound or grounded as they should be and will therefore end up damagingly distorted. The dialogue between theory and practice, where each informs the other, is fundamental in order to make sense of the conceptualisation and implementation of intercultural responsibility within a framework of intercultural competence. Intercultural competence, due to the current controversy brought about by the notion of 'competence' itself (already discussed in the introduction to this book), is a general goal that may be implemented in many different ways. The commitment to developing intercultural responsibility within a theoretical and practical framework puts training in intercultural competence on a track that is distinctive, audacious, serious and urgent. Secondly, dealing with complex ideas and *complexity (b)* itself and expressing them in a simple, organised and clear way, was also a major requirement and goal of this project, that of creating practical materials for the development of intercultural responsibility. Trainees can be quick to reject ideas that seem abstract, inaccessible or even disturbing. It is always a challenge to attempt to deconstruct and uncover ideas, feelings and behaviours that are generally taken for granted or are often hidden from view and to invite trainees to address and manage them. Trainees may feel inspired and stimulated, as they often do, but can also withdraw and turn away. Although difficult, dealing with complex ideas and complexity is not only cognitively stimulating, but also an inspiration to one's performance and, while it can make the whole exercise more demanding, it can also encourage intercultural communication and interaction.

However, it is easy to *slip into a humanitarian, patronising and even demagogic tone (c)* while working on the development of intercultural responsibility. Focusing on the ethical angle of issues can mislead us into adopting an intrusive moral stance and distract us from our initial good intentions, leading us to adopt overprotective and, paradoxically, self-centred attitudes. The real meaning of 'responsibility' in the term 'intercultural responsibility' is then at stake here, since it is as much about responsibility for others in relation to oneself as it is about responsibility for oneself in relation to others. Material designers and trainers must be aware, as well as make their trainees aware, of such risks and be cautious about them. Encouraging solidarity and ethical co-responsibility, without being condescending or invasive, can represent a step ahead in the development of intercultural competence. Nevertheless, stimulating *reflection upon meaningful individual experiences, needs and interests (d)* is a significant and indispensable strategy in intercultural education, by and large, and can provide rich resources for discussion and help stimulate debate. However, making the most of this opportunity requires a vast amount of knowledge, competence and experience of the material designer and the educator/trainer or such wealth may simply be spoilt or wasted. Firstly, there is a need to *provide a safe context (e)* to enable discussion of pleasurable, intimate, sensitive, perplexing or uncomfortable issues. However, such a safe context is not necessarily cosy, harmonious or tranquil, but needs to be supportive, stimulating, reassuring, genuine and committed. Then, a *capacity to grasp the significance of the moment (f)* that is transitory, changeable, relative... also gives an opportunity, that cannot be missed, of grasping the moment in a full and far-sighted perspective. Training for intercultural competence, and within it on intercultural responsibility, if it goes beyond mere technical and functional training, helps develop a sharp, to some extent intuitive and automatic, but exercised and informed capability to more quickly seize the various strengths that coexist in a given situation. Finally, *exploring the implicit as well as the explicit implications (g)* of our cultural behaviours leads us beyond the visible, immediate, obvious and often deceitful aspects that may generate hasty and incorrect judgements. Indeed, appearance may be as misleading in monocultural as in multicultural settings because, in the former, thinking and behavioural patterns seem to be consensual, but hidden details can misguide us. However, in multicultural settings, our perceptions can nevertheless betray our resolutions, if we follow mistaken assumptions, although here difference is more exposed and expected.

There are other risks we may encounter in the process of formally developing intercultural responsibility, such as *the danger of taking an 'anything goes' approach (h)*, which may appear shrouded in a strong veil of flexibility. The issue here is where to draw the line. The question must nevertheless be asked and remains critical. Coherence and sensibility may again prove very helpful and prevent exaggerated positions from being adopted. In connection to this, it is important *not to go astray, while 'crossing borders' (i)*. Although it is impossible to engage in intercultural communication and interaction without being flexible and ready to 'cross borders' – cultural, social, psychological, epistemological, political, geographical or other – setting limits is as fundamental as getting started. This aspect is particularly sensitive when it comes to intercultural responsibility since this is all about ethical and moral, as well as ideological principles, beliefs and values. Furthermore, because it requires *that common-sense and taken-for-granted assumptions are challenged (j)*, but without causing offence, and *that even basic and essential principles are questioned (k)* without being threatened, this process – that of developing intercultural responsibility – demands that sensitivity, perspicacity, discernment and wisdom grow alongside one another, that is, intercultural responsibility is not about a single and homogeneous competency, but rather involves a coherent combination of various qualities endowed with a specific focus and direction. This process also needs *to promote a sense of detachment without preventing a sense of belonging (l)*, since while the former allows for a critical view of relations, principles and standards, the latter enables the establishment of relationships, commitments and solidarities. Although this coexistence and balance may seem paradoxical and infeasible, it is nonetheless vital and sound.

In addition to the points mentioned above, there are other aspects that should not be overlooked in designing materials on intercultural responsibility, such as *the acknowledgement of the various cultural representations present in a given social context, without forgetting the underrepresented as well as the unrepresentable (m)*. Neither diversity nor discrimination at different levels can be ignored. Ideas, knowledge and, therefore, people can be discriminated against for motives other than material conditions, for example for not corresponding or adjusting to dominant criteria and standards. Diversity and discrimination can emerge in a very subtle way, linger beyond immediately obvious evidence and go unnoticed to most, except those who enjoy their attributes or suffer their consequences. However, material designers and educators/trainers, in their position as intercultural experts, need not only be alert but also deepen their knowledge and understanding of such sensitive and subtle aspects. *Ongoing relations of power cannot be disregarded (n)* either. Trainees need to be educated on how to challenge them, while remaining aware of the possible consequences they may suffer while resisting or even defying the *status quo*. In sum, material design and education/training in intercultural responsibility is expected to *generate 'reflection-in-action' without restraining spontaneity or emotional involvement (o)*. Intercultural responsibility is therefore achieved through checks and balances, and also by running risks and taking challenges. Such an undertaking, that of designing materials and carrying out workshops on this matter, is therefore not an easy project, although it is both feasible and rewarding.

Putting Theory into Practice in Intercultural Responsibility

The development of intercultural responsibility, within a framework of intercultural competence, mainly involves taking a specific look at various aspects of identity and life rather than focusing on the topic per se. Trainees should, nevertheless, at some point reflect upon the meaning of the term and critically consider the implications of this notion for individual intercultural behaviour and commitments. For example, trainees may be asked:

- *Tell your colleagues about an experience which was, in some way, related to Intercultural Responsibility;*

In the following example, trainees are asked to articulate the concept with previous intercultural experiences in a self-critical manner:

- *To what extent do you think you acted in a culturally responsible/ irresponsible way?*

Antonyms and synonyms are helpful tools for stimulating discussion of abstract terms, since trainees are indirectly led to discuss the limits of their understanding of the concept. However, this may only be a step into the very definition of the concept 'intercultural responsibility' and the considerations about various possibilities of including such preoccupations into everyday communication and interaction.

- *Critically analyse the definition and application of the concept 'Intercultural Responsibility';*

This is only one step away from contextualising the concept within some aspect of intercultural communication and interaction. Therefore, the focus gradually moves from the philosophical discussion of the concept itself into real-life situations, decisions and conclusions. Trainees are challenged and stimulated intellectually to illuminate *realia* with academically grounded philosophical reflections. Then, they may be asked:

- *Try to recognise one's limits in dealing with unknown situations and cultures* (Activity title: 'Been there, done that...')

Linking intercultural responsibility with other concepts relevant to intercultural competence is also a possibility:

- *Now, re-write the description of your nationality as if it were seen by a member of one of the other nationalities;*
- *...how you describe another nationality in opposition to features you ascribe to your own;*
- *Organise these nationalities into as many groups as you find suitable; then, exchange your findings with those of another colleague and critically examine your colleague's decisions and vice-versa...;* (Activity title: 'Oh! I have heard about them')

Strategies like identifying opposites and exploring mirror-like reciprocities are helpful in intercultural education/training. In addition, other abstract concepts may be brought into the discussion about intercultural responsibility, such as trust:

- *In order to build a relationship of trust, it is important...;*
- *What is their [common values] importance for building trust in multicultural teams?* (Activity title: 'Alternative ending')

The key is to promote discussion about finding common values while, at the same time, being able to understand and negotiate different perceptions of these values in the context of building relationships of trust. It may also be important to consider to what extent and in what terms it is sensible to develop relationships, in general, and intercultural relationships in particular, in professional contexts. Are there different paradigms in different organisational structures or is it a matter of personality or both?

- *Establishing personal relationships can also help, for when people find themselves in a difficult situation, a crisis, they help each other in such a way that would be impossible, if they weren't friends.* (This statement is quoted from an interview with an NGO worker); (Activity title: 'Friends')
- *I mean, for example, my colleagues at my level, we rarely go out together, because we don't all have the same preferences, uhm, and this leads to... there may be factors that are not in our control, like A doesn't get along with B, or A's wife doesn't get along with B's, who doesn't get along with C, and this eventually affects our professional relationships.* (Quoted from an interview with a businessman) (Activity title: 'Friends')

There are basic issues concerning the development of intercultural responsibility within multicultural team/group work that should be discussed. One such issue involves the different types of relationships – personal, social, professional – and their various implications, risks and potential, as well as the limits to combining them. Decision-making is, to a greater or lesser extent, another aspect that most workers will have to deal with in their everyday activities. They may sometimes even be requested to select their co-partners for a team task:

- *Please choose two of your colleagues with whom you would like to work more closely and justify your choice;*
- *Think about to what extent your choice was influenced by their (a) nationality; (b) race; (c) gender; (d) language; (e) culture; (f) status; (g) personality; (h) professional competence;*
- *Discuss to what extent first impressions can be right or wrong and their weight in decision making;* (Activity title: 'Pick me, pick me')

It is impossible to deal with the concept of intercultural responsibility without also considering the problem of discrimination as a whole, as well as its various degrees and subtle forms. More than that, it is the responsibility of educators/trainers and material designers to unveil the process of judgement making in intercultural relationships for their trainees and help them in dealing with other cultures in a non-judgemental way, which cannot be absolute, nor would it be desirable that it were. Therefore, trainees need to be encouraged to become conscious of this process and consequently of the effects that ethnocentric statements and attitudes may have on people who work with them:

- *Are there any statements you find particularly irritating? Why?*
- *What reactions may his/her attitude cause in a multicultural team?* (Activity title: 'A cultural superiority complex')

An ethnocentric attitude, either overt or covert, can be very detrimental to team climate and making hidden value judgements visible is essential for the deconstruction of discriminatory practices. Covert discrimination, determined by preconceptions and misconceptions that are unspoken, can equally result in offence and mistreatment. Furthermore, discrimination is firmly grounded on power relations, not only at the individual level, but also at an organisational level. The increasingly global economy brings with it shifts in the relations of power and responsibility. For example, the relations between the headquarters of an organisation and its subsidiaries around the world mirror unequal power relations. The power of the subsidiaries, which are often strategically located where wages are lower, is limited by strategic decisions taken by the parent units, whereas legal responsibilities towards states and workers lie in the subsidiaries or are diluted somewhere between the boundaries. A glass ceiling in the career ladder of managers based in the subsidiaries also reinforces the power gap between them. There are several aspects to be considered in such a relationship:

- *What serious consequences can a financial crisis at the parent bank have on the host country of one of its subsidiaries?*
- *How do you think international/intercultural responsibility could work between the parent bank and its subsidiaries?*
- *What can host-country stakeholders expect from their national government during the establishment of subsidiaries and whenever a crisis arises?*
- *Can different cultural patterns increase the gap between the home and host-country supervisors?*

- What sorts of conflicts are likely to occur in meetings between them?
- Discuss how issues of face (Ting-Toomey & Kurogi, 1998) can occur in such meetings? (Activity title: 'Global power, local responsibility')

Issues of face have a strong impact on intercultural relations and have given way to a complete theory of 'face-work' and 'intercultural conflict', both linked to intercultural identity-based competence, developed by Ting-Toomey (see Part I, Chapter 2). Face-work and intercultural responsibility are inextricably linked, since both involve sensitive issues of dignity and therefore education/training aimed at the development of intercultural competence needs to focus on preparing trainees to deal with sensitive issues of face negotiation.

The construction of identity often implies the affirmation of certain values, considered one's own, in contrast to other values, considered as belonging to the Other. This 'binary' mindset can be unconscious or intentional, and generally determines the positive and negative connotations of each situation. Such situations not only have an individual scope, but also a collective one and, therefore, both social and political implications. Trainees are, therefore, expected to become aware of what is being silenced in the construction of identities, and the consequences of individual judgements based on such opposing binaries.

The activity *Black is not White*, given below as an example, focuses on the process of identity construction and the exclusion mechanisms that it implies, although these mechanisms are not always made evident. The strategy here largely involves approaching the fears that may arise when deconstructing such mechanisms and bringing them into the light where they can be reviewed. Group learning dynamics play an important role here in that, on the one hand, the group situation implies an exposure of oneself in a context where we may want to appear interculturally competent, but on the other hand, once started, the group dynamics may generate not only a stimulating discussion but eventually also fruitful ground for further learning.

In the first stage of this activity, trainees reflect, write down and discuss some aspects of their identity, as identified and viewed by themselves, described both from an affirmative point of view – what they are – and from the perspective of what they are not. They also discuss whether 'being something' implies not being something else and *vice versa*. Conclusions should be shared and discussed with the whole group and are meant to lead trainees to question whether such attributes must be mutually exclusive. At a later stage, they are encouraged to question the meaning and validity of a list of concepts given in order to determine

Intercultural Responsibility 91

whether they accept the fact that their having certain attributes implies that they lack others. The purpose here is to get trainees to think about how they perceive and conceptualise otherness, how their own cultural setting may lead to biased results and how this process is a permanent feature of everyday life.

Sample Activity

BLACK IS NOT WHITE

I

When we think of ourselves as individuals, and our individual identity, the basic question we ask is 'Who/what am I?'

Try to think of three 'things' you are:

- _____
- _____
- _____

However, we can also turn this question around and ask 'Who/what am I <u>not</u>?' Again, list three 'things' you think you are not:

- _____
- _____
- _____

Looking back at what you consider yourself to *be* and to *not be*, do you think each of the items you listed may also have one or more counterparts? In other words, do the things you 'are' imply that you 'aren't' one or more other things? Likewise, is it possible that 'not being' the items you listed means that you 'are' certain other things?

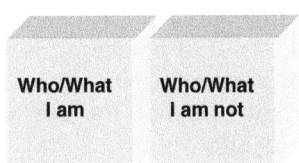

Read the following text:

« Contamination is always at work in establishing the sequence of oppositions that shape our political imaginary as well as our identities, collective and individual ones. Our idea of being a man implies the sense of not being a woman; our sense of belonging to the

West, to civilization, to democracy, depends on acknowledging at the same time that we are not Eastern, savage or politically irrational and unruly. The determination of these "positive" identities relies therefore on the simultaneous production of a set of oppositional concepts. The emergence of these "positive" identities to which we lay claim involves an operation of what Derrida terms "violence"; it is based on the suppression and denigration of one set of terms for the sake of the elevation of the other. But this mechanism also involves another type of suppression – a "forgetting" of the fact that our own identity and sense of belonging is premised on a lack, on not being somebody else, but also, perhaps, on simultaneously desiring that otherness which we do not have or maybe even comprehend, but which we attempt to make fit into our own conceptual spectrum. »¹

For discussion:

(1) The author describes a process of the construction of identity. Sum up this process in your own words.
(2) Above, you mentioned characteristics that are or are not part of your identity as an individual. Now think of three 'binaries' present in your construction of identity that are part of the culture you consider yourself to belong to.
(3) The author refers to 'our sense of belonging to the West, to civilization, to democracy'.
 (a) Do you identify with this thought?
 (b) According to the author, how is this collective identity constructed?
(4) Consider the following statement, taken from the text: 'this mechanism also involves (…) a forgetting of the fact that our own identity and sense of belonging is premised on a lack…', and that sometimes we may even desire the 'attributes' we lack.
 (a) Can you find any evidence for this statement in your own construction of identity?
 (b) Do you think that your culture looks up to certain aspects of other cultures?
(5) The author refers to 'that otherness which we do not have or maybe even comprehend, but which we attempt to make fit into our own conceptual spectrum'.
 (a) What do you think the author means by this?
 (b) Although this process is not very evident, it is present in everyday life. Can you think of an example?

(c) What may be the consequences (positive as well as negative) of this process of 'fitting otherness into our own conceptual spectrum'?

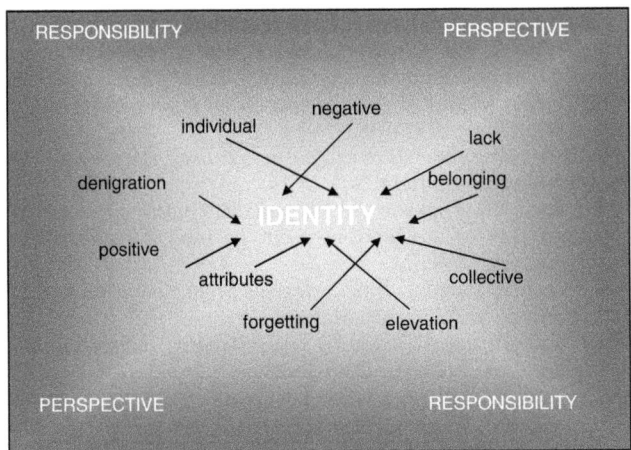

Notes
1. Zylinska, J. (2005) *The Ethics of Cultural Studies*. New York: Continuum.

References

Agar, M. (1994) The intercultural frame. *International Journal of Intercultural Relations* 18 (2), 221–237.
Agne, R.R. (2007) Reframing practices in moral conflict: Interaction problems in the negotiation standoff at Waco. *Discourse & Society* 18 (5), 549–578.
Asante, M.K. and Davis, A. (1989) Encounters in the interracial workplace. In M.K. Asante and W.B. Gudykunst (eds) *Handbook of International and Intercultural Communication* (pp. 374–391). Newbury Park, CA: Sage.
Buskens, V., Corten, R. and Weesie, J. (2008) Consent or conflict: Coevolution of coordination and networks. *Journal of Peace Research* 45 (2), 2005–2222.
Byram, M. (2008) *From Foreign Language Education to Education for Intercultural Citizenship*. Clevedon: Multilingual Matters.
Dinsbach, A.A., Feij, J.A. and de Vries, R.E. (2007) The role of communication content in an ethnically diverse organization. *International Journal of Intercultural Relations* 31, 725–745.
Ferrell, O.C., Fraedrich, J. and Ferrell, L. (2005) *Business Ethics: Ethical Decision Making and Cases* (6th edn). Boston, MA: Houghton Mifflin Co.
Fine, R. and Boon, V. (2007) Cosmopolitanism: Between past and future. *European Journal of Social Theory* 10 (1), 5–16.

Ibarra-Colado, E., Clegg, S.R., Rhodes, C. and Kornberger, M. (2006) The ethics of managerial subjectivity. *Journal of Business Ethics* 64, 45–55.

Luitjers, K., van der Zee, K. and Otten, S. (2008) Cultural diversity in organizations: Enhancing identification by valuing differences. *International Journal of Intercultural Relations* 32, 154–163.

Modood, T. (2007) *Multiculturalism: A Civic Idea*. Polity: Cambridge, UK.

Odysseos, L. (2003) On the way to global ethics? Cosmopolitanism, 'ethical' selfhood and otherness. *European Journal of Political Theory* 2 (2), 183–207.

Palacios, J.J. (2004) Corporate citizenship and social responsibility in a globalised world. *Citizenship Studies* 8 (4), 383–402.

Phipps, A. (2007) *Learning the Arts of Linguistic Survival: Languaging, Tourism, Life*. Clevedon: Multilingual Matters.

Resick, C.J., Hanges, P.J., Dickson, M.W. and Mitchelson, J.K. (2006) A cross-cultural examination of the endorsement of ethical leadership. *Journal of Business Ethics* 63, 345–359.

Risager, K. (2007) *Language and Culture Pedagogy: From a National to a Transnational Paradigm*. Clevedon: Multilingual Matters.

Ting-Toomey, S. and Chung, L.C. (2005) *Understanding Intercultural Communication*. Los Angeles, CA: Roxbury Publishers.

Ting-Toomey, S. and Kurogi, A. (1998) Facework competence in intercultural conflict: An updated face-negotiation theory. *International Journal of Intercultural Relations* 22 (2), 187–225.

Chapter 5
Emotional Management: Expressing, Interpreting and Making Meaning of Feelings in Multicultural Teams

ALEXANDRA KAAR

Introduction

Intercultural training helps individuals develop cultural self-awareness, culturally appropriate behavioural responses and a positive orientation towards other cultures (Levy, 1995). In developing intercultural competence, it is not sufficient to assess the interpersonal dynamics at the cognitive level. One also needs to address the affective level of intercultural interactions. As any other social encounter, intercultural interactions prompt emotional responses as well as a cognitive appraisal of the events happening around us. Together, they help interpret the event and form appropriate courses of action (Brown, 2003; Garcia-Prieto et al., 2003). The diversity dimension adds complexity to these processes. Chen and Starosta (1996) consider affective competence as an important skill of effective interculturalists. They define it as the ability to 'project and receive positive emotional responses before, during, and after intercultural interactions' (Chen & Starosta, 1996: 362). It is thus important to recognize emotions in oneself and others, understand their causes and effects, and manage them effectively.

In multicultural teams, specific demands exist with regard to expressing, interpreting and making sense of the emotions and feelings of individual team members. This chapter addresses the issue of emotions and emotional management in the particular context of multicultural teams. It starts out by providing a brief overview of research findings on emotions in general and their role in teams. It then explains how cultural diversity impacts the formation of emotional responses. The chapter concludes by highlighting the particular role of trust and perceptions of trustworthiness in generating positive emotional states in individual team members, particularly at the beginning of teamwork. An exemplary activity on this topic is provided.

Emotions in the Workplace

The issue of emotions in the workplace has long been overlooked because a rational paradigm dominated organisation research and the social and behavioural sciences until the 1990s (Ashkanasy et al., 2002; Mowday & Sutton, 1993). Only recently, a growing body of literature in the field of organisational behaviour and social psychology acknowledges the role of affect in the workplace. Studies confirm the impact of emotions on creativity, motivation, helping behaviour, job satisfaction and performance at individual, group and organisational levels (e.g. Ashforth & Humphrey, 1995; Ashkanasy, 2003; Averill et al., 2001; Brief & Weiss, 2002; Connolly & Viswesvaran, 2000; Fisher & Ashkanasy, 2000). It is increasingly recognised that individuals cannot elude their emotions and the impact they have on interactions and behaviour. In making sense of what is going on around individuals, they do not only engage their 'rational mind', but also their 'emotional mind' (Goleman, 1995). Brown (2003: 123) contends that 'feelings and moods affect our attitudes, motivation, behaviours, and interactions with people around us, virtually all our waking hours'. For Fineman (2003: 29), 'emotions permeate all organizational processes'. Emotions structure interactions and relationships, and guide the courses of action and thought (Ashkanasy et al., 2000; Salovey & Mayer, 1990).

The major concepts developed in the field of emotion research are mood theory, emotional labour, affective events theory and emotional intelligence (Ashkanasy et al., 2002). These concepts formed the basis for the development of the activities for the topic of emotion management. Most activities build on findings from emotional intelligence, as this is the most prominent concept in the field. It was originally developed by Salovey and Mayer (1990) and further expanded on by Goleman (1995). In their conception of emotional intelligence, Mayer et al. (1999) focus on abilities specifically related to emotions. The factors identified encompass (a) the ability to identify emotions in self and others, as well as to express them accurately; (b) the ability to understand how emotions influence information seeking and induce behavioural responses; (c) the ability to analyse emotions and give meaning to them; and (d) the ability to regulate and manage one's own and others' emotions.

The emotional competency inventory described in Goleman et al. (2002) takes a broader stance towards emotional intelligence by including personality traits. In developing their self-assessment tool, the authors organised the competencies reflecting emotional intelligence into four clusters. The first cluster, self-awareness, encompasses emotional self-awareness, accurate self-assessment and self-confidence. The second cluster is termed self-management and includes measures of emotional self-control, trustworthiness, conscientiousness, adaptability, optimism, achievement orientation and initiative. In a third cluster, the authors group empathy, organisational awareness and service orientation under the topic of social awareness. The fourth cluster is made up of developing others, inspirational leadership, influence, communication, acting as a change catalyst, conflict management, building bonds, and teamwork and collaboration, all of them measuring relationship management.

Emotion Management in Multicultural Teams

Emotional intelligence is particularly important in teams as there is great interdependence between the members involved. Druskat and Wolff (2001) suggest that in order to develop effective interaction processes in the team, one has to understand the role of emotions in these processes. However, only a few studies to date have empirically examined the effects of emotions in a team context. Offermann et al. (2004) show that emotional intelligence is a critical skill in social and interdependent settings. Similarly, Schutte et al. (2001) find that emotional intelligence is associated with empathic perspective taking, self-monitoring, social skills and cooperation, all of them facilitating interpersonal relations. Other studies confirm the positive relationship between emotional competence and team processes, team effectiveness, team performance and conflict resolution (e.g. Feyerherm & Rice, 2002; Jordan & Troth, 2004; Peslak, 2005; Rapisarda, 2002). Saavedra and Van Dyne (1999) reveal that emotional investments of individual team members increase relationship commitment and hence facilitate team survival. Emotions influence the degree of effort exerted in the team, and determine the willingness to commit oneself to the team.

As reported in a number of studies (e.g. Barsade, 2002; Bartel & Saavedra, 2000), emotions are contagious and spread in teams. A combination of individual-level affective states and group- and contextual-level factors shapes the affective experience of the team, leading to group emotion (Kelly & Barsade, 2001). Positive emotions trigger an upward spiral of excitement, which enhances personal involvement and produces positive attitudes towards the task at hand. Conversely, negative feelings have deteriorating effects on the team spirit. They create conflict, distrust and fear, and may eventually lead to mediocre or poor team outcomes. Totterdell *et al.* (1998) found that high levels of team commitment and a good team climate enhance this contagion effect. Effective emotion management therefore helps to avoid a culture of mutual expression of dissatisfaction.

In line with the above-mentioned concept of emotional intelligence, the following questions have to be addressed by individuals in a multicultural team environment:

(1) How do individuals express emotions in the team?
(2) How do individuals perceive and interpret their own and other team members' emotions?
(3) What are the effects of emotions on the behaviour of individual team members, and subsequently on team processes and outcomes?
(4) What are appropriate ways for individual team members to manage their own and other team members' feelings in order to facilitate cooperation as well as to improve satisfaction and overall team performance?

It is two mechanisms that merit closer attention. First, the display of emotions is culturally determined. This causes difficulties when it comes to accurately recognising, interpreting and judging emotions in other people. Second, perceptions of dissimilarity provoke emotional reactions that can either enhance or limit team performance. Frequently, negative emotions of individual team members lead to tensions and conflict in the team, which affects team performance.

Emotion Display and Culture

In multicultural team settings, a major difficulty of recognising others' emotions results from diverse ways of expressing emotions around the globe (Ekman, 1972). While emotions are culture-general in their underlying dimensions, they become manifest in different behaviours. This is because every culture disposes of emotion display rules, prescribing which emotions are shown in which situations and how. These rules are learned and based on cultural norms and values (e.g. Ekman, 1972; Matsumoto *et al.*, 1998; Tsai & Chentsova-Dutton, 2003). The important questions are how much emotion is appropriately revealed to others in social situations, as well as when and how such emotion expression gets sanctioned or rewarded. The study by Renjun and Ziang (2005) on work group emotions in Chinese culture settings illustrates this. It shows how the cultural values of harmony, face concerns and the instrumental need of goal achievement impact on emotion regulation. In order to maintain harmony and face, people must not lose their balance and temper. Showing anger and direct confrontation are viewed as inappropriate and unacceptable behaviour. According to Trompenaars (1993), one can distinguish between neutral and affective cultures, which vary in the extent of emotions displayed to other people. While some cultures are very expressive, making extensive use of body language, people from other cultures are conditioned to suppress certain emotions right from infancy on.

These distinct emotion expression rules make it difficult to interpret someone else's emotional state because the behavioural cues normally used for decoding emotions and their intensity are misleading (Matsumoto et al., 2002). Hence, people have to develop intercultural emotion perception skills, allowing them to determine antecedents of emotions in other people, to recognise and decode emotions, and anticipate and understand the resulting behaviour. With regard to their own emotion display, individuals have to develop an awareness of when it is appropriate to show particular emotions openly. This helps to avoid offending other team members unintentionally and contributes to maintaining a positive team climate.

Emotions and Diversity

The experience of diversity can evoke a state of emotional arousal in team members as individuals are confronted with unfamiliar behaviours and attitudes. According to Garcia-Prieto et al. (2003: 413), 'diversity is a subjective experience of social categories to which members "feel" they belong'. Among the most frequently cited visible diversity attributes are gender, age, race and ethnicity. Individuals identify with a particular group based on these categories, and derive a sense of belonging from them (Ashforth & Mael, 1989). At the same time, these categories serve as the basis for differentiating between in-groups and out-groups. As indicated by Williams (2007), individuals may perceive other people's social identities as a threat to their own, especially when they hold different values. Social identities may provoke negative emotions such as anxiety, hostility or animosity, and hinder effective cooperation between members from different social groups (Tajfel & Turner, 1986).

In a group of diverse people starting to work together as a team, individuals are strangers to each other. Cultural identities may be more salient than the team identity, leading to perceived social distance (Tsui *et al.*, 1992). As individuals have only little information about each other, they evaluate and judge other team members based on social group membership. Feelings and emotions serve as the basis for these judgements when other more rational sources of information are not available. The categorisations and feelings may be biased due to previously held prejudices and stereotypes. Stereotypes are beliefs about characteristics, attributes and behaviours of members pertaining to other groups. They are frequently non-conscious and immediate, and based on real or perceived group differences (Hilton & von Hippel, 1996; Jussim *et al.*, 1995). At worst, the evaluation of another's social identity creates emotional tension, inhibits the development of trust and hinders integration and identification with the team (Barsade *et al.*, 2000; Milliken & Martins, 1996; O'Reilly *et al.*, 1998; Tsui *et al.*, 1992).

Watson *et al.* (1993) show that as teams work together, over time the initial negative feelings decrease. Hence, in order to make multicultural teams work, special attention must be paid to the initial phases of team development. At this stage, the interaction between self-categorisation, social identity formation and stereotyping on the one hand, and emotional arousal on the other is most paramount and threatening to team interaction processes. Being aware of these processes allows individuals to better understand and interpret their own and other people's affective states.

Trust in Multicultural Teams

Emotions and feelings seem to play an important role in the development of trust and assessment of other people's trustworthiness (Williams, 2001). McAllister (1995) and Lewis and Weigert (1985) for instance show the effects of people's affective states on the evaluation of other people's trustworthiness. This is important, as a number of studies have consistently shown the positive effects of interpersonal trust on cooperation and interaction (e.g. Blau, 1964; Druskat & Wolff, 2001; Jones & George, 1998). Especially in the initial stages of team formation, attention must be paid to the development of trust between team members as it forms the basis for team identity, effective interaction and integration. Trust in other people is defined as 'the willingness of a party to be vulnerable to the actions of another party based on the expectation that the other will perform a particular action important to the trustor, irrespective of the ability to monitor or control that other party' (Mayer *et al.*, 1995: 712). It is based on perceptions of the others' ability to bring about positive outcomes, and the others' willingness to act in accordance with one's values and in the best interest of the people involved in the interaction.

The cultural diversity inherent in multicultural teams may impede the development of trust, as perceptions of social distance and different group membership reduce perceptions of trustworthiness and the willingness to trust (e.g. Buchan et al., 2002; Zolin et al., 2004). Thus, intercultural competence also entails the ability to build trust between people with different cultural backgrounds, thereby facilitating relationship building in the multicultural team. Similar to emotion expression, differences exist between cultures with regard to non-verbal symbols indicating trust and trustworthiness. Hence, individuals also need to develop an understanding of trust-eliciting behaviour and actions signalling trustworthiness, and how these behaviours and actions differ across cultures.

ICOPROMO Activity 'Why do I trust you?'

In the activity 'Why do I trust you?' students become aware of the factors determining perceived trustworthiness, and how they differ across cultures. Following a short introduction when participants present themselves in front of a small group of trainees, they select at least two factors from the worksheet (Exhibit 5.1) that make the person trustworthy in their eyes.

The results are compared in the small groups. A class discussion follows during which the facilitator draws attention to the question, why factors such as age, gender, social status and education may influence the level of initial trust granted to a 'stranger'. This discussion creates an awareness of the fact that unfamiliar behaviour, dissimilar appearance and different social conventions may inhibit the formation of initial trust. Furthermore, participants become alert to the importance of being open to the unfamiliar and offering a leap of faith to what is unknown to them. In the subsequent discussion, the trainees reflect on behaviours that, in their view, help to build trust in a multicultural team (Exhibit 5.2).

Training Objectives and Approach

The purpose of the activities designed for emotion management is to explore the role of emotions in organisational life in general, and multicultural teams in particular. Participants have the opportunity to reflect on their own positive and negative emotions they bring to multicultural settings and the resulting behaviour. Empathy is increased

Worksheet: Why do I trust you? – Part I

Trust Factors

Trust is an important prerequisite for working in multicultural teams. When meeting a person for the first time, we usually develop initial trust based on certain characteristics a person displays. These characteristics may vary across cultures. Try to find out in your team whether there are any cultural differences related to initial trust.

Based on the previous activity, indicate for each member of your group the factors that render this person trustworthy. Mark a minimum of two and a maximum of four characteristics.

Name					
Pleasant physical appearance					
Age					
Gender					
Perceived similarity					
Education and experience					
Social status					
Family background					
Ability, know how and expertise					
Social competence					
Friendliness					
Communication Skills					
Openness					
Appreciation and respect					
Credibility					
Positive feelings / likeability					
Voice					
Persuasiveness					

Additional remarks:

_____

_____

_____

_____

Exhibit 5.1: Why do I trust you? – Part I

Emotional Management

> **Worksheet: Why do I trust you? – Part II**

Trustworthy Behaviours

It is widely mentioned in the bibliography focused on teamwork that there are specific factors that contribute to building trust in a multicultural group (and therefore help it turn into a team). The most widely mentioned, directly or indirectly, are the following:

- focus on the task
- share information
- express feelings
- share values
- reach conclusions via consensus
- agree on procedures
- make sure everyone understands what the tasks and procedures are all about
- develop personal/social relations within the group/team
- take responsibility on one's task
- share new ideas
- write down all decisions and relevant participants' contributions
- encourage communication
- avoid conflict
- establish rules of interaction between group/team members
- strong leadership
- other(s) _____

1. Single out which of the above factors you didn't mention.
2. Complete the list with other factors you mentioned but are not included in the list above.
3. Select five factors, amongst them all, which you find most important. In your small group, explain your choice.

Select those five you find least relevant. Again, explain the choice to your fellow group members.

Exhibit 5.2: Why do I trust you? – Part II

as individuals learn to sense others' emotions and understand where they are coming from. In comparing their own emotional responses and affective behaviours to those of people from other cultures in similar situations, they can identify culturally learned patterns of emotion regulation and become aware of the cultural differences that exist with regard to emotion expression. In addition, they discuss alternative ways of responding to emotionally charged situations.

The main objective of the activities developed for the topic of emotion management is therefore to create awareness and understanding of these issues among participants, to develop emotion recognition and management skills, as well as coping mechanisms for dealing effectively with emotions in multicultural team settings. Most importantly, cultural influences on emotions and emotion management are addressed, making individuals aware of the ways in which cultural diversity adds complexity to effective emotion management in teams.

The activities in this section employ a variety of experiential learning methods with the aim of getting individual participants involved. Apart from journal assignments, self-awareness inventories are used alongside small group discussions. As suggested by Brown and Knight (1999), self-awareness inventories serve as a starting point to bring to the surface latent issues such as behavioural styles in expressing certain emotions. Furthermore, role plays, simulation games and critical incidents are employed and allow for experiencing and expressing emotions in the training setting. Based on the insights gained, individuals are motivated to change; they can experiment with and develop alternative responses. This training approach should encourage interpersonal sensitivity and self-reflection (McCaffery, 1995; Wight, 1995).

Dealing with emotions in a training setting is of course not without risk. The issues addressed are highly personal and in themselves evoke strong emotional responses that the trainers need to understand and cope with. In order to develop the necessary skills to deal with emotions in multicultural teams effectively, individuals have to experiment, be open to feedback and analyse their own and others' behaviour. A great amount of emotional self-awareness and openness on the part of the participants and also the trainers is thus required. This openness will be rewarded as participants find out that others share similar experiences and the accompanying feelings, such as frustration, anxiety, fear or joy.

The activities on emotion management frequently involve self-reflection as well as interpersonal reflection, incorporating the need to share personal and emotional experiences in small and possibly diverse groups. This may make people feel uncomfortable and vulnerable (Khuri, 2004). Hence, the facilitator has to create a safe environment characterised by high levels of trust between the facilitator and the participants, as well as among participants. Individuals must have equal status within the group and develop respect and appreciation for each other.

In addition, great responsibility lies with the trainer as she/he structures, manages and guides the discussions. Thus, it is essential that the trainer possesses strong facilitation and process skills as well as sensitivity to the trainees' needs. When emotions surface, the trainer has to display sensitive behaviour in order to avoid resistance and frustration on the part of the trainees. Although the success of the activities frequently depends on the participants' ability and willingness to express their individual views openly, the facilitator has to acknowledge and accept an individual's decision not to share specific experiences.

Conclusion

Emotion management in multicultural teams is an important topic for the development of intercultural competence. Interpreting and making sense of emotions is difficult because of culturally determined emotion display rules. In addition, adapting to new and unfamiliar cultural values, practices and behaviour can be emotionally challenging. Social categorisation processes and stereotyping may also bring about negative attitudes in individual team members and thus create resistance and conflict. This impacts the performance of the team. Individuals have to learn to understand the sophisticated processes underlying affective responses in intercultural interactions and have to develop ways to deal with them effectively.

Team members need to be able to interpret others' and their own emotions accurately and take appropriate action. By means of experiential learning, team members manage to identify and challenge their own and other participants' emotional responses in multicultural team settings, thereby increasing their confidence when dealing with their own and others' emotions.

References

Ashforth, B.E. and Humphrey, R.H. (1995) Emotion in the workplace: A reappraisal. *Human Relations* 48 (2), 97–125.

Ashforth, B.E. and Mael, F. (1989) Social identity theory and the organization. *Academy of Management Review* 14 (1), 20–39.

Ashkanasy, N.M. (2003) Emotions in organizations: A multi-level perspective. *Research in Multi-Level Issues* 2, 9–54.

Ashkanasy, N.M., Härtel, C.E.J. and Daus, C.S. (2002) Diversity and emotion: The new frontiers in organizational behavior research. *Journal of Management* 28 (3), 307–338.

Ashkanasy, N.M., Härtel, C.E.J. and Zerbe, W.J. (2000) Emotions in the workplace: Research, theory, and practice. In N.M. Ashkanasy, C.E.J. Härtel and W.J. Zerbe (eds) *Emotions in the Workplace: Research, Theory, and Practice* (pp. 3–18). Westport, CT: Quorum Books.

Averill, J.R., Chon, K.K. and Hahn, D.W. (2001) Emotions and creativity, East and West. *Asian Journal of Social Psychology* 4 (3), 165–183.

Barsade, S.G. (2002) The ripple effect: Emotional contagion and its influence on group behavior. *Administrative Science Quarterly* 47 (4), 644–675.

Barsade, S.G., Ward, A.J., Turner, J.D.F. and Sonnenfeld, J.A. (2000) To your heart's content: A model of affective diversity in top management teams. *Administrative Science Quarterly* 45, 802–836.

Bartel, C.A. and Saavedra, R. (2000) The collective construction of work group moods. *Administrative Science Quarterly* 45 (2), 197–231.

Blau, P.M. (1964) *Exchange and Power in Social Life*. New York: Wiley.

Brief, A.P. and Weiss, H.M. (2002) Organizational behavior: Affect in the workplace. *Annual Review of Psychology* 53, 279–307.

Brown, C. and Knight, K. (1999) Introduction to self-awareness inventories. In S.M. Fowler and M.G. Mumford (eds) *Intercultural Sourcebook: Cross-Cultural Training Methods* (Vol. 2) (pp. 19–30). Yarmouth, ME: Intercultural Press.

Brown, R.B. (2003) Emotions and behavior: Exercises in emotional intelligence. *Journal of Management Education* 27 (1), 122–134.

Buchan, N.R., Croson, R.T.A. and Dawes, R.M. (2002) Swift neighbors and persistent strangers: A cross-cultural investigation of trust and reciprocity in social exchange. *American Journal of Sociology* 108 (1), 168–206.

Chen, G.M. and Starosta, W.J. (1996) Intercultural communication competence: A synthesis. *Communication Yearbook* 19, 353–383.

Connolly, J.J. and Viswesvaran, C. (2000) The role of affectivity in job satisfaction: A meta-analysis. *Personality and Individual Differences* 29 (2), 265–281.

Druskat, V.U. and Wolff, S.B. (2001) Building the emotional intelligence of groups. *Harvard Business Review* 79 (3), 80–90.

Ekman, P. (1972) Universal and cultural differences in facial expressions of emotion. In J. Cole (ed.) *Nebraska Symposium on Motivation, 1971: Vol. 19* (pp. 207–283). Lincoln, NB: University of Nebraska Press.

Feyerherm, A.E. and Rice, C.L. (2002) Emotional intelligence and team performance: The good, the bad and the ugly. *International Journal of Organizational Analysis* 10 (4), 343–362.

Fineman, S. (2003) *Understanding Emotion at Work*. London: Sage.

Fisher, C.D. and Ashkanasy, N.M. (2000) The emerging role of emotions in work life: An introduction. *Journal of Organizational Behavior* 21 (2), 123–129.

Garcia-Prieto, P., Bellard, E. and Schneider, S.C. (2003) Experiencing diversity, conflict, and emotions in teams. *Applied Psychology: An International Review* 52 (3), 413–440.

Goleman, D. (1995) *Emotional Intelligence*. New York: Bantam Books.

Goleman, D., Boyatzis, R. and McKee, A. (2002) *Primal Leadership: Realizing the Power of Emotional Intelligence*. Boston, MA: Harvard University Press.

Hilton, J.L. and von Hippel, W. (1996) Stereotypes. *Annual Review of Psychology* 47 (1), 237–271.
Jones, G.R. and George, J.M. (1998) The experience and evolution of trust: Implications for cooperation and teamwork. *Academy of Management Review* 23 (3), 532–546.
Jordan, P.J. and Troth, A.C. (2004) Managing emotions during team problem solving: Emotional intelligence and conflict resolution. *Human Performance* 17 (2), 195–218.
Jussim, L., Nelson, T.E., Manis, M. and Soffin, S. (1995) Prejudice, stereotypes, and labeling effects: Sources of bias in person perception. *Journal of Personality and Social Psychology* 68, 228–246.
Kelly, J.R. and Barsade, S.G. (2001) Mood and emotions in small groups and work teams. *Organizational Behavior and Human Decision Processes* 86 (1), 99–130.
Khuri, L.M. (2004) Working with emotion in educational intergroup dialogue. *International Journal of Intercultural Relations* 28, 595–612.
Levy, J. (1995) Intercultural training design. In S.M. Fowler and M.G. Mumford (eds) *Intercultural Sourcebook: Cross-cultural Training Methods* (Vol. 1) (pp. 1–15). Yarmouth, NB: Intercultural Press.
Lewis, D.J. and Weigert, A. (1985) Trust as a social reality. *Social Forces* 63 (4), 967–985.
Matsumoto, D., Consolacion, T., Yamada, H., Suzuki, R., Franklin, B., Paul, S., Ray, R. and Uchida, H. (2002) American-Japanese cultural differences in judgements of emotional expressions of different intensities. *Cognition and Emotion* 16 (6), 721–747.
Matsumoto, D., Takeuchi, S., Andayani, S., Kouznetsova, N. and Krupp, D. (1998) The contribution of Individualism vs. Collectivism to cross-national differences in display rules. *Asian Journal of Social Psychology* 1 (2), 147–165.
Mayer, J.D., Caruso, D.R. and Salovey, P. (1999) Emotional intelligence meets traditional standards for an intelligence. *Intelligence* 27 (4), 267–298.
Mayer, R.C., Davis, J.H. and Schoorman, D.F. (1995) An integrative model of organizational trust. *Academy of Management Review* 20 (3), 709–734.
McAllister, D.J. (1995) Affect- and cognition-based trust as foundations for interpersonal cooperation in organizations. *Academy of Management Journal* 28 (1), 24–59.
McCaffery, J.A. (1995) The role play: A powerful but difficult training tool. In S.M. Fowler and M.G. Mumford (eds) *Intercultural Sourcebook: Cross-cultural Training Methods* (Vol. 1) (pp. 17–25). Yarmouth, NB: Intercultural Press.
Milliken, F.J. and Martins, L. (1996) Searching for common threads: Understanding the multiple effects of diversity in organizational groups. *Academy of Management Review* 21 (2), 402–433.
Mowday, R.T. and Sutton, R.I. (1993) Organizational behavior: Linking individuals and groups to organizational contexts. *Annual Review of Psychology* 44, 195–229.
Offermann, L.R., Bailey, J.R., Vasilopoulos, N.L. and Seal, C. (2004) The relative contribution of emotional competence and cognitive ability to individual and team performance. *Human Performance* 17 (2), 219–243.
O'Reilly, C.A.I., Caldwell, D.F. and Barnett, W.P. (1989) Work group demography, social integration, and turnover. *Administrative Science Quarterly* 34 (1), 21–37.

Peslak, A.R. (2005) Emotions and team projects and processes. *Team Performance Management* 11 (7/8), 251–262.

Rapisarda, B.A. (2002) The impact of emotional intelligence on work team cohesiveness and performance. *International Journal of Organizational Analysis* 10 (4), 363–379.

Renjun, Q. and Ziang, Z. (2005) Work group emotions in Chinese culture settings. *Singapore Management Review* 27 (1), 69–86.

Saavedra, R. and Van Dyne, L. (1999) Social exchange and emotional investment in work groups. *Motivation and Emotion* 23 (2), 105–123.

Salovey, P. and Mayer, J.D. (1990) Emotional intelligence. *Imagination, Cognition and Personality* 9 (3), 185–211.

Schutte, N.S., Malouff, J.M., Bobik, C., Coston, T.D., Greeson, C., Jedlicka, C. and Rhodes, E. (2001) Emotional intelligence and interpersonal relations. *Journal of Social Psychology* 141 (4), 523–536.

Tajfel, H. and Turner, J.C. (1986) The social identity theory of intergroup behavior. In S. Worchel and W.G. Austin (eds) *Psychology of Intergroup Relations* (pp. 7–24). Chicago, IL: Nelson-Hall.

Totterdell, P., Kellett, S., Teuchmann, K. and Briner, R.B. (1998) Evidence of mood linkage in work groups. *Journal of Personality and Social Psychology* 74 (6), 1504–1515.

Trompenaars, F. (1993) *Riding the Waves of Culture: Understanding Cultural Diversity in Business*. London: Nicholas Brealey Publishing.

Tsai, J.L. and Chentsova-Dutton, Y. (2003) Variation among European Americans in emotional facial expression. *Journal of Cross-Cultural Psychology* 34 (6), 650–657.

Tsui, A.S., Egan, T.D. and O'Reilly, C.A.I. (1992) Being different: Relational demography and organizational attachment. *Administrative Science Quarterly* 37 (4), 549–579.

Watson, W.E., Kumar, K. and Michaelsen, L.K. (1993) Cultural diversity's impact on interaction process and performance: Comparing homogeneous and diverse task groups. *Academy of Management Journal* 36 (3), 590–602.

Wight, A.R. (1995) The critical incident as a training tool. In S.M. Fowler and M.G. Mumford (eds) *Intercultural Sourcebook: Cross-cultural Training Methods* (Vol. 1) (pp. 127–139). Yarmouth, NB: Intercultural Press.

Williams, M. (2001) In whom we trust: Group membership as an affective context for trust development. *Academy of Management Review* 26 (3), 377–396.

Williams, M. (2007) Building genuine trust through interpersonal emotion management: A threat regulation model of trust and collaboration across boundaries. *Academy of Management Review* 32 (2), 595–621.

Zolin, R., Hinds, P.J., Fruchter, R. and Levitt, R.E. (2004) Interpersonal trust in cross-functional, geographically distributed work: A longitudinal study. *Information and Organization* 14 (1), 1–26.

Chapter 6
Intercultural Interaction: A Sense-making Approach

TERENCE MUGHAN and GREG O'SHEA

Introduction

Intercultural interactions are events where people from different cultures communicate, either face-to-face or using technology. Since the early 1990s, they have significantly increased in volume because of the increased mobility of products, services and labour and will do so in the future given the on-going globalisation of business ventures, immigration patterns and other social changes. The patterns of intercultural interaction in the workplace today are no longer characterised by the expatriation model that informed so much intercultural thinking in the past. Foreign direct investment, labour mobility at all levels and electronic communication have all increased massively since the collapse of the Berlin Wall (Wall & Rees, 2004). In a global environment characterised by complexity and ambiguity, one certainty about the future of organisations is that they are becoming increasingly multicultural and people will need to know more about culture and cultural differences to be effective in their everyday working lives by working in communities, groups or teams of other colleagues or professionals. The social context in which we live makes the understanding of intercultural interaction a prerequisite for those who aspire to successful careers.

Theoretical Rationale

In designing training materials for the ICOPROMO project, the authors interpreted intercultural interaction as a theme involving teleological processes and based on real situations in the workplace. These situations often feature problems or misunderstandings and require of individuals the ability to communicate effectively to solve the problem. In interacting, the learner is required to demonstrate the ability to draw on and select from the knowledge and skills accumulated in learning and training to produce an appropriate response to interlocutors and other stimuli, such as problems or dilemmas. ICOPROMO was a comprehensive training programme that included all the cognitive, affective, linguistic and social preparation necessary in accompanying modules. The purpose of this theme was to plunge the learner into situations where they have to produce the appropriate intellectual and behavioural response to complex stimuli. Therefore, the training activities for intercultural interactions were integrative in nature and often included elements of many of the accompanying themes, as well as other key issues in the workplace, such as strategy, leadership and change. This holistic approach is somewhat at odds with earlier forms of intercultural training. In this approach, the concept of cultural difference is interpreted as a sovereign one that has to be considered as a critical, independent factor in communication and interaction. If there is a misunderstanding between a British person and a German person, cultural difference must be the cause of it. The weaknesses in this assumption are evident yet often overlooked. Such misunderstandings can just as easily be attributed to personality, power, role or financial differences between the parties, to name just a few of the possibilities.

Of course, organisational experience and theory exist as generic concepts independently of (and some would say pre-date) the intercultural era and reality. The training activities dealing with interaction should reflect this holistic theoretical and experiential reality in order to be relevant to learners. As the ICOPROMO project developed, it came to incorporate additional theoretical perspectives on communication. The process of interacting with other cultures in a work environment takes place in a context that is defined by commercial, organisational or professional goals and structures. The individual and his/her objectives and needs are framed by this and the need to reconcile personal considerations with organisational messages and imperatives. In order to act appropriately, the individual needs to make sense of these messages and imperatives and that is not always straightforward or shared with other individuals (Adler, 2001).

Sense making

One element of organisational theory that has received much attention in recent decades is sense making. We hold that sense making has much to offer the field of intercultural theory and has much in common with it. Weick *et al.* (2005) posit that sense making is an issue of language, talk and communication, and that situations, organisations and environments are talked into existence. Moreover, sense making is particularly located in experience and interaction and the individual's responses to unexpected stimuli or incomprehensible events. Sense making is about the interplay of action and interpretation and in this respect forms an important element of intercultural interaction, where individuals are required to adjust to data and events that are not part of their expectations (Weick et al., 2005). This chapter will examine the role of sense making in intercultural interactions within the newly formed management and production teams of the BMW/Rover organisation in the second half of the 1990s and its place in the training activity designed for the ICOPROMO programme.

The underlying approach to the development of the training activities was a social constructivist one, whereby learning is an active process where learners should learn to discover principles, concepts and facts for themselves (Ackerman, 1996; Brown et al., 1989). In learning to interact with other cultures, principles of early learning are replicated at least in part and individuals make meanings through interactions with each other and with the environment they live in. Knowledge is thus a product of humans and is socially and culturally constructed (Ernest, 1991; Prawat & Floden, 1994). This approach, combined with the formative experiences encountered in the other sections of the project, acknowledges that each individual would have a unique response to the data (in the form of text, case study, video, etc.), drawing on personal experience and knowledge of theory. The BMW-Rover training activity is designed to encourage this and allow students to exchange interpretations and share meaning as part of the exercise.

In individuals, sense making is the largely cognitive activity of constructing a hypothetical mental model of the current situation and how it might evolve over time, what threats and opportunities for each action are likely to emerge from this evolution, what potential actions can be taken in response, what the projected outcomes of those responses are and what values drive the choice of future action. In organisations, sense making is a collaborative process of creating shared awareness and understanding out of different individuals' perspectives and varied interests (Weick, 2000). The process of moving from situational awareness in individuals to shared awareness and understanding to collaborative decision making can be considered a socio-cognitive activity in that the individual's cognitive activities are directly impacted by the social nature of the exchange and vice versa.

Klein et al. (2006) have presented a theory of sense making as a set of processes that is initiated when an individual or organisation recognises the inadequacy of their current understanding of events. Sense making is an active two-way process of fitting data into a frame (mental model) and fitting a frame around the data. Neither data nor frame comes first; data evoke frames and frames select and connect data. When there is no adequate fit, the data may be reconsidered or an existing frame may be revised. This description resembles the recognition-metacognition model (Cohen *et al.*, 1996), which describes the metacognitive processes that are used by individuals to build, verify and modify working models (or 'stories') in situational awareness to account for an unrecognised situation. Weick *et al.* (2005) identify the key characteristics of sense making. It:

- Organises flux – sense making starts with chaos in the form of overwhelming data and the individual's need to begin to order it.
- Starts with noticing and bracketing – the individual encounters phenomena that have no name and needs to create a framework for it.
- Is about labelling – these phenomena have to be given labels to permit communication and plausible acts of management.
- Is retrospective – when we encounter a problem, we observe then act. Understanding comes later.
- Is about presumption – to make sense is to connect the abstract and the concrete.
- Is social and systemic – the environment influences norms among groups.
- Is about action – uncertainty is met by action – what is going on? What do I do next?
- Is about organising through communication – communication is central to organisational sense making.

We see here clear areas of interface between sense-making theory and intercultural theory. The role of communication, generalisation, ambiguity, reflection and adaptation are present in both fields, as are the surrounding phenomena of the environment and the influence it exerts on the choices and actions of the individual. This framework provides a useful support for the theory of intercultural interaction in organisations. Gudykunst (1991) stated that, as communities become ever more complex, it is essential that we go beyond an emphasis on increasing knowledge about individual cultures to an emphasis on increasing knowledge concerning intercultural interaction. The ability to deal with the tasks, problems and opportunities that organisations and society will face in the future requires not only knowledge that many cultures exist, but also knowledge of how cultures interact with each other and how this interaction can occur in a positive, productive manner. A basic goal is to encourage learners to think carefully, in an in-depth manner, about the influences of culture in their own lives and in the lives of other people. People can prepare themselves by learning to deal with understanding cultural differences and with communication across cultural boundaries.

Tools for doing this include identifying cultural influences on their own behaviour, searching for culturally based reasons in their intercultural encounters, to analyse critical incidents that depict people in intercultural encounters that involve a misunderstanding or a difficulty. These processes entail the development of cognitive and affective attributes, such as tolerance of ambiguity, active listening and mindfulness (Gudykunst *et al.*, 1996).

One of the guidelines to understanding culture is that it becomes clear in 'well-meaning clashes' (Brislin, 2000). People from different cultures come together and want to interact in a sensitive and effective manner. They may have the reputation of possessing considerable social skills in their own culture. Yet after an intercultural encounter, people feel that the interaction did not go smoothly. The difficulties people face during intercultural interactions can be captured in critical incidents and then used as a highly effective communication tool. Critical incidents are short stories that describe individuals and give some background about them. A plot line is developed, and there is an ending to the incident that involves a misunderstanding among people and/or the feeling that the intercultural interaction did not proceed as smoothly as people hoped. Learners are asked to identify reasons for the misunderstanding and to identify the cultural difference that may be involved. People can learn to think about their own cultures and to identify aspects of their cultures that have provided guidance for selected behaviours. With this important set of self-insights, they can look on the behaviour of other people in other cultures in a more sophisticated manner. While observing other people's behaviour, we make attributions, i.e. based on our cultural background and past experiences we give meaning to these behaviours as part of the sense-making process. Because we all have a unique background and set of experiences, meaning is relative and therefore sense making is relative. The same behaviour can be given different meanings by different people, and sometimes we may attribute a wrong meaning to the behaviour we have observed. Interactions of all kinds generate the need to make sense and this process is even more complex when different cultures are involved in the interaction.

The BMW/Rover case study was therefore designed to develop awareness of sense-making tools that improve interaction in intercultural working situations. The activity, which was classified as an 'experiential-culture-specific' one by Cushner and Brislin (1997), provides evidence of how the employees of BMW and Rover, in interacting across cultures, behaved in the face of data and phenomena that made little sense to them. These characteristics will be used to discuss the training activity and the place of sense making in intercultural interaction.

The Training Activity

The purpose of this activity is to enable students to test their sense-making abilities on a real company case. The case presents a multi-layered set of data within which aspects of cultural difference are embedded alongside strategic, financial and political issues. Students are asked to unpack these issues and weigh intercultural issues appropriately in order to develop sense-making skills. Participants will apply earlier learning to an integrated case illustrating intercultural behaviour within a complex organisational and management situation. They will learn to assess the relationship between personal, organisational and national perspectives. The role of concepts such as communication styles, power relationships and personal mobility will be assessed as elements in a complex professional situation.

THE CASE OF BMW/ROVER (abridged)

Introduction

In 1994 BMW purchased the Rover Group from British Aerospace for £800 million. In 1999 it sold Rover to the Phoenix Group for £10. In between, many discussions and conflicts took place within the new organisation and with the British government to make the new organisation commercially viable. The suspicion that it could never be so, and the historical distrust of Germans by many sections of the British population and media, made this a very unhappy alliance. Speculation and rumours flourished on the political, organisational and interpersonal levels as German and British politicians, executives, engineers and apprentices tried to work together productively. The daily reality these people experienced cannot be properly understood without a knowledge of the cultural and organisational background that impinged so directly on the tasks and problems they faced. At the same time, their fate was being influenced by considerations of global corporate strategy and competition in a highly competitive industry.

Company Culture

In many ways the two companies were opposites of each other. The Rover Group has a long and chequered history. It itself began life in the early twentieth century as an independent company making mid to upper range cars. In the post-war years it was merged in with a number of other brands in an inefficient and politically driven nationalised organisation. Years of inefficiencies and labour unrest followed.

At the end of the 1970's, Britain underwent a political sea-change as the Conservative government of Margaret Thatcher set about dismantling the post-war industrial settlement. Rover was sold off to British Aerospace for £150 million as the Government tired of trying to make the company efficient and viable. Another was a partnership with the Japanese company Honda, which went a long way to improving engine quality and production efficiency. The company focussed its efforts on the volume car market, small to mid-range saloons competing with the likes of Ford, Toyota, Renault and Fiat.

The origins of BMW trace back to 1913 when Karl Friedrich Rapp, a Bavarian who had been a well-known engineer in a German aircraft company, formed Rapp Motoren Werke in a suburb of Munich. The company specialized in airplane engines. However, Rapp found that they were problematic and suffered from excessive vibration. Nearby, Gustav Otto, also an airplane specialist, set up his own shop, Gustav Flugmaschinenfabrik, building small aircraft.

In 1959 the company was ailing and Daimler-Benz made a bid for it. Herbert Quandt, the Chairman, increased his holding and retained family control of the company. What is still essentially a family company has, since the 1970's, become a leading world-brand from a German base with all of the features of a German organisation. Quality of engineering is at the core of its processes and it now rivals Mercedes-Benz at the top end of the market in Germany and across the world. The company's desire to extend its reach beyond its manufacturing centres in Germany continued with its bid to buy the Rover Group in 1994.

The reasons for BMW's acquisition of Rover have been much discussed. The German company's desire to exend its product range and geographical dealer network had a lot to do with it. BMW appeared however to under-estimate the capital required to make Rover viable and Rover gradually became disillusioned, particularly the Longbridge plant.

Review of the final days

After much negotiation, within BMW and with the British and German governments, BMW decided to sell Rover at a nominal fee in order to rid itself of the chronically loss-making parts of the 'English Patient'. It also claimed the high value of the pound had contributed to the failure to make Rover succeed. However, BMW held on to many prize assets, including the Land Rover, Mini, MG and Triumph brands and the efficient Cowley plant. It would go on to sell Land Rover to Ford for more than twice the amount it paid for Rover in 1994 and to manufacture a new model Mini at the Cowley plant.

EVIDENCE OF INTERACTION

The following quotations are taken from a transcript of a BBC broadcast which followed the course of the BMW acquisition of the Rover group. They are not meant to be an authoritative representation of either reality or of the BBC transmission. This particular episode was entitled 'Bonding' and depicted what happened on three levels of the organisation when executives, engineers and apprentices began to interact with their foreign partners. In spite of some notable exceptions, the picture painted is one of an organisation in crisis where attempts to build a common culture on the shopfloor and in the research labs are undermined by the failure of top management to give or make sense to each other. Some talk of integration while others appear more intent on separation from or subordination of the partner.

Views of BMW and Rover employees expressed during their exchange programmes or in daily relations with their foreign partners: All the quotations that follow were uttered in English, which was by far the dominant language of communication at all levels.

British Executive
(After handling a telephone call from a German newspaper wanting to know why Rover Chief Executive John Towers had resigned). "That's interesting. They are coming at it from the angle that he was forced to resign. I explained he wanted to spend more time with his family."

German Executive
"BMW-Rover is a match made in heaven. One day they will see how obvious it was."

British Engineer
"As British company, when faced with a problem as an engineer, we are used to finding a quick, cheap solution. The Germans do it differently. They look for the best solution, no matter how much it costs."

German Engineer
"The British are flexible, that's true. We Germans look for rules. If we don't find any, we make some. But now we are working together and that is good. Yes, the British are beginning to become a little German and vice versa."

German Apprentice
"We wanted the British apprentices to do the computer design work but they couldn't handle it, so we had to do it."

British Apprentice
(i) "The German apprentices don't have as much fun as we do. We like taking the Mickey out of each other but they are too serious."
(ii) "We tried to follow the talk but it was all in German. I understood a couple of words like 'franchising' but that was all."

Points for Discussion

(1) Why did BMW purchase Rover?
(2) In HR terms, was BMW's exchange programme well-intended? What were its probable benefits and drawbacks?
(3) Which cultural differences emerge in this story (on the political, organisational and interpersonal levels)? Discuss the importance of the following concepts and others you think play a part:
- foreign language competence and use;
- national stereotypes;
- awareness of the Self and the Other;
- relationship-building;
- power in relationships and communication.

> (4) Which factors, apart from cultural difference, might explain the tensions between the companies and the countries?
> (5) Given what we now know about this case, rank all factors (cultural, political, business) in terms of their importance in explaining the failed merger. Explain your decisions.
> (6) Reflect on the role of training (language, intercultural etc) in an organisation such as BMW/Rover. What, as a training consultant, would you consider to be realistic aspirations in undertaking such work? What obstacles to the achievement of your objectives would you anticipate and how would you respond when you encounter them?

The training activity required students to gain a factual knowledge of the case by reading the materials and conducting further research on-line and in the library. They then read the above quotations from the video and, in groups, discussed the situation and views of the employees with a view to understanding how the latter were perceiving events around them. They were asked to identify and categorise intercultural issues and place them within a broad context of interaction. This entailed attributing communication and relationship problems to either cultural difference or to other causes, such as strategy, leadership, politics or personality.

Our experience of piloting and using this activity for training has been very satisfactory. Students have enjoyed the experience of 'picking out' intercultural phenomena from real-life exchanges and discussing the relative role of culture in making sense of complex events in a large business organisation. Great sympathy for employees of the BMW-Rover organisation was expressed. The difficulty they were having adapting to the new structure was clear for all to see, as was their genuine energy and effort to do so. The complexity of the causes was also evident. The strategic changes at the top of BMW, the poor foreign language skills of the British employees, the differing approaches to engineering standards and the varying levels of personal commitment to the project on the part of key BMW and Rover executives all played a part in creating mixed messages and values. Culture (including language) was just one of the reasons for the incidences of poor intercultural interaction. This 'relativisation' of culture within the business sphere as one of many possible causes of misunderstandings or disruption of the work of cross-national organisations and teams has been the key learning point on all occasions when the activity has been used. When students are asked to explore training solutions for the problems they have witnessed, they address both individual and organisational levels of the problem, proposing actions at all levels of the company.

Conclusions

Data about intercultural interaction in organisations can be difficult to obtain and present in such a way as to replicate the experience of the real BMW-Rover employees. At best it will be documented in written and video form drawn from a variety of sources. Sometimes key data will be confidential and cannot be reproduced for training purposes. This may lead to reservations about the validity of the interpretation of events and the value of the exercise. However, this is quite normal in case study-based learning and one needs to remember that it is the concepts that form the key learning points, not the case (or the company) itself.

The BMW-Rover case illustrates an important fact about organisations in the global era. Where intercultural action takes place, the interaction is not only intercultural. The organisation is subject to a range of other stimuli, constraints and imperatives that are interlaced with intercultural factors, influencing and being influenced by them. Understanding intercultural interaction and training people to do so entails a recognition of this larger picture by incorporating data and concepts that frame or are framed by the intercultural perspective. In the case of BMW-Rover, these data are strategic (BMW as a global player in the automotive industry), political (Rover and the history of government intervention in the industry), financial (as a driver of different behavioural practices) and personality-oriented (executives as leaders and rivals). Some degree of comfort with these concepts is therefore required to place intercultural interaction in context and make sense of a complex situation. In this respect, intercultural training has moved on from the controlled and limited situations (hotel, family, office, restaurant) portrayed in manuals of the 1970s and 1980s to the multi-layered, integrated kinds of situations we witnessed at BMW-Rover. In portraying and preparing people for intercultural interaction in complex organisations, it is not possible or indeed desirable to present interaction as being exclusively intercultural and eliminating all surrounding cognitive stimulus that is not primarily 'intercultural' by nature. When the personality, the political, the financial and the strategic interfere, additional tools are required to enable the employee to interpret events and behaviour. We argue that sense-making theory offers the potential for the development of tools that are compatible with intercultural theory and add value to it. More research and effort is required to develop integrated training materials in this field, but our work on ICOPROMO would suggest that we could start by:

(1) Incorporating organisational background into the scenario, in the form of strategic, historical and leadership data.
(2) Drawing on a range of sources, primary and secondary, written and video.
(3) Promoting an understanding of tools (drawn from human resources and organisational theory) to understand and improve organisational development and individual performance.
(4) Within this framework, valorising and relativising intercultural theory as a key dimension of sense making.

References

Ackerman, P.L. (1996) A theory of adult intellectual development: Process, personality, interests, and knowledge. *Intelligence* 22 (2), 227–257.
Adler, N. (2001) *International Dimensions of Organizational Behavior*. Boston, MS: PWS-Kent.
Brislin, R. (2000) *Understanding Culture's Influence on Behavior*. Fort Worth, TX: Harcourt.
Brown, J.S., Collins, A. and Duguid, P. (1989) Situated cognition and the culture of learning. *Educational Researcher* 18, 32–42.
Cohen, L.B., Gilbert, K. and Brown, P.S. (1996) Infants' understanding of solidity: Replicating a failure to replicate. *Infant Behavior and Development* 19 (1), 206–219.
Cushner, R. and Brislin, K. (eds) (1997) *Improving Intercultural Interactions: Modules for Cross-cultural Training Programs* (Vol. 2). Thousand Oaks, CA: Sage.
Ernest, P. (1991) *The Philosophy of Mathematics Education*. London: Falmer Press.
Gudykunst, W.B. (1991) *Bridging Differences. Effective Intergroup Communication*. Newbury Park, CA: Sage.
Gudykunst, W.B., Guzley, R.M. and Hammer, M.R. (1996) Designing intercultural training. In D. Landis and R.S. Bhakat (eds) *Handbook of Intercultural Training* (pp. 61–80). Thousand Oaks, CA: Sage.
Klein, G., Moon, B. and Hoffman, R.F. (2006) Making sense of sensemaking: A macrocognitive model. *IEEE Intelligent Systems* 21 (5), 88–92.
Prawat, R.S. and Floden, R.E. (1994) Philosophical perspectives on constructivist views of learning. *Educational Psychologist* 29 (1), 37–48.
Wall, S. and Rees, B. (2004) *International Business* (2nd edn). New York: Prentice Hall/Financial Times.
Weick, K.E. (2000) *Making Sense of the Organization*. Oxford: Blackwell Publishing Professional.
Weick, K.E., Sutcliffe, K.M. and Obstfeld, D. (2005) Organizing and the process of sensemaking. *Organization Science* 16 (4), 409–421.

Chapter 7
Communicative Interaction: Intercultural Verbal and Nonverbal Interaction

MARÍA LUISA PÉREZ CAÑADO and
MARÍA DEL CARMEN MÉNDEZ GARCÍA

Introduction

Working adequately in multicultural teams is fast becoming 'the sine qua non for global success', as Marquardt and Horvarth (2001: 4) put it. An important number of factors come into play in guaranteeing success in the multicultural workplace, all of which have been examined in depth in the ICOPROMO Project and are explored through the different chapters of this second section. Communicative interaction is crucial in multicultural team dynamics, alongside other aspects such as sense making, perspective taking, awareness of the self and other or assuming social responsibility, all included in the transformational model of intercultural development designed by Glaser *et al.* (2007). Indeed, 'direct contacts with dissimilar others' (Ting-Toomey, 1999: 7) are fast becoming a common part of our lives with the interlinked world economy, advances in telecommunication and technology, increased travel and worldwide movement of immigrant workers. Thus, it becomes essential in the global workplace to learn to interact with international co-workers and to acquire the necessary knowledge and skills to be competent in intercultural communication, as this is 'a necessary first step in becoming a global citizen of the 21st century' (Ting-Toomey, 1999: 5).

The aim of the present chapter is precisely to examine, from both a theoretical and a practical perspective, the factors involved in successful intercultural communication. To this end, it begins by providing a theoretical framework, where the concept of communicative interaction is defined, its importance is highlighted and the main elements it involves are examined. This theoretical overview is then complemented from a practical perspective by outlining the different subtopics and activities designed by the ICOPROMO team to work on communicative interaction and by providing an in-depth description of a sample activity.

Communicative Interaction in the Global Workplace: Some Theoretical Considerations

Definition and importance

Communication is a complex process that requires the successful implementation of numerous skills and devices. In simple terms, it can be defined as the mode or method by which we exchange ideas or information. In order for communication to be effective, there needs to be interaction between the participants in the exchange; we cannot say that communication has occurred unless one person speaks and the other person understands what has been said.

The complexity involved in communication is greatly increased if the latter is intercultural, that is, if it takes place 'between people from different national cultures' (Gudykunst, 2002: 179). As Andersen *et al.* (2002: 90) signal, 'Intercultural interactions are always problematic. Linguistic barriers in many intercultural interactions are compounded by differences in nonverbal behavior'. However, despite the difficulties inherent in intercultural communication, its study becomes essential at the outset of the 21st century, as a notable number of authors (e.g. Ting-Toomey, 1999; Andersen *et al.*, 2002; Wiseman, 2002; Gudykunst *et al.*, 2005) highlight. Like no time before in history, we are finding ourselves in contact with culturally diverse people, thanks to an interlinked world economy, advances in telecommunication and technology, increased travel and worldwide movement of immigrant workers. In Ting-Toomey's (1999: 7) words, 'As we enter the 21st century, direct contacts with dissimilar others in our neighborhoods, schools, and workplace are an inescapable part of our life'.

Thus, it becomes essential in the global workplace to learn to interact with international co-workers and to acquire the necessary knowledge and skills to be competent in intercultural communication. This is necessary to become, what Ting-Toomey (1999: 5) terms, a 'global citizen of the 21st century'.

It is not surprising that, given its increased significance, there have been great advances in the conceptualisation of intercultural communicative competence, particularly over the course of the past two decades (Wiseman, 2002; Gudykunst *et al.*, 2005). And what exactly does intercultural communicative competence involve? To begin with, an adequate conceptualisation of this construct requires a broader formulation of the traditional concept of communicative competence, as Alptekin (2002: 63) forcefully upholds: 'The conventional model of communicative competence... would appear to be invalid in accounting for learning and using an international language in cross-cultural settings. A new pedagogic model is urgently needed to accommodate the case of English as a means of international and intercultural communication'. In fact, Peterson (2004: 87) goes as far as to propose substituting the term 'competence' for the more encompassing word 'intelligence', which, in his view, 'suggests more highly developed abilities'.

More specifically, Gudykunst (1998) and Wiseman (2002) consider that competent intercultural communication involves three conditions: *knowledge* (about the people, context, communication rules or expectations), *motivation* (the needs, feelings and drives involved in the interaction process) and *skills* (related also to an important set of attitudes such as mindfulness, empathy or adaptability).

For Peterson (2004), successful intercultural interaction boils down to having at least some basic notions of the interlocutor's language, possessing knowledge of nonverbal aspects and of one's own cultural style, and knowing how the latter meshes with the cultural style of others.

Finally, Ting-Toomey's (1999: 16) definition of intercultural communication is as follows: 'the symbolic exchange process whereby individuals from two (or more) different cultural communities negotiate shared meanings in an interactive situation'. Thus, the transactional, give-and-take nature of the intercultural exchange is here emphasised, together with its use of both verbal and nonverbal symbols.

Intercultural verbal communication

What seems incontrovertible after examining the different ways in which intercultural communicative interaction can be conceptualised is that numerous variables need to come into play in order to guarantee its success. And which are these all-important elements that are involved in intercultural interaction?

Naturally, verbal aspects are at the top of the list. Within them, language mastery is, to begin with, essential for successful communication to take place; that is, mastery of what Canale and Swain (1979) term *grammatical competence*, which is viewed by these authors as comprising knowledge of lexis, morphology, syntax, phonology and graphology (spelling). As Gudykunst (1998: 215) stresses, 'the greater our cultural and linguistic knowledge, and the more our beliefs overlap with those of the strangers with whom we communicate, the less the likelihood there will be misunderstandings'.

However, in addition to linguistic aspects, an important number of verbal communication styles also need to be taken into consideration to guarantee successful intercultural communication (Gudykunst, 1998; Ting-Toomey, 1999; Andersen *et al.*, 2002; Gudykunst & Lee, 2002; Lim, 2002; Peterson, 2004). These can be articulated in terms of the following series of binary distinctions.

Talk versus silence

Whereas, in the West, silence is merely something to be filled in and may be regarded as emptiness, ignorance or blank in communication, in Asia, it is viewed as a valuable and important part of it, becoming a control strategy for cultures such as the Chinese or Japanese. Certain communities thus have a greater tolerance of silence, as it can convey from truthfulness to social discretion (e.g. in Japan). Differences in the perception of silence are caused by factors such as ethnicity, high or low context or individualism-collectivism (Gudykunst, 1998; Ting-Toomey, 1999; Lim, 2002). Thus, we need to be aware of the fact that 'Silence can serve various functions, depending on the type of relationship, the interactive situation, and the particular cultural beliefs held' (Ting-Toomey, 1999: 11).

Topic management and turn-taking

Awareness of when, how and whom to interrupt and knowledge of the conventions governing turn-taking across cultures is also necessary to guarantee successful intercultural verbal communication. The length of the turns taken, their distribution, the organisation of the topic and the use of repetition, feedback devices or backchannelling all vary depending on the culture. This variation seems to be reliant particularly on individualism-collectivism (Gudykunst, 1998).

Elaboration/animation

The degree of elaboration and animation also varies across cultures (Gudykunst, 1998; Lim, 2002). Expressiveness, assertion and exaggeration are characteristic of Arabic cultures and of certain ethnicities, such as the African-American one. This contrasts with the under-assertiveness and under-expressiveness of certain Asian communities and with the more restrained verbal style of European Americans.

Direct versus indirect verbal styles

The distinction between these next two verbal styles is to be found in 'the extent to which communicators reveal their intentions through their tone of voice and the straightforwardness of their content message'

(Ting-Toomey, 1999: 103). Direct cultures clearly reveal their intentions and formulate their messages in a forthright tone of voice. They are often linear thinkers who prefer to get straight to the point in conversations. On the other hand, in indirect verbal styles, what is left unsaid may be as important as what is expressed outright, actual intentions may be hidden and the tone of voice employed is subtler. Formalities and protocols are followed and circular thinking is favoured.

Individualism versus collectivism and person-oriented versus status-oriented verbal styles

Individualism versus collectivism, or person-oriented versus status-oriented verbal styles, in Ting-Toomey's (1999) terms, differ in the degree to which the verbal style is more individual-centred or role-centred. Members of individualistic cultures are more focused on affect and on the achievement of inclusion than those of collectivistic ones, who pay more attention to the behaviour and status of others.

Self-enhancement versus self-effacement

Related to the former dichotomies is this next one, which deals with the extent to which a verbal style emphasises or de-emphasises one's achievements and skills. Modesty, humility and even self-deprecation are characteristic of certain Asian cultures (e.g. Japan) versus the self-enhancement patterns followed in many Western cultures (e.g. the USA).

Low- versus high-context communication

The last dichotomy worthy of consideration within intercultural verbal communication is among the most often cited, as it intersects with all the aforementioned ones. In general, low-context communication is characterised by being direct, explicit and open. It conveys messages verbally. High-context communication, on the other hand, is indirect, subtle and understated. It expresses meaning through context and nonverbal channels. By and large, Eastern societies are considered high-context cultures and Western ones, low-context cultures (Lim, 2002).

The relationship between language, culture and thought

Throughout the previous headings, we have observed how all the aforementioned aspects of verbal communication are used differently across cultures; that is to say, these elements are 'sensitive to cultural diversity' (Lim, 2002: 83). Or, as Gudykunst (1998: 181) phrases it, 'Individuals' communication styles are dependent upon the degree to which they have internalized the values of the culture in which they are socialized...'.

Without doubt, this points to the triadic relationship between language, culture and thought, which is of paramount importance within our examination of intercultural communicative interaction (Nisbett, 2005). Indeed, research on intercultural communication in the workplace (Knapp *et al.*, 1987) has evinced that taking universality for granted is one of the major sources of multicultural clashes.

From Boas (1911/1966), to Sapir (1924/1929), to Whorf (1956) (all quoted in Lim, 2002), it has traditionally been held that a fluid continuum exists among the three, with each element influencing the others. Thus, for instance, in this sense, the Sapir-Whorf hypothesis maintains that structural differences between language systems are paralleled by nonlinguistic cognitive differences and that the structure of one's native language strongly influences or fully determines the world view that a person acquires while learning the language. Thus, this hypothesis contains two propositions: *Linguistic Determinism* (the belief that language determines thought) and *Linguistic Relativity* (difference in language equals difference in thought). Research on the ethnography of speaking (Lim, 2002: 73) has also revealed that 'languages are closely tied to the values and ideologies of their users, and syntactic structures and lexical items inevitably reflect the idiosyncratic experiences of the speech communities'.

Culture is also thought to influence language. In Gudykunst's (1998: 172) words: 'Culture and language are highly interrelated. Our cultures influence the languages we speak, and how we use our languages influences our cultures'. Ting-Toomey (1999: 112) even refers to this '*necessary* tie between language and culture' with a specific term: 'languaculture'.

Intercultural nonverbal communication

Culture not only influences language, however; it is also believed to have an impact on nonverbal aspects of communication. 'If language is the key to the core of a culture, nonverbal communication is indeed the *heart* of each culture. Nonverbal communication is omnipresent throughout a culture – it is everywhere' (Ting-Toomey, 1999: 120). Indeed, as both Ting-Toomey (1999) and Andersen *et al.* (2002) stress, although nonverbal interaction has innate or cultural-universal elements, it is also affected by culture-specific ones.

The significance of such nonverbal aspects in general is incontrovertible. As Revell and Norman (1999: 91) point out, 'Communication is *more* non-verbal than verbal' (emphasis in the original). Indeed, current neuro-linguistic programming (NLP) beliefs maintain that only 7% of what is communicated is done by means of the actual words we use, while as much as 55% is communicated bodily and 38% through our tone of voice. Ting-Toomey (1999: 115) is no less emphatic: 'Many nonverbal experts (e.g., Birdwhistell, 1955; Mehrabian, 1981) estimated that in every social encounter, nearly two-thirds of the interaction meaning is derived through nonverbal messages'. As this author holds, it can complement, emphasise, substitute or contradict what is expressed verbally. It is everywhere and thus has 'interaction primacy' (Ting-Toomey, 1999). And it becomes even more crucial in intercultural contexts, as Andersen et al. (2002: 90) point out: 'beyond language, multichannelled problems exist in interpreting nonverbal behavior of people from other cultures'.

Ting-Toomey (1999: 115) defines nonverbal communication as 'the nonlinguistic behaviors (or attributes) that are consciously or unconsciously encoded or decoded via multiple communication channels'. And all these channels or mediums need to be considered to render a complete account of intercultural nonverbal communication.

Kinesics

Kinesics, or facial, bodily and gestural movement, is important for the expression and recognition of emotions across cultures, as well as for conversational management (Gudykunst, 1998; Ting-Toomey, 1999). According to the neuro-cultural theory of facial expression of emotion (Ekman, 1972), certain emotional facial expressions are innate, but culture also influences the expression of emotions by providing display rules that are learned culturally and that determine when and how such emotions can be expressed. In turn, within conversational management, it is particular hand gestures and bodily movements that come into play.

Oculesics

Oculesics or eye contact has already been mentioned as an important nonverbal regulating device in conversational management. It is necessary to be aware of the differences that exist across cultures in terms of when and how much eye contact to maintain. Certain communities engage in more eye contact than others or do so more when listening than when speaking (individualistic cultures). Acknowledging such differences can help avoid intercultural miscommunication.

Vocalics

This next nonverbal medium refers to vocalic behaviour related to speech, including accent, pitch range and intensity, volume, articulation, resonance or tempo (Ting-Toomey, 1999). Whereas for certain cultures (e.g. Arab ones) loudness has positive connotations of sincerity, and softness of speech is viewed as a sign of deviousness, other communities associate positive traits to speaking softly (Gudykunst, 1998). Tone (paralinguistics) is also closely related to this third nonverbal aspect.

Haptics

Different cultures also have diverse expectations of when and whom it is appropriate to touch. High-contact cultures (generally found in warmer climates) tend to engage in more touching behaviour than low-contact ones (which tend to be located in cooler regions) (Hall, 1976; Gudykunst, 1998). The former type of culture also tends to have greater needs of other sensory exposure, such as olfactory (smell) involvement (Ting-Toomey, 1999).

Proxemics

Haptics, along with proxemics (space), contribute to interpersonal spatial boundary regulation (Ting-Toomey, 1999). There are also differences between high- and low-contact cultures in terms of how far people stand from each other. What may be an adequate personal distance for one community may be perceived as a violation of spatial boundaries by another, which may even result in aggressiveness in certain individualistic cultures.

Chronemics

A final significant form of nonverbal communication is chronemics, or the interpretation and understanding of time. Hall (1984) distinguished between two time patterns that differentiate individualistic from collectivistic cultures: the monochronic time schedule (M-time) and the polychronic time schedule (P-time). M-time (individualistic) cultures tend to do one thing at a time and to separate task-oriented and social time. P-time (collectivistic) cultures typically engage in several simultaneous activities and have more flexible attitudes towards blending task-oriented and social time.

Thus, this brief overview of intercultural nonverbal aspects has led us to confirm what Andersen's (2002) research reveals, namely, that the differences in intercultural nonverbal communication lie along the nonverbal codes of kinesics, oculesics, vocalics, haptics, olfactics, proxemics and chronemics.

Strategic competence

The previous heading has evinced that nonverbal interaction is a powerful resource (and not merely a number of linguistic aspects) to convey messages. It is part of *strategic competence*, yet another element to be borne in mind within communicative interaction. Initially, its definition is narrow in scope, as Canale and Swain (1979: 30) characterise this component as comprising the verbal and nonverbal communication strategies that are activated in order to compensate for breakdowns in communication caused by either performance variables or insufficient competence. However, Canale (1983: 10–11) subsequently expands this definition by adding that strategic competence can also be called into action in order to 'enhance the effectiveness of communication (e.g. deliberately slow and soft speech for rhetorical effect)'. This broader conception is upheld by Tarone and Yule (1989) and by Brown (1994: 228), who defines strategic competence in a comprehensive manner, as 'the way we manipulate language in order to meet communicative goals'. *Communication strategies* (Brown, 1994; Larsen-Freeman & Long, 1993; Oxford, 1990) or *production strategies* (Skehan, 1998) can, in turn, be subdivided into *achievement strategies*, which range from code-switching or literal translation to paraphrasing and appeal for repair and confirmation, and *reduction strategies*, which involve topic avoidance and nonverbal communication (Johnstone, 1989; Bygate, 2000).

Skills

Finally, as Ting-Toomey (1999: 141) indicates, 'Mindful verbal and nonverbal communication requires the application of flexible, adaptive interaction skills'. These skills are well summarised by Gudykunst (1998) as directly related to managing uncertainty and anxiety. They involve six main abilities that are in line with important attitudes necessary to communicate effectively in intercultural contexts.

The first ability is the *ability to be mindful*, which involves being able to put oneself in the interlocutor's shoes and to display sensitivity to other frames of reference. The second ability mentioned by Gudykunst (1998) – *tolerance of ambiguity* – is directly related to the third one – *management of anxiety* – as the greater the tolerance of ambiguity, the less anxiety experienced in intercultural communication. The attitudes of sensitivity, understanding and learning to truly listen all come into play in the *ability to empathize*, while adaptability and flexibility are at the core of the *ability to adapt our communication*. Finally, all the aforementioned skills and attitudes – empathy, adaptability, mindfulness – need to come together in order to have the *ability to make accurate predictions and explanations*, the final one to which Gudykunst (1998) alludes.

Communicative Interaction in the ICOPROMO Project

A general introduction to the activities within 'communicative interaction'

In line with the foregoing, the ICOPROMO Project acknowledges the paramount importance of communicative interaction in a global context and thus seeks to provide training and practice in the intercultural communicative interaction strategies, skills and attitudes that foster success in the multicultural workplace. This specific thematic block also strives to raise general awareness of the significance of communicative interaction and of the factors it involves by focusing on each of the elements that have been mentioned in the theoretical introduction as affecting it. In this sense, the project basically develops the intercultural competence of communicating across cultures in all its facets: verbal and nonverbal communication and language awareness.

The project does so by means of ten activities subdivided into two modules: Module A (basic-intermediate level) and Module B (intermediate-advanced level). The first of the modules begins by considering the general components that the literature deems necessary for competent communicative interaction (Activity 1: 'Communication on Earth') and focuses on the process of communication and on its verbal and nonverbal components by asking participants to do the following observation activity:

You are going to conduct a study in which observation skills and analysis and reflection of data are required. Imagine you come from another planet and you have been asked to write a report on how human beings communicate on Earth. You communicate by means of telepathy, so you are not familiar with human communication. Go to a cafeteria/restaurant and to a market. Observe what happens in each place for thirty minutes and write down all the relevant aspects in a notebook.

At home with the same peer, analyse and interpret the data and fill in the following table. Prepare a 5–10 minute report on human communication on the basis of the information contained in the table. Remember that you will be reporting to people from your planet who use telepathy and who do not know anything at all about human communication. This means that you will have to explain even the most basic aspects in great detail.

It then narrows the scope to focus on aspects of verbal communication and strategic competence (Activity 2: 'Myself as a language user') by encouraging reflection upon the importance of language through focus on the following aspects:

(a) Languages spoken
(b) When you learnt them and whether this determines your command of the languages.
(c) Circumstances under which you use each of them.
(d) Mother tongue and its world-wide relevance.
(e) Foreign language/s and their world-wide relevance.
(f) Examples in which mastery of a particular language has been paramount (either in the native culture or abroad).
(g) Any other instances which support some or all of the quotes.
(h) Examples in which lack of linguistic proficiency has been overcome by the use of other devices.

The question of language, culture and thought, and the way they help us categorise the world around us is also probed in greater depth via another activity (Activity 3: 'Language, culture, and thought' – see **the following section** – and Activity 4: 'Mañana'). Finally, intercultural nonverbal communication is also devoted attention in this initial module with an activity that explores its different mediums, as well as universal versus culture-bound behaviours (Activity 5: 'Pleased to meet you'). Here, immediacy, kinesics, oculesics and proxemics, together with the abilities to be mindful, adapt our communication and make accurate predictions, all come into play through an enlightening role-play:

SAMPLE ROLE CARD

SPAIN:

In Spain, men usually shake hands with other men and kiss women on both cheeks. Women usually kiss men/women on the cheek if they know each other or if the atmosphere is more informal. In formal terms, people usually shake hands and smile, thus showing friendliness.

When speaking, people usually stay close to each other and keep eye contact. There is no problem in looking at each other's eyes or face.

> This usually implies that you are paying attention to your interlocutor. Touching is certainly not discarded, especially if you meet a friend or one of your relatives. 'Lack of eye contact' or 'detachedness' may indicate that somebody is not really interested in talking to you or that he/she does not care about you at all.
> Use either the formal or the informal pattern.

Nonverbal communication is again examined in Module B, with special emphasis on vocal segregates in this case (Activity 7: 'Real English sounds'). However, the stress in this second module is on the skills and attitudes necessary for effective intercultural communication (Activity 6: 'How well do you know me?') and on applying what has been previously learned to the specific context of multicultural teamwork (Activity 8: 'Multicultural team dynamics', Activity 9: 'The written feedback', and Activity 10: 'HTH'). In this sense, the thematic block proceeds with a sieve-like structure, from the general components of intercultural communicative interaction to their application in the global workplace. Thus, practice in the strategies, attitudes and skills offered in this chapter is geared at achieving successful communicative interaction and at working towards effective multicultural teamwork.

A sample activity: 'Language, culture and thought'

Let us now illustrate in greater depth how some of the concepts of communicative interaction that have been examined theoretically and corroborated practically are worked on explicitly through the ICO-PROMO activities. The sample exercise selected – 'Language, culture and thought' – as its name indicates, seeks to encourage reflection on the relationship among these three elements. Through it, the learner is expected to attain a clear picture of the mutual influence that language, culture and thought exert upon each other and to contrast the way in which culture affects the way we behave, think and talk across cultures. Awareness-raising of linguistic aspects and of similarities and differences is crucial here.

Over the course of approximately 70 minutes and preferably with multicultural participants, the activity develops with a combination of individual study, group work and whole class discussion. It should be introduced by highlighting the relationship among language, culture and thought and by explaining the *Sapir-Whorf hypothesis* and the concepts of *Linguistic Determinism* and *Linguistic Relativity*. The brief theoretical introduction presented in the following worksheet can be used as a starting point for this first step. Students' opinions should be elicited in this respect.

> The relationship between **language, culture,** and **thought** has originated heated debate. It has traditionally been held that a fluid continuum exists among the three, with each element influencing the others. Thus, for instance, in this sense, the **Sapir-Whorf hypothesis** (Whorf, 1956: 212–214) maintains that structural differences between language systems are paralleled by non-linguistic cognitive differences and that the structure of one's native language strongly influences or fully determines the world view that person acquires while learning the language. Thus, this hypothesis contains two propositions: *Linguistic Determinism* (the belief that language determines thought) and *Linguistic Relativity* (difference in language equals difference in thought). Culture is also thought to influence language, a classic example being the way in which Eskimos employ 12 to 15 different words for snow.
>
> In this exercise, we are going to reflect precisely on the relationship among language, culture, and thought. Below are examples of how **culture** can influence the **way we behave** (13 cases), **think** (5 instances), and **talk** (6 situations). Fill in the slots beside each one with the answers that would apply to your specific culture. Afterwards, compare and contrast your results with those of a partner from a different nationality and fill in the table with the outcomes you have found most striking in terms of similarities or differences.

The participants should then be asked to fill in the slots in the following table individually, while the facilitator monitors performance and makes himself/herself available to answer questions related to meaning and content.

Ways in which we differ	
Ways in which we behave	1. How and when we greet each other
	2. How closely we stand to each other
	3. The holidays we celebrate and how we celebrate them

Ways in which we differ	
	4. How we show respect and disrespect
	5. What, when, and how we eat and drink
	6. How and when we use means of transportation
	7. If, how, and when we touch each other
	8. The roles of men and women, and how each should behave
	9. The roles of parents and children, and how each should behave
	10. How time is understood and used
	11. How often we smile, whom we smile at, and what it means when we smile
	12. Relationships and obligations between friends
	13. How or whether we take turns, stand in line, etc.
Ways in which we think	1. What's polite or impolite
	2. What makes us feel good, and what depresses us
	3. What makes us proud, and what shames us
	4. What we find funny or sad
	5. How we see old age, and how we value elders
Ways in which we talk	1. What should be communicated directly, and what indirectly
	2. What language, dialect, and tone of voice we use
	3. Whether conversation should be formal or informal
	4. What should be said, and what should be left unsaid
	5. Whether, when, how, and with whom we make small talk
	6. How open or guarded we are with information

Subsequently, the participants should be grouped in pairs (or groups of three if there is a limited number of students from different nationalities) with someone from a different nationality and asked to compare their outcomes, filling in the second table in the process. If the pairs/groups are from the same nationality, they can be asked to look for striking similarities and differences in their own answers. Group formation and performance should be monitored by spending a few minutes with each pair/group.

Comparison of outcomes	
Similarities	Differences
–	–
–	–
–	–
–	–
–	–

The activity should be concluded with a debriefing phase, where interesting findings are discussed with the whole class. It is interesting to ask participants explicitly whether they consider culture influences thought, language and behaviour, on the basis of the outcomes obtained in the exercise. The discussion is more focused if each pair/group is asked to select three to five categories under each heading where they have observed the most striking similarities or differences across cultures.

Conclusion

This chapter has allowed us to examine the topic of communicative interaction in connection to the different phases of the 2003–2006 ICOPROMO Project, among which a great harmony has been discerned. Indeed, all the theoretical aspects examined in the introductory section have been worked on practically via a well-defined batch of activities designed for its two modules.

Both the theory and practice on this topic confirm that there is a clear-cut set of elements that need to be considered in order to guarantee successful intercultural communication in the multicultural workplace. These include variables of verbal communication (involving especially *language mastery, talk versus silence, turn-taking and topic management, direct and indirect verbal interaction styles* and *low versus high-context communication*); the relationship between *language, culture* and *thought*; factors affecting nonverbal communication (particularly *paralinguistics, oculesics, haptics* and *proxemics*); communication or production strategies (of both *reduction* and *achievement* type); and certain skills or attitudes (involving above all the *ability to be mindful*, the *ability to empathize* and the *ability to adapt our communication*). Both modules of the ICOPROMO Project seek to raise awareness of all these factors that are involved in successful communicative interaction across cultures, a task definitely worth undertaking for its positive repercussions both at a professional and personal level, since, as Ting-Toomey (1999: 8) puts it, it will 'help us to uncover our own diversity and "worthiness"' and will 'ultimately enrich the depth of our own life experiences'.

References

Alptekin, C. (2002) Towards intercultural communicative competence in ELT. *ELT Journal* 56 (1), 5–64.
Andersen, P.A., Hecht, M.L., Hoobler, G.D. and Smallwood, M. (2002) Nonverbal communication across cultures. In W.B. Gudykunst and B. Mody (eds) *Handbook of International and Intercultural Communication* (pp. 89–106). Thousand Oaks, CA: Sage.
Brown, H.D. (1994) *Principles of Language Learning and Teaching*. Englewood Cliffs, NJ: Prentice Hall Regents.
Bygate, M. (2000) *Speaking*. Oxford: Oxford University Press.
Canale, M. (1983) From communicative competence to communicative language pedagogy. In J.C. Richards and R.W. Schmidt (eds) *Language and Communication* (pp. 2–27). London: Longman.
Canale, M. and Swain, M. (1979) Theoretical bases of communicative approaches to second language teaching and testing. *Applied Linguistics* 1 (1), 1–47.
Ekman, P. (1972) Universal and cultural difference in the facial expression of emotion. In J.R. Cole (ed.) *Nebraska Symposium on Motivation* (pp. 207–23). Lincoln, NB: University of Nebraska Press.
Glaser, E., Guilherme, M., Méndez García, M.C. and Mughan, T. (2007) *Intercultural Competence for Professional Mobility*. Strasbourg: Council of Europe.
Gudykunst, W.B. (1998) *Bridging Differences. Effective Intergroup Communication*. Thousand Oaks, CA: Sage.
Gudykunst, W.B. (2002) Intercultural communication. Introduction. In W.B. Gudykunst and B. Mody (eds) *Handbook of International and Intercultural Communication* (pp. 179–182). Thousand Oaks, CA: Sage.
Gudykunst, W.B. and Lee, C.M. (2002) Cross-cultural communication theories. In W.B. Gudykunst and B. Mody (eds) *Handbook of International and Intercultural Communication* (pp. 25–50). Thousand Oaks, CA: Sage.
Gudykunst, W.B., Lee, C.M., Nishida, T. and Ogawa, N. (2005) Theorizing about intercultural communication. In W.B. Gudykunskt (ed.) *Theorizing About Intercultural Communication* (pp. 3–32). Thousand Oaks, CA: Sage.

Hall, E.T. (1976) *Beyond Culture*. Garden City, NY: Doubleday/Anchor.
Hall, E.T. (1984) *The Dance of Life: The Other Dimension of Time*. Garden City, NY: Doubleday/Anchor.
Johnstone, R. (1989) *Communicative Interaction*. London: CILT.
Knapp, K., Enninger, W. and Knapp-Potthoff, A. (1987) *Analyzing Intercultural Communication*. Berlin: Mouton de Gruyter.
Larsen-Freeman, D. and Long, M.H. (1993) *An Introduction to Second Language Acquisition Research*. London: Longman.
Lim, T. (2002) Language and verbal communication across cultures. In W.B. Gudykunst and B. Mody (eds) *Handbook of International and Intercultural Communication* (pp. 69–88). Thousand Oaks, CA: Sage.
Marquardt, M. and Horvath, L. (2001) *Global Teams: How Top Multinationals Span Boundaries and Cultures with High-speed Teamwork*. Mountain, CA: Davies-Black.
Nisbett, R. (2005) *The Geography of Thought*. London: Nicholas Brealey.
Oxford, R.L. (1990) *Language Learning Strategies: What Every Teacher Should Know*. Boston, MA: Heinle and Heinle.
Peterson, B. (2004) *Cultural Intelligence. A Guide to Working with People from Other Cultures*. Yarmouth, ME: Intercultural Press.
Revell, J. and Norman, S. (1999) *In Your Hands. NLP in ELT*. London: Saffire Press.
Skehan, P. (1998) *A Cognitive Approach to Language Learning*. Oxford: Oxford University Press.
Tarone, E. and Yule, G. (1989) *Focus on the Language Learner: Approaches to Identifying and Meeting the Needs of Second Language Learners*. Oxford: Oxford University Press.
Ting-Toomey, S. (1999) *Communicating Across Cultures*. New York: The Guilford Press.
Wiseman, R.L. (2002) Intercultural communication competence. In W.B. Gudykunst and B. Mody (eds) *Handbook of International and Intercultural Communication* (pp. 207–224). Thousand Oaks, CA: Sage.

Chapter 8
Ethnography: The Use of Observation and Action Research for Intercultural Learning

KATALIN ILLES

Introduction

Intercultural learning has gained considerable popularity in higher education over the past 20 years. It is now a standard part of general and subject-specific introduction programmes in most disciplines and it has become an integral part of the curriculum of business education both in Europe and in other parts of the world.

Research into the pedagogical and methodological aspects of intercultural learning are continuously preparing the ground for more multidisciplinary research initiatives. The challenges, the current levels of achievement and the general impact of effective intercultural learning and intercultural communication are observed, measured and reported through research publications. The general interest in the subject encourages both academics and course participants to use more innovative, less mainstream approaches to learning in order to enhance the impact of intercultural learning on the overall sense making of both organisations and classroom environments.

In this chapter, we shall focus on ethnography, a less frequently used method of intercultural learning. Ethnography refers to a research methodology that was originally developed in the context of culture studies. It is a methodology that is useful for sense making in the broadest sense, both in organisations and in social interactions. It incorporates observation, action learning and reflection.

Ethnography has its roots in phenomenological methodology, which stems from anthropology (Hammersley, 1990). Anthropology is the study of people, especially of small foreign communities, their societies and customs. Ethnography is an approach in which the researcher uses socially acquired and shared knowledge to understand the observed patterns of human activity. It is a style of research rather than a single method and uses a variety of techniques to collect data. *Ethno-* means folk and art – *graphy* – means description. Werner and Schoepfle (1987) claim that ethnography means any full or partial description of a group.

Although it has been a feature of social science research throughout most of the 20th century, and has been used across a wide range of disciplinary applications, ethnography escapes a ready summary definition.

In recent years it has become a site of debate and contestation within and across disciplinary boundaries. 'The main aim of the ethnographers... [is] to observe how people interact with each other and with their environment in order to understand their culture' (Eriksson & Kovalainen, 2008: 138).

> Ethnographers seek to gain an **emic** perspective, or the "native's point of view" of what happens in a culture. This means that they try to perform research without imposing their own conceptual frameworks on the empirical world at the beginning of the research process. According to our experience, understanding the emic perspective is often the most difficult feature of ethnographic research for a business researcher who is more familiar with what is called the **etic** perspective. The "emic" world-view is part of the anthropological research tradition and rather different from the "etic", or the outsider's perspective, which is more common in business research. However, some ethnographers also claim that it is necessary to learn to combine the emic and the etic views in the same study (Barley, 1996). (Eriksson & Kovalainen, 2008: 138)

For our purposes, we define this style of research as:

> The study of people in naturally occurring settings or fields by means of methods which capture their social meanings and ordinary activities, involving the researcher participating directly in the setting, if not also the activities, in order to collect data in a systematic manner but without meaning being imposed on them externally. (Brewer, 2000: 10; for other explications of ethnography see: Atkinson *et al.*, 2001; Burgess, 1984; Davies, 1999; Fetterman, 1998; Hammersley & Atkinson, 1995)

This method of research must permit access to people's social meanings and activities. But it does not necessarily mean actual participation in the setting, so ethnography's repertoire of techniques includes in-depth interviews, discourse analysis, personal documents and vignettes and also participant observation. Visual methods, like video, photography, film and the internet are now also joining the list (Brewer, 2004).

These methods are also used in other non-ethnographic research, but here they are employed to meet objectives that distinguish it as a style of research that explores the social meanings of people in the setting by close involvement in the field. The other prominent feature of ethnography is that the above-listed methods are not used in isolation.

Ethnography routinely incorporates triangulation of method because it involves the use of multiple methods of data collection.

A further complication is that there is an interpolation of method and methodology in ethnography. It presupposes certain methods of data collection and it is also closely associated with a particular philosophical framework that validates its practice. This framework is called *naturalism* and also the *humanistic, hermeneutic* or *interpretative paradigms*.

Naturalism is an orientation concerned with the study of social life in natural settings. Social life is studied as it occurs independently of experimental manipulation. Its fundamental premise is that the main aim of social sciences is to understand people's actions and their experience of the world, and the ways in which their motivated actions arise from and reflect back on these experiences. According to naturalism, we can only be objective in our description if we minimise our influence on the activities of the people that we study.

The main method of collecting data is participant observation where the researcher becomes a full working member of the group being studied. The research normally takes place over a long period of time, often many months, in a clearly defined location such as a factory floor, and involves direct participation in the activities of that particular workplace.

The aim of the method is to be able to interpret the social world in the way that the members of that particular world do. Bogdan and Taylor (1975) and Patton (1990) offer a number of suggestions for researchers conducting ethnographic research, which can be summarised in the following stages.

- Build trust as early as possible.
- Become as involved as you can with the phenomena, but maintain an analytical perspective.
- Develop strong contacts with a few key informants.
- Gather data from as many different sources as possible, using multiple methods.

- Capture participants' views of their experiences in their own words, but remember the limitations of their perspectives.
- Write up field notes as soon as possible after leaving the setting and do not talk to anyone until you have done so.
- Be descriptive when taking your field notes and draw diagrams of physical layouts.
- Include your own experiences, thoughts and feelings as part of your field notes.
- As field work draws to a close, concentrate on making a synthesis of your notes.

A considerable number of disciplines have used an ethnographic approach. There are many factions and schisms and ethnography is perhaps the most hotly contested site in qualitative research today (Denzin & Lincoln, 1994). A number of different styles of ethnography are emerging. These styles depend on the skills and training of the researcher and the nature of the group with which the ethnographer is working. Whatever the type of ethnography adopted, it 'provides insights about a group of people and offers us an opportunity to see and understand their world' (Boyle, 1994).

It is useful to consider the following points before embarking on ethnographic research:

- You need to find an organisation that is open and ready to support your research.
- You have to develop a high degree of trust in those you are working with to ensure that you will be able to collect relevant data.
- If you are fully participating in the group, you must cope with being a full-time member of a working group as well as doing the research.
- You need to decide whether the particular setting or group best reflects the research interests and whether it will be possible to generalise from the findings.

Despite all the difficulties, ethnography is a very rewarding method because it gives an opportunity to the researcher to gain first-hand experience, to understand and interpret the phenomenon better.

Business-related ethnographic research has a long but rather thin history. A number of studies have focused on people in the workplace and how they make sense of their daily life in organisations (e.g. Dalton, 1959; Kunda, 1992; Watson, 1994; Barley & Kunda, 2004) and Schwartzman (1993) talks about 'organisational ethnography'.

The danger of all kinds of ethnography is that when the researcher has preconceived ideas, theoretical frameworks and concepts in mind, then she/he will easily miss the distinctive features and underlying issues of the group or community that she/he studies. It is a more fruitful starting point when the researcher has a general interest in the group, community or culture and approaches the research with an open mind and a willingness to take on board and record all aspects and dynamics as they naturally or unexpectedly occur or evolve without making judgements or evaluations in the process.

Illustrating the Theory

It is rather difficult to give a practical feel for ethnography in the classroom. Ideally, we would like to design a field trip or a set of interviews and observations where students of ethnography could apply the techniques and concepts and gain new insights into a culture and experience the depth, richness and insight that ethnography has to offer.

Unfortunately, many courses are limited to classroom-based activities, so we suggest a couple of tested activities that add practical value to understanding the use of ethnography in culture studies and are suitable for use in a classroom. In these exercises, all participants are observers and observed at the same time.

Before embarking on the activities with our participants, it is important to make a clear conceptual distinction between the functionalist and constructivist theoretical frameworks for studying different cultures.

Most students of culture find it easy to understand the relatively simple functionalist concepts of Hofstede (1997), Hampden-Turner and Trompenaars (2000) and the myriad of others who replicated their research in different cultures. Although the functionalists have made a major contribution to culture studies by calling attention to the impact of cultural differences on productivity and business relationships internationally, the negative side of this framework is that when it is applied in isolation, it can lead to a rather narrow and stereotypical view of people who are outside the individual's own culture.

It is more meaningful and more challenging to consider, for example, Gullestrup's (2006) constructivist model of culture (Figure 8.1). Gullestrup uses the functional aspects of culture as a starting point for his exploration. His model consists of horizontal cultural segments and vertical cultural layers. The horizontal cultural segments include the social segment, the security-creating segment, the identity-creating segment, the integration segment, the conveyance segment, the management and decision segment and the distribution segment. The vertical cultural layers are the immediately perceivable process layer, the difficult to perceive structural layer, the formalised layers of norms and rules, the non-perceivable existence, the basic value layer and the fundamental world conception.

This model combines the more immediately accessible horizontal segments of culture with the vertical culture dimension that defines the inner direction of influence in a given culture.

Gullestrup approaches culture from an anthropological starting point and studies culture in its complexity, offering different cultural

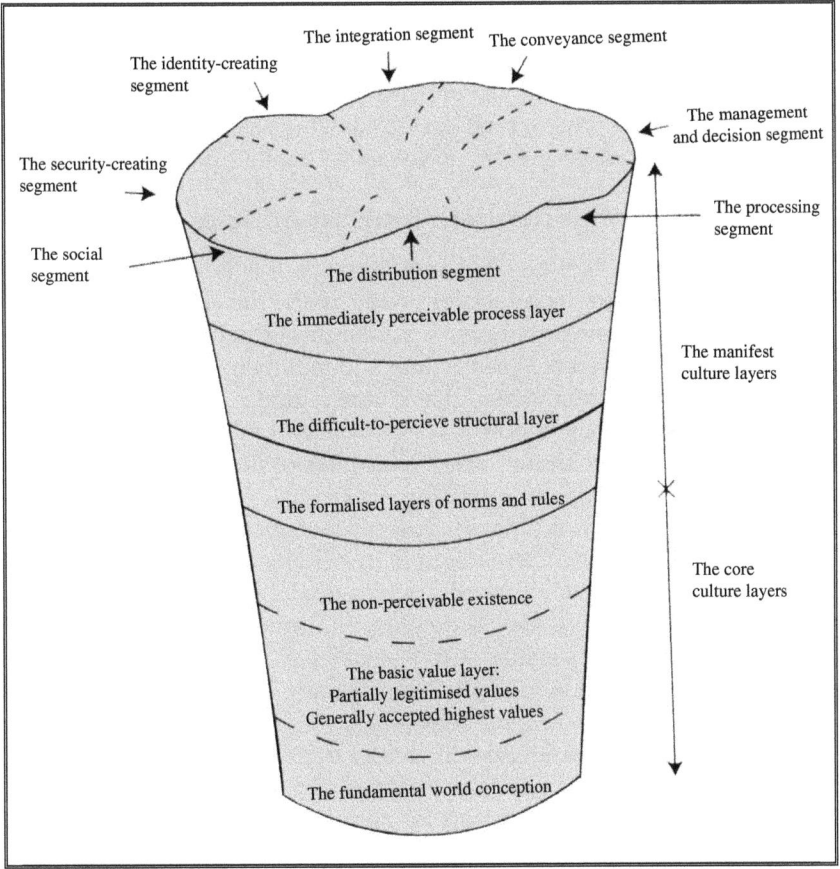

Figure 8.1 Culture as a complex entity consisting of culture segments and culture layers. The semi-static model (Gullestrup, 2006: 101).

segments and layers for consideration. His semi-static model invites both researchers and observers to reflect on the complex, interrelated and dynamic nature of cultures.

The philosophical underpinning of constructivism is that we are continuously creating our own reality. It is a helpful starting point when we work in multi-cultural teams because individuals can easily find their personal reference points for different cultural influences in their personal lives. It is a useful aid for sense making and intercultural dialogue both in the classroom and in the workplace. The constructivist models invite us to monitor our own behaviours and thought processes and actively observe how we contribute to or influence the outcome of multi-cultural interactions. This approach will also encourage us not to jump to stereotypical conclusions about others without making an effort and distinguishing between the abstract concepts of a particular culture and the individual who we observe and who has been influenced to some extent (but not necessarily exclusively) by that particular culture.

Preparation for the Decision-making Activity

Before using the 'Making Decisions' activity, it is important to ensure that participants are comfortable with both the functionalist and constructivist concepts of culture. It is also important to check the level of self-awareness, personal reflection and ability of non-judgemental observation of the participants. A basic understanding of ethnography as a research methodology and how it can be used in the daily activities of intercultural interactions will also be an important prerequisite for the successful use of the decision-making activity.

There are a number of Jungian type psychological exercises available. Some of them are particularly effective in helping people to understand that there are distinctly different personality types within the same culture who will behave very differently in a multi-cultural interaction (a very thorough personality test is available for example at www.insights.com, for those who want to incorporate cultural awareness into their broader personal development plans).

The 'Risks We Take' exercise will give an initial opportunity to observe and understand personal preferences of self and others. It also serves as a first step that prepares participants for non-judgemental observation and intercultural dialogue where different suggestions need to be considered and a group consensus has to be achieved to complete the exercise.

This exercise can be used on its own, but it can also be followed by the 'Making Decisions' exercise that builds on the observations and learning experiences of the 'Risks We Take' exercise. In the second exercise, participants are first asked to reflect on their personal decision-making processes, and then they are invited to discuss with others in pairs and in small groups the outcome of their reflections. In the final part of the exercise, participants are asked to reflect on decision making in organisations.

Risks We Take Exercise

Rationale

The purpose of this activity is to help participants to familiarise themselves with the key concept of Jungian personality types and appreciate how personality types influence our decision making and the level of risk we are comfortable with.

Learning outcomes

- Recognising different personality types.
- Appreciating the advantages and limitations of own personality type.
- Recognising and appreciating the features of other people's personality type.
- Learning to negotiate with different personality types.

Time required

10–15 minutes individual personality type test.
20–30 minutes discussion in groups of the same personality type.
20–30 minutes preparing a small group presentation.
20–30 minutes for group discussion and preparing a group presentation in mixed personality type groups.
20–30 minutes group presentations.
30 minutes for class discussion and comparison of different experiences.

Brief

Task 1. Read through the following 40 statements. Which group of 10 statements describe you best? Which is the second and third best description of you? Which set of statements is the least true about you?

Jungian personality types

Identify the set of statements that best describe your overall preferences. Which of the set of 10 statements would you feel most comfortable with? Put the sets in order of preference, starting from the closest and finishing with the least attractive proposition for describing your style of behaviour and action.

Set 1 (red)

- Bold and energetic.
- Evaluates people on their results.
- Outgoing and direct.
- Frank, honest and natural leader.
- Embracing change readily.
- Self-disciplined, confident and convincing.
- Enthusiastic leader – drives for results.
- Constantly strives towards self-improvement.
- Dynamic negotiator.
- Competitive and wants to win at all costs.

Set 2 (yellow)

- Seeking variety in both tasks and relationships.
- Articulate and active in communication.
- Has an outgoing nature and builds relationships quickly.
- Often charming and persuasive.
- Approachable and affectionate with friends.
- Effective and flexible in relationships.
- High profile and visibility.
- Becomes involved in many activities.
- Grasps opportunities quickly.
- Imaginative problem solver.

Set 3 (green)

- Dependable.
- Remains calm under pressure.
- Prefers a 'hands-on' approach to problem solving.
- Trustworthy.
- Open-minded and tolerant of others.
- Sensitive to the needs of others.
- Trusting and tolerant of others' actions.
- Happy to serve and help others.
- Good listener. Can help others achieve their goals.
- Solid organisational abilities.

Set 4 (blue)

- Logical thinker.
- Quiet and conscientious.
- Perfectionist.
- Analytical and detached.
- Responsible.
- Quietly supportive.
- Disciplined and precise.
- Pays great attention to detail.
- Neat, tidy and thorough.
- Brings order and structure through good organisation.

Task 2. In your group, you are asked to organise a birthday party for your best friend. Please discuss and prepare a detailed plan for the party including all the preparations and actions you intend to take to guarantee the success of the event.

Task 3. In your group of mixed personality types, you receive £100,000. It is your money that you can share equally between group members and make individual decisions about it; team up with another member of the group and choose a joint investment opportunity in pairs; keep the whole amount together and set up a business together. Discuss the options, make a choice and present a detailed plan to the class.

Ideally, it would be beneficial to complete tasks 1–3 before starting the 'Making Decisions' activity.

Activity: Making Decisions

Rationale

The purpose of this activity is to discover how participants have experienced decision making in organisations or social units that they have been part of. A decision-making model is then proposed that seeks to include a variety of preferences as they are described for example in Jungian psychological typologies. The activity also encourages participants to reflect on culture-specific aspects of decision making.

Learning outcomes

(1) Identify different decision-making frameworks.
(2) Self-evaluation of what makes sense for me in decision making in organisations.

(3) Reflecting on the different frameworks of decision-making in organisations.

Time required

60 minutes.

Process

Participants are initially asked to reflect and think on their own and write down some ideas about the following questions:

- How do I personally make decisions... do I spend much time on analysis of data or facts, on creating ideas/solutions/alternatives, on making a rational choice among alternatives, based on my feelings or value systems?
- If you had 30 minutes to make a decision... what would you spend your time on?

Participants then work with a partner, explaining their reflections on their own decision-making... the pair then connect with another pair... they share more briefly their reflections and then attempt to make a summary of where the four participants spend their time based on the above questions. They present the summary to the larger group and the facilitator draws some conclusions on the several small group presentations, highlighting how our personalities and personal preferences influence our decision-making.

Participants then return to their individual reflective thinking mode and think about the following questions:

- How would I summarise the way of making decisions in companies in my culture? Analysis... ideas... choosing... feelings...
- How much participation is expected in a group... is there an autocratic decision... some input from the group to the leader and then the leader decides... or consensus based on democratic inputs...?
- Are decisions made quickly or slowly?
- Are they made in public or in private?

The participants then work in pairs and then fours and summarise their findings.

The facilitator then presents some decision-making models and asks the participants which models resonate with experiences in their own culture and situations.

Which ones do they personally now feel comfortable with... if they wished for a decision-making process that made sense to them, what would be their wish?

Participants think on their own and complete the following sentence on a blank sheet of paper... 'it would be great if....... were part of the decision-making process where I work or live....'

The participants return to their pair working and prioritise key wishes as part of the collective sense making... the facilitator collects the list...

Discussion

This activity gives plenty of opportunities for participants to reflect on their individual decision-making processes and identify personal patterns and develop a conscious recognition of the process. Being mindful of one's own decision-making process is the first step in appreciating that although there are similarities between individual processes, there are also differences. These differences stem partly from the individual's culture and partly from the personality type, education and life experiences of the person.

Through dialogue, observation, comparison, discussion and feedback throughout this activity, participants will notice and articulate personal preferences. Clearly articulated personal preferences form a starting point for observing and acknowledging organisational decision-making processes. When it is done through the emic form of ethnography it provides a useful diagnostic tool for the decision-making culture of an organisation.

The wish list at the end of the activity signals an etic approach of how things should be according to the individual observer. By comparing the two lists, participants can prepare recommendations for a new decision-making process that would make sense for a larger number of individuals in the organisation or group.

Conclusion

In this chapter, we outlined the value of introducing some form of ethnography in the classroom and in the workplace. The use of observation and action research for intercultural learning was discussed. Observation and personal reflection provide valuable opportunities for participants to compare, contrast and relate current experience to past events and observations. Gullestrup's semi-static model of culture was introduced. This constructivist model highlights the complex and dynamic nature of intercultural interactions.

Two activities were used to illustrate how course participants can gain first-hand experience of their own personal preferences and decision-making processes. These exercises also provide opportunities to observe others and how they might have totally different preferences and decision-making processes.

References

Atkinson, P., Coffey, A., Delamond, S., Lofland, J. and Lofland, L. (2001) *Handbook of Ethnography*. London: Sage.
Barley, S. and Kunda, G. (2004) *Gurus, Hired Guns, and Warm Bodies: Itinerant Experts in a Knowledge Economy*. Princeton, NJ: Princeton University Press.
Brewer, J.D. (2000) *Ethnography*. Buckingham: Open University Press.
Brewer, J.D. (2004) Ethnography. In C. Cassell and G. Symon (eds) *Essential Guide to Qualitative Methods in Organisational Research* (p. 312). London: Sage.
Bogdan, R. and Taylor, S. (1975) *Introduction to Qualitative Research Methods*. New York: John Wiley.
Boyle, J.S. (1994) Styles in ethnography. In J.M. Morce (ed.) *Critical Issues on Qualitative Research* (p. 159). Thousand Oaks, CA: Sage.
Burgess, R. (1984) *In the Field*. London: Routledge.
Dalton, M. (1959) *Men Who Manage*. New York: John Wiley.
Davies, C.A. (1999) *Reflexive Ethnography*. London: Routledge.
Denzin, N.K. and Lincoln, Y.S. (eds) (1994) *Handbook of Qualitative Research*. Thousand Oaks, CA: Sage.
Eriksson, P. and Kovalainen, A. (2008) *Qualitative Methods in Business Research*. Newcastle-upon-Tyne: Sage.
Fetterman, D. (1998) *Ethnography*. London: Sage.
Gullestrup, H. (2006) *Cultural Analysis – Towards Cross-cultural Understanding*. Copenhagen: Business School Press.
Hammersley, M. (1990) *Reading Ethnographic Research: A Critical Guide*. New York: Longman.
Hammersley, M. and Atkinson, P. (1995) *Ethnography: Principles and Practice*. London: Routledge.
Hampden-Turner, C. and Trompenaars, F. (2000) *Building Cross-cultural Competence*. Chichester, UK: John Wiley.
Hofstede, G. (1997) *Cultures and Organizations: Software of the Mind*. Columbus, OH: McGraw-Hill.
Kunda, G. (1992) *Engineering Culture, Control and Commitment in a High-Tech Corporation*. Philadelphia, PA: Temple University Press.
Patton, M. (1990) *Qualitative Evaluation and Research Methods*. Newbury Park, CA: Sage.
Schwartzman, H. (1993) *Ethnography in Organisations*. London: Sage.
Watson, T. (1994) *In Search of Management: Culture, Chaos and Control in Managerial Work*. London: Routledge.
Werner, O. and Schoepfle, G. (1987) *Systematic Fieldwork: Foundations of Ethnography and Interviewing*. Newbury Park, CA: Sage.

Chapter 9
Biography: The Role of Experience in Intercultural Learning

MARÍA DEL CARMEN MÉNDEZ GARCÍA and
MARÍA LUISA PÉREZ CAÑADO

Introduction

The reflective analysis on personal experience possibly becomes one of the best starting points towards the development of intercultural competence. Indeed, it could be said that an informed reflection on the self turns out to be a *sine-qua-non* for intercultural communication, a particular type of interaction characterised by the need to make sense of otherness and to truly understand others.

In a multicultural teamwork context and on the basis of research, the ICOPROMO team has identified the importance of proceeding to the informed exploration of the self and of personal experience together with other key aspects for multicultural dynamics, such as the role of feelings and emotions, the relevance of observation and action research, the need to cope with all shades of diversity, the significance of verbal and non-verbal communication issues, the necessity to cope with unknown or ambiguous contexts, or the balance between power and ethics in a multicultural work setting.

My Biography: The Rediscovery of Identity on the Basis of Reflective Observation on Experience

'My Biography' favours the exploration of elements that are inherent in human beings and that pertain to their unique life experience. These elements are inevitably shaped by external forces, of which culture stands out.

Who am I? The Spanish philosopher Ortega y Gasset states 'Yo soy yo y mis circunstancias' [I am myself plus my circumstances]. Indeed, human personality is moulded by the perception human beings have of their self, which is, in turn, determined by personal biographies – that is to say, life experiences and the familiar, socio-economic, educational and professional backgrounds in which each individual is born, raised, educated and where the professional activity is carried out. Additionally, personality is influenced, to a certain extent, by the perception that the people around the individual have of himself/herself.

Society and culture definitely help shape people's worldview, values, beliefs, expectations and behaviours. It has been said that without a culture it is impossible to 'see', but that this culture also blinds human beings forever. What does this, in principle, contradictory statement mean? Learning starts at the moment of birth and is a life-long process. Human beings have to be taught how to learn, how to look at the world and how to handle the complex reality around them. An essential element in this process of learning how to deal with the world is, without doubt, the stance the individual takes, the 'glasses' worn in order to be able to see. From the moment of birth, human beings are progressively taught how to build the glasses that, once constructed, will partly remain unchanged throughout their lives and will invariably filter reality. These glasses are 'manufactured' by the experience in the first culture, even though they also contain a great deal of personal ornaments, the ones humans extract from their own personal experience.

In the ICOPROMO framework, My Biography constitutes the foundations of multicultural group dynamics. This thematic unit rests on the assumption that a critical exploration of the self must necessarily precede the process of facing and truly understanding otherness. The never-ending dialogue that is established between the (inner) self and the other equates the continuous discovery of other cultural patterns on the basis of the native culture. In this sense, awareness raising of the individual's identity, of the main standpoints implicit or explicit in his/her cultural background and how they interrelate, surface as a precondition before meeting otherness. And it is precisely in intercultural contexts, when the individual faces difference, that she/he starts to delve into and question all the assumed aspects of his/her own social groups and begins to see them in the light of a completely different perspective.

My Biography addresses diverse elements of the self, considered the centre of experience, versus the person, the publicly recognised human being (Pavlenko & Lantolf, 2000: 163). There is an initial focus on the self in order to discover the main features that make up the way she/he is portrayed and contemplated in society. The analysis of the nature of the relationship that holds between the self and the person represents one of the main goals of My Biography.

Identity and biographical narratives

The notion of identity provides an insightful framework for the analysis of key features of both, the self and the person. As stated above, human identity is built on the combination of personal and socio-cultural characteristics. In fact, the creation of identity emerges as an outstanding element in an overarching conception of culture (Gullestrup, 2006: 101).

In the collective sphere and closely related to the notion of the person, social identity theory contemplates the individual as a member of specific in-groups versus other out-groups or, as Tajfel (1972: 292) puts it, identity is 'the individual's knowledge that he belongs to certain social groups together with some emotional and value significance to him of this group membership'. Hogg (2006: 115) contrasts this social definition with the notion of personal identity, which correlates with the idea of the self as 'a self-construal in terms of idiosyncratic personality attributes that are not shared with other people ("I")'. Hogg (2006: 115) acknowledges that even though the construction of personal identity differs from the social sphere, 'group life often frames the development of personal identities and interpersonal friendships and enmities... People have as many social and personal identities as there are groups they belong to and personal relationships they are involved in'. As a result, the self and the person, the personal and the social, even though dissimilar, materialise as complementary shades of identity.

For Brewer and Gardner (1996), the individual self (with personal characteristics that make him/her unique) and the collective self (the self in his/her different group ascriptions) do not possibly reflect the complex reality. This is why they propose a triadic concept of identity in which the relational self (the individual in constant dialogue with the significant others) mediates between the personal attributes and the roles and behaviours displayed in society.

There are probably as many identities as groups the individual belongs to and she/he identifies with. The individual's multiple identities are usually 'conveyed to others in the form of a narrative' (Wodak *et al.*, 2009: 14). In this 'narrative identity' 'the narrated self, however, is also an "other" to the extent that at least a part of an individual narrative arises from the internalised attitudes, values, behavioural dispositions and patterns of action taken from important role models' (Wodak *et al.*, 2009: 14). Both communities and individuals create their own narratives. All societies have momentous narratives that are passed onto the next generation and that can be considered as a symbol of collective identity, as a product that reflects the main values of the society, as the glue that keeps the whole community together.

As to personal stories, autobiographic narratives become a privileged tool to understand how individuals make sense of their experiences in their everyday life. Shore (quoted by Pavlenko & Lantolf, 2000: 160) considers that it is through narratives that 'experience is literally talked into meaningfulness' and 'the strange and the familiar achieve a working relationship'. The narratives need to be related to an existing category or mode of thinking even though, sometimes, the story changes or reformulates the existing theory, category or hypothesis. Either with or without reformulation of previous categories, the whole process demands a great dose of coherence; otherwise instability and insecurity will arise (Norton, 2000: 160).

Narratives facilitate the inner dialogue of the self. First person accounts in the form of narratives have indeed become a remarkably revealing source of data about the process of second language and intercultural learning (Pavlenko & Lantolf, 2000). Narratives play a fundamental role in the reconstruction of the self when individuals move to another community and have to cope with the uncertainty implicit in conveying through terms in the non-native language – at the beginning an empty code void of life and emotions (Hoffman, 1989; Norton, 2000; Pavlenko & Lantolf, 2000) – ideas that were easily put into words in the mother tongue by means of terms that evoke, which are full of meaning and loaded with a whole life experience.

In sum, narratives emerge as an indispensable instrument in the analysis of human identity, facilitating the discovery and rediscovery of individual experiences, and helping individuals appreciate and comprehend these experiences.

Identity creation, personal experience and intercultural communication

Personality, although relatively stable, is not fixed; it changes throughout time and across circumstances or events. As 'Shrek' states in the first film of this world-famous story, individuals are like 'onions'; they have layers (see Utley's metaphor of the 'culture onion'; Utley, 2004). In spite of these unavoidable changes, the inner layers, those that form the core of personal identity, are much more stable. According to social identity theory, they are the layers delimited and shaped by the process of socialisation, which is defined as 'the comprehensive and consistent induction of an individual into the objective world of a society or sector of it' (Berger & Luckmann, 1966: 150). Socialisation, the process that turns a 'biological being' into a 'social one', makes the child learn 'to classify the world in which it lives, and to impose a system of values upon it' (Hendry, 1987: 38). The whole process of socialisation and the promotion of a particular worldview that accompanies it rest upon language, rituals enacted and the symbolic system of a given society (Hendry, 1987: 38) and seem to be an everlasting and highly determining phenomenon in individuals' life and experience.

Closely related to the process of socialisation is the need to belong, to feel a member of a group. Accordingly, group inclusion (Hinton, 2000; Vivian & Brown, 1995) turns out to be paramount in this process of becoming a social being, determining to a large extent individual behaviour, viewpoints and values. In the process of socialisation, the person realises that she/he is a member of different in-groups (at the church, at school, etc.). This need for group/s ascription and for group assertion appears in the literature as the basis for inter-group conflict both within and across cultural groups.

What occurs when, for whatever reason and in whichever circumstances, the individual comes across otherness either at home or abroad? A certain degree of uncertainty underlies the intercultural experience and clashes are likely to appear, since all the taken-for-granted values, practices and abilities that have required long years of learning in the individual's first cultural background, language included, are called into question and are no longer applicable or useful in another society.

To sum up, culturally relative values, beliefs and assumptions are thought to be normal or universal until there happens to be a contact with members from a different (ethnic, linguistic, socio-economic, national, etc.) group. It is at this stage of confrontation with otherness that an analysis of one's identity and experience proves essential for the development of intercultural competence.

In this context, personal biographies or, as it is termed, 'awareness of the self and the other' is explicitly contemplated as one of the competences in the Transformational Model of Intercultural Development, designed by Glaser et al. (2007). The duality of the self-other movement in the paradigm brings to the foreground the relevance of critically analysing individual experiences and stories from at least five different angles. First, the intercultural competence of awareness of the self and the other implies being able to assess and reflect on one's own social constructs in view of a critical cultural awareness and stance, a kind of inward journey. Second, an explicit analysis of things that are the same and that differ across cultures, peoples and individuals gives way to the recognition of the existence of similarities and differences among human beings. Third, there is a need to be willing to find out about the other in order to reach real intercultural understanding. Fourth, awareness of the self and the other entails being capable of dealing with culture-shock and reverse culture-shock, which rests on the development of the skills to manage the anxiety or impact that individuals experience when they lose the familiar aspects of reality in, for example, entering a new culture or, even more unexpectedly, when they return home after a considerable span of time spent in a different society. Fifth, individuals seem to benefit from an explicit and implicit analysis of stereotypes and generalisations. Stereotypes (cf. Gudykunst, 2004; Tajfel, 1981) are related to human cognition, to the way human beings categorise and interpret reality, and they seem to be present in communication, either with members of one's own culture or, even more acutely, with people from other cultural backgrounds. Moreover, stereotypes are usually linked to prejudices, which are affective in origin. Their affective nature is probably the chief reason why they may become so powerful and dangerous (Allport, 1954). Stereotypes and prejudices are presented not only as existing categories in the human mind, but also as almost unavoidable, since they are 'in the air'; they just impregnate the environment in which the person grows up and develops.

The inward journey necessitates the critical review of one's culture-bound beliefs, values, behaviours and assumptions and becomes a fascinating experience of discovery and rediscovery, of learning, relearning and unlearning (Glaser et al., 2007). The intercultural experience, either at home or away, is unique in that it has the potential to help individuals see the world from the multiple perspectives and dimensions necessary to undergo this inward journey.

Learning from experience in an intercultural work setting

Learning from experience or experiential learning has been defined as 'education that occurs as a direct participation in the events of life' (Houle, 1980: 221). Kolb (1984) distinguishes formal learning from experiential learning. The importance of this dichotomy lies in the awareness that cognitive (formal) learning is only one side of the coin, learning being equally dependent upon experiencing things and situations and being involved in them with the five senses. In a circular model, Kolb (1984) establishes a never-ending link between concrete experience, reflective observation and abstract conceptualization and knowledge. Experience is translated into learning outcomes as the result of the abstract conceptualization that is produced when reflective observation on a particular concrete experience has taken place and it all becomes the basis for action (active experimentation).

Experience, observation, analysis and action (Kolb, 1984) are the roots of learning and, needless to say, of intercultural learning. What characterises intercultural learning is the constant personal change it implies as the individual develops strategies to deal with otherness and difference (Amorim, 2001). As a matter of fact, questioning one's assumptions and viewpoints seems to be a constant element of intercultural learning.

Ng et al. (2009) deem that experiential learning entails the display of conscious behaviours to translate experience into learning outcomes. For them, this provides a very interesting framework to understand why different individuals learn differently from the same intercultural experience. Ng et al. (2009) uphold that only some individuals are able to engage completely in the intercultural experience, and these are the ones that make the most of experiential learning.

Intercultural competence or cultural intelligence (Ng et al., 2009), the abilities to function satisfactorily in intercultural settings (Early & Ang, 2003), appears as a relevant construct for experiential learning. According to Ng et al. (2009), cultural intelligence works at four levels: metacognitive (which involves consciousness and awareness at culturally diverse backgrounds), cognitive (related to the knowledge of norms, practices and conventions in intercultural situations), motivational (the willingness to learn from intercultural exchanges) and behavioural (apparent in verbal and non-verbal behaviour).

Ng et al. (2009) link the constructs of what they call cultural intelligence with the key elements of Kolb's experiential learning paradigm. In terms of concrete experience, it is propounded that individuals with a high motivational and behavioural cultural intelligence will look for concrete experiences in their intercultural practices. In the phase of reflective observation, individuals showing high cognitive and metacognitive cultural intelligence will be prone to cross-cultural reflection. To reach abstract conceptualisation successfully, the implementation of cognitive and metacognitive cultural intelligences are required. The four elements of cultural intelligence (cognitive, metacognitive, motivational and behavioural) are at the heart of active experimentation. To put it in a nutshell, the level of cultural intelligence seems to have an effect on the degree of experiential learning obtained in intercultural work contexts (Shaffer et al., 2006; Ng et al., 2009).

Global or multicultural team members are likely to develop their intercultural competence as a result of formal learning (and here is where the value of the ICOPROMO Project lies) and as a result of informal or experiential learning in their everyday lives in general and in multicultural contexts and/or teamwork. As Kolb (1984) points out, people have prior ideas and knowledge of what culture is and this has very interesting implications for experiential learning given that, being or not aware of it, experience is interpreted in the light of preconceived ideas and previous knowledge. As a consequence, personal upbringing, culture and experience are all linked in intercultural learning through teamwork.

In their identification of the main competences that need to be developed by multicultural teamwork leaders, Chang and Tharenou (2004: 65–70) distinguish five main areas: cultural empathy, communicative competence, generic managerial skills, personal style and learning on the job. Learning on the job is paired with attitudes such as flexibility or adaptability, being curious, having a willingness to learn, tolerance for ambiguity and being observant.

The development of intercultural competence in general and in a multicultural teamwork setting in particular, largely depends on personal attributes (such as cultural awareness, curiosity and respect), personal skills (such as observation and reflection or communicative competence) and, above all, the individual's readiness to learn on the spot (Wills & Barham, 1994), which is highly determined by his/her previous experiences in other cultures or backgrounds. To a large extent, intercultural respect and understanding seem to stem from personal experiences and attributes, together with the individual's experiences with otherness. All these characteristics correlate with the degree of experiential learning achieved; a high display of intercultural competences being a precondition for an intense and fruitful experiential learning.

From Theory to Practice. My Biography: A Sample of the Exploration of the Self and Personal Experiences for Intercultural Learning

A general introduction to the activities within My Biography

My Biography invites the participant to reflect overtly and explicitly on a wide array of elements of their personal biographies as a starting point towards understanding otherness.

At the basic-intermediate level, initial activities such as *My Objective and Metaphorical Profile* make personal data converge as a passport to identity from a double perspective, an objective and a more metaphorical definition, which help individuals become aware of the qualities, features and characteristics they purposely choose to represent themselves in society at the same time as they consider to what extent their personal profile is determined by their experiences. The focus of these activities is the exploration of personal and social identity that, hopefully, will help understand participants' relational identity.

A subsequent set of activities, namely, *My Foundations* and *The Bricks*, delve into the process of socialisation. They develop the intercultural competence of awareness of the self and the other by assessing and reflecting on one's own social constructs. Multicultural team players need to understand the relevance of the traces left by the process of socialisation. As a consequence, in this set of activities there is a scrutiny of the individual's assumed values, beliefs, knowledge, behaviour, skills and practices with a view to critically analysing where they originate from and how determining they are when forging the individual's personality. Notions of 'subjectivity' and 'objectivity' spring here. In this respect, special attention is paid to the role formal education plays in the development of individuals, how it moulds their identities and prepares them to become successful citizens of a particular community. In this cluster of activities, there is a balance in the consideration of the personal, social and relational selves. Other tasks (i.e. *The Roof*) concentrate on the individual's intercultural experiences and how these experiences are approached and processed in the person's culture-bound mind with an emphasis on collective identity.

At the intermediate-advanced level, social identity theory is again dealt with in connection with aspects such as group ascription, the creation of in-groups and out-groups, inter-group conflict and prejudice (Vivian & Brown, 1995), in-group favouritism and the threat of out-group discrimination (Hinton, 2000: 105–125). All these elements are intertwined with crucial issues such as individuals' perception and stereotyped images of otherness in a comprehensive set of tasks on collective and relational identities named *Group Membership*.

In *Europeans, what do you expect?*, the phenomenon of stereotype is likewise related to human cognition, as categorising and even stereotyping turn out to be one of the ways in which the human mind works in order to cope with the mass of information received every day. Spanish cartoons and newspaper clippings that portray a wide array of European groups have been used for this purpose.

Further tasks, such as *Behavioural Norms*, use examples of autobiographies extracted from films for the analysis of personal and cultural behavioural patterns. They help participants ponder the fact that members from different cultures exhibit a wide range of behavioural norms, often misunderstood and misinterpreted by outsiders. Lastly, a collection of activities combine most of the factors seen above in a professional setting. For instance, in *The CV vs. Communication Display Portfolios*, personal characteristics appear as a relevant criterion in the selection of staff members in multicultural teamwork; personal data is linked to job-related processes such as the preparation of CVs both for monocultural and intercultural team contexts. Finally, in *Critical Incidents*, intercultural encounters at work are seen according to a variety of possible misunderstandings that are likely to spring up in multicultural professional environments.

One of the main goals of My Biography is to help individuals come to terms with the fact that there is no single way of interpreting reality. In spite of the inherent value of My Biography for the exploration of the more personal side of intercultural competence, parts of specific activities may not work in a professional and/or competitive setting in which participants tend to be very careful with personal information they are willing to share and may object to unveiling personal data and circumstances.

A sample activity: *A new institution, a new group, a new 'me'*

Berger and Luckmann (1966) distinguish two steps in individuals' social learning: primary and secondary socialisation. For them, primary socialisation is 'the first socialization an individual undergoes in childhood, through which he becomes a member of society' (Berger & Luckmann, 1966: 150). It involves the cultural foundations laid by family and relatives in the person's early childhood; in spite of its subtle, progressive and unconscious nature, primary socialisation constitutes an everlasting process because it permeates the individual through his/her five senses for an extended and highly determining period of time: his/her childhood. Secondary socialisation, which follows primary socialisation, is 'a subsequent process that inducts an already socialized individual into new sectors of the objective world of his society' (Berger & Luckmann, 1966: 150). It starts with school entrance, and consists of a much more conscious type of learning regulated by the educational institutions and laws of a particular community.

As discussed above, inevitably, secondary socialisation involves the personal ascription to different in-groups. The values, norms, beliefs and behaviours acquired or learnt in the diverse institutions of secondary socialisation are usually deeply ingrained and determine, to a large extent, the social and personal self. Examining the process of secondary socialisation and being aware of what it means for the individual is valuable in that it provides him/her with the clues to become acceptable members of a given community. However, the individual is not usually aware of how culture-bound this process is and will only begin to question it when she/he encounters people from other cultures or spends some time in other cultures and realises that his/her social learning is no longer adequate to the new environment.

A new institution, a new group, a new 'me' is an elementary-intermediate level activity designed to be mainly used in multicultural learning settings. On the basis of two narratives (see Norton, 2000; Pavlenko & Lantolf, 2000; Wodak *et al.*, 2009), this task aims at making possible the inner dialogue that occurs in the process of creating personal stories. In particular, it encourages participants to reflect upon their secondary socialisation; to assess the relevance of the values, beliefs, norms and behaviours learnt or acquired in different institutions of secondary socialisation; and to ponder all these elements in connection with in-group ascription. Reflection and cultural flexibility underlie this activity.

Two texts have been used as samples. The trainer is free to choose similar extracts from literature, magazines or even films to conduct the activity. Text 1 has been written by a young American female and represents her review of her secondary socialisation, with very little attention to the aspects promoted during her primary socialisation. A narrative from the insider's perspective, it gives a detailed account of the values, beliefs, norms and behaviour that she learnt or acquired during this phase in different institutions. The multiple ascriptions to diverse in-groups, with the corresponding aspects endorsed by each and the social status ascribed to each are outstanding topics in the narrative. Likewise, the issue of national identity is raised.

Text 2 (Hendry, 1987: 45–48) presents the male outsider's perspective on one of the earliest institutions of secondary socialisation in Japan, kindergarten. Comparison of the values, norms and behaviours promoted both during primary socialisation and in the beginning of the secondary socialisation process are made explicit in the excerpt. Much importance is given to the new in-group and emphasis is laid on the collective versus the individual.

The two samples display parallel and dissimilar elements in both cultural backgrounds. It is apparent that all these elements influence the individual's identity. Relevant factors arise that have an impact on multicultural teamwork.

The first passage is reproduced below (to read the original version of the second text see Hendry, 1987: 45–48).

Text 1

I grew up in a rural part of Mississippi where just visiting one of my playmates was a grand ordeal because our parents had to drive us wherever we went. There was never a lack of woods to explore or hay bales to jump on or fields to play in, but one made friends with the few kids who lived relatively nearby, because convincing your parents to drive to the next town to pick up a friend was highly unlikely. For this reason, the largest factor in my socialization was elementary school.

Almost all of my extracurricular activities revolved around school. After living for a few years in Vicksburg, Mississippi, my parents moved back to my father's hometown of Moselle when I was in the first grade. I finished kindergarten in Vicksburg, of which I remember very little. The first big social impact that I remember in my life was when I had to begin the first grade in Moselle. I distinctly remember being petrified in front of my peers, and being furious at my mother for making me wear a dress when everyone else was dressed in t-shirts and shorts. From that point on I knew that I never wanted to wear nice clothes to school, because kids wearing nice clothes had to be sure to not get dirty on the playground, so they never had as much fun and didn't fit in as well.

The friends I made at school encouraged me to join the Girl Scouts when I was eight or nine. We met at a local restaurant, which would eventually become my first place of employment. We went on a lot of nature walks, fed the ducks, did arts and crafts; all the typical Girl Scout activities. We also put on mini-plays for each other in which I was always chosen to be the prince, the knight in shining armor, etc. This was because I was the tallest, and it was only natural that the tallest of us would be the one chosen to play the boy part.

Girls Scouts eventually gave way to cheerleading, which was crucial to social status in the fourth grade (I was about ten or eleven). Girls couldn't be cheerleaders and boys couldn't play (American) football until the fourth grade, so it was a considerable stepping stone in our lives. As much as I enjoyed doing the cheers and shouting and cutting flips, what I truly desired more than anything was to wear the uniform. With the uniform came a sense of pride and popularity that was unmatched by any other group association. As we got older, it became a trend for a boy to let a girl wear his football jersey if he liked her, so a girl wearing both the cheerleading uniform and a football jersey was practically a star. I never quite made it to that level because I was taller than all the boys throughout elementary school, and no boy wanted a girlfriend who was taller than he was. When I got to high school I tried out for cheerleading and didn't make it (due to an embarrassing fall during tryouts) so I quickly had to find a new group to associate with, the Technology Student Association (definitely not as 'cool' as cheerleading).

One thing I learned about gender roles in elementary school was that football was not a girl's sport. I distinctly remember an incident in the fifth grade when a group of girls and I got in trouble for playing football at recess with the boys. When the teacher saw us playing she immediately stopped us and told us that the girls should go play a different game. I told the teacher that I didn't think that was fair and that I would play football with the boys if I wanted to. That got me a quick trip to the principal's office. He explained to me that girls could get hurt playing football and that we should play a sport like basketball. I explained to him that being pushed down on the jagged rocks of the outdoor basketball court hurt a lot worse than the soft grass of the football field, and that I had the scars to prove it. His response was that I would either stop playing football or I would spend the rest of my recesses sitting by the fence. That was the end of my football career.

In addition to cheerleading, I also joined the basketball team in the fourth grade. This was my first group to join in which black girls were members. Black girls didn't want to be cheerleaders or Girl Scouts, but they all wanted to play basketball. Basketball was also a sport for tall girls, so I fit right in. I had great coaches in elementary school so I excelled, which gave me a feeling of achievement and taught me a lot of valuable lessons about hard work and teamwork. I continued to play basketball with those same girls up until high school, when I quit in the ninth grade (at fifteen or sixteen).

This is when I became aware of racial differences. Children from a number of local elementary schools went on to attend one high school in a central location, so at the age of twelve we started school with a new group of peers. I joined the basketball team at the high school, but I soon realized that my black friends that I had played with in elementary school acted differently when they were around the new black kids. They didn't speak the same and they didn't treat me the same. As I look on it in retrospect, I see clearly that they were trying to fit into a new social group, but at the time it angered me, and I soon formed stereotypes about them.

In elementary school my ideas of nationalism were formed. We recited the pledge to the flag every morning before class. Each year the

> fourth grade class put on a play in which they recited the preamble to the Constitution, sang the national anthem, and sang all the hymns for each branch of the armed forces. I even remember that I held the first letter 'E' in the word 'preamble' and I recited the phrase 'establish justice, ensure domestic tranquility.' However, as strong as my national identity was enforced, my identity as a Southerner was just as ingrained.
>
> In high school we were given extensive teaching of the American Civil War, even more than the American Revolution. We studied the war in depth from both sides, and though the atrocities that were committed in the South (such as slavery) were never glossed over, our teachers made sure we knew the other factors involved (such as states' rights).
>
> The only other institution that had a big impact on my socialization was the church. After my parents moved back to Moselle they took some time choosing a church, and for a long time I remember being a little embarrassed when people would ask me what church I attended and I didn't have an answer. Eventually they began to attend my father's parent's old church (his family was Methodist), but the congregation was mainly older people so my sister and I started to attend a Baptist church nearby that had a large youth group. The youth group took lots of trips and had lots of activities so it attracted a large number of young people in the area. The people who owned the local restaurant where I attended Girl Scout meetings went there, so it was through them that I got my first job as a waitress.
>
> A. Price

The activity is conducted in pairs. Each participant is asked to read a different text on secondary socialisation (either in the USA or in Japan) with a view to creating an information gap. In class, the pairs proceed to the worksheet partially reproduced below and start by comparing and contrasting the two texts. The following questions are used to prompt the answers, which are jotted down in the table below:

> (1) What institutions of secondary socialisation are described in the texts?
> (2) Is there an explicit reference to 'secondary socialisation'? What about 'primary socialisation'? If so, how are they related?
> (3) What values, norms, beliefs and behaviours are emphasised and promoted in the institutions?
> (4) How does becoming a member of a new in-group affect the individual?

Text 1	Text 2
Q1.	Q1.
Q2.	Q2.
Q3.	Q3.
Q4.	Q4.

Taking any of the sample excerpts as a model, participants then write a parallel text on the institutions that have had a say in their secondary socialisation process and the in-groups that have shaped their personality. Explicit mention could be made of the relevance of the following (or other) institutions in connection with values, norms, beliefs and behaviours enhanced: kindergarten, primary school, secondary school, university, church, etc.

In pairs or in groups of four, participants analyse the texts they have produced individually by answering the four questions shown above. Alternatively or additionally, participants could conduct interviews with a person from their own and another cultural background and report on their findings in small groups or to the rest of the class.

Finally, the debriefing of the activity is done with the whole group. To the previous issues, a further topic for discussion is added: relevant conclusions that can be drawn for multicultural teamwork dynamics.

CONCLUSIONS FOR MULTICULTURAL TEAMWORK DYNAMICS

My Biography and in particular *A new institution, a new group, a new 'me'* scrutinize the individual's biography as regards the acquisition of his/her own cultural practices and how they become determining elements in the way of perceiving and dealing with otherness. Without doubt, they will give participants food for thought and, hopefully, help them become aware of the importance of these factors in their sense of identity as a prerequisite for real intercultural communication and understanding when the encounter with the other happens.

To conclude, the activities making up My Biography smooth the progress of the inward journey so that individuals' intercultural competence can map out outwards again.

Conclusion

A starting point towards awareness of intercultural dynamics in multicultural group work, My Biography favours the exploration of experiences both in the construction of the self and in the work context.

Like any other factor, circumstance or activity that contemplates personal elements, some of the tasks in My Biography may encounter the reluctance of certain participants to reveal aspects that they may consider to be too personal or which they understand may make them vulnerable. What individuals have to value is to what degree this vulnerability and the possible interest in not dealing overtly with personal issues is compatible with creating an atmosphere of confidence and trust in the work context.

Multicultural teamwork has the potential to bring about a profound change in the individual's worldview, personality and ways of understanding and doing things. In this context, intercultural learning seems to rest on both the analysis and awareness of personal experiences and 'on the spot' experiences with otherness in a global work setting. The chief value of the activities within My Biography is the possibility they offer to make the most of experiential learning in the work setting for prospective multicultural team players and/or raising awareness of relevant issues of identity and personality so that current multicultural team members can enhance their experiential learning on the job.

References

Allport, G. (1954) *The Nature of Prejudice*. Cambridge, MA: Addison-Wesley.
Amorim, L. (2001) Intercultural learning A few awareness tips for US and European Fellows & Host Community Foundations. On WWW at http://www.efc.be/ftp/public/cpi/TCFF%20Intercultural%20Learning.pdf.
Berger, P. and Luckmann, T. (1966) *The Social Construction of Reality*. Penguin: Harmondsworth.
Brewer, M.B. and Gardner, W.L. (1996) Who is this 'we'? Levels of collective identity and self representations. *Journal of Personality and Social Psychology* 71, 83–93.
Chang, S. and Tharenou, P. (2004) Competencies needed for managing a multicultural workgroup. *Asia Pacific Journal of Human Resources* 42 (1), 57–74.
Early, P.C. and Ang, S. (2003) *Cultural Intelligence: Individual Interactions across Cultures*. Palo Alto, CA: Stanford University Press.
Glaser, E., Guilherme, M., Méndez García, M.C. and Mughan, T. (2007) *Intercultural Competence for Professional Mobility*. Strasbourg: Council of Europe.
Gudykunst, W.B. (2004) *Bridging Differences. Effective Intergroup Communication* (4th edn). Thousand Oaks, CA: Sage.

Gullestrup, H. (2006) *Cultural Analysis – Towards Cross-cultural Understanding.* Copenhagen: Business School Press.
Hendry, J. (1987) *Understanding Japanese Society.* London: Croom Helm.
Hinton, P.R. (2000) *Stereotypes, Cognition and Culture.* London: Psychology Press.
Hoffman, E. (1989) *Lost in Translation.* Hardmondsworth: Penguin Books.
Hogg, M.A. (2006) Social identity theory. In P.J. Burke (ed.) *Contemporary Social Psychological Theories* (pp. 111–136). Palo Alto, CA: Standford University Press.
Houle, C. (1980) *Continuing Learning in the Professions.* San Francisco, CA: Jossey-Bass.
Kolb, D.A. (1984) *Experiential Learning.* Englewood Cliffs, NJ: Prentice Hall.
Ng, K.Y., Van Dyne, L. and Ang, S. (2009) From experience to experiential learning: Cultural intelligence as a learning capability for global leader development. *Academy of Management Learning and Education* 8 (4), 511–526.
Norton, B. (2000) Eva and Mai: Old heads on young shoulders. In B. Norton (ed.) *Identity and Language Learning. Gender, Ethnicity and Educational Change* (pp. 60–74). Harlow: Longman.
Pavlenko, A. and Lantolf, J.P. (2000) Second language learning as participation and the (re)construction of selves. In J.P. Lantolf (ed.) *Sociocultural Theory and Second Language Learning* (pp. 155–178). Oxford: Oxford University Press.
Shaffer, M.A., Harrison, D.A., Gregersen, H., Black, J.S. and Ferzandi, L.A. (2006) You can take it with you: Individual differences and expatriate effectiveness. *Journal of Applied Psychology* 91, 109–125.
Tajfel, H. (1972) La catégorisation sociale. In S. Moscovici (ed.) *Introduction à la psychologie sociale* (Vol. 1) (pp. 272–302). Paris: Larousse.
Tajfel, H. (1981) Social stereotypes and social groups. In J. Turner and H. Giles (eds) *Intergroup Behaviour* (pp. 144–167). Chicago, IL: University of Chicago Press.
Utley, D. (2004) *Intercultural Resource Pack: Intercultural Communication Resources for Language Teachers.* London: Cambridge University Press.
Vivian, J. and Brown, R. (1995) Prejudice and intergroup conflict. In M. Argyle and A.M. Coleman (eds) *Social Psychology* (pp. 105–125). London: Longman.
Wills, S. and Barham, K. (1994) Being an international manager. *European Management Journal* 12 (1), 49–58.
Wodak, R., De Cillia, R., Reisigl, M. and Liebhart, K. (2009) *The Discursive Construction of National Identity* (2nd edn). Edinburgh: Edinburgh University Press.

Chapter 10
Diversity Management: Negotiating Representations in Multicultural Contexts

CLARA KEATING, MANUELA GUILHERME and
DANIEL HOPPE

Introduction

The need to search for a different kind of education, aimed at flexible and open-minded individuals who are prepared to live with cultural differences, was one of the central ideas that inspired us to work on this theme. This implied creating atmospheres of complicity, respect and creativity, as well as reinforcing the need to look at the co-habitation of different cultural backgrounds as a source of professional competence. 'Co-habitation of difference' as a 'source of professional competence' is a starting point to get us thinking about ways in which we can realistically manage diversity and in whose terms we are undertaking such a challenge. It may entail many positive aspects, but it can also lead to misunderstandings, exclusions, conflicts, tensions or violent confrontations in the public space – be it the workplace, the market or the street. To 'manage' usually implies acting according to interests located on broader scales and in organisational discourses, reinforcing rationales of productivity and making business, situated in what Gee *et al.* (1996) call the 'new work order'. In this sense, it is imperative that we reflect critically on concepts such as *diversity* and *management*, as well as on the full implications of what *managing diversity* might (or needs to) mean for the ways in which professional worlds are being configured hegemonically throughout the globe.

This chapter develops the key idea that the management of diversity implies critical awareness of two crucial aspects. Firstly, the situated development of *spaces of multicultural intersubjectivity*. We will reflect on the construction of such spaces as dynamic and unstable arenas permeated by hegemonic representations in conflict with each other. One way of looking at these spaces is by developing critical awareness of language, languages and the semiotic representations at play in individual, group and institutional interaction. Secondly – and as a way of expanding Ting-Toomey and Chung's (2004) notion of a 'creative mindset' – the construction of a *critically creative mindset*, i.e. the development of attitudes towards diversity that celebrate partiality and difference, in the dialogic sense of these terms. Our aim is to assume a position of modesty and mutual respect towards the multiple stances from which authorities of various natures can, ideally, be legitimised. This implies critical reflection on the foundations that motivate constraints and generate contradictions that emerge in this space of multicultural intersubjectivity. This understanding might be used as a resource for effective, creative and transformative management of diversity, not only at a local, but also at a global level.

The last part of the chapter is an attempt to put some of these ideas into practice in the field of intercultural training. It discusses the development of analytic instruments that will allow us to make visible the power mechanisms involved in the dynamics of multicultural teams, at the personal, group and institutional levels. Understanding the ideological work involved in the very definition of these levels is crucial and it will help us understand what is made visible and what is being erased by the ongoing distribution of powers (of various natures) in multicultural teams.

Space of Intercultural Intersubjectivity

To explain the theoretical approach underlying the activities, we first focus on the construction of 'diverse diversities'. What does it mean to be 'diverse' and who is defining this diversity? Issues of sameness and difference, of stereotypes and prejudices, as well as what was considered new and known were seen as being negotiated in interaction and in intercultural encounters. We explored ways in which particular points of view affected intercultural relations and we reflected on these in terms of broader discourses and ideologies, most of them naturalised in the ways individuals saw the world and had experienced it in the past. Issues of power and hegemony were intrinsically affecting the construction of difference and diversity. To manage diversity thus implied a broader process of negotiating representations that were being constructed in sites of cultural conflict, as well as concrete decision-making processes, situated in the rationales brought about by the organisational structure – and their actors – that were a constitutive part of these sites of negotiation. How were things being represented in the minds of individuals and social groups? What were the mechanisms underlying these acts of representation? How was something being constructed as a resource in a context permeated by cultural conflict and tension? Who, in the end, was defining something as a resource?

Negotiating representations in multicultural contexts can best be understood if we posit the creation of *spaces for multicultural intersubjectivity*. Such a concept implies two crucial aspects: firstly, an emphasis on situated learning and development, that must be brought to the fore when thinking about inter- and multicultural awareness; secondly, a systematic reflection on the workings of power and dominance taking place in the multiple layers at play in intercultural encounters.

Workings of power and dominance maintain the structural existence of organisations and institutions, derived from particular naturalised narratives, discursive orders and discursive formations (Foucault, 1969); they determine the scope of action by the actors at play in particular settings and events, each one with its own trajectory of socialisation; they sustain the regimes of social and verbal interaction that work in situated meaning-making activities and events. These are some of the multiple layers that arise in intercultural encounters. Others can be found. For this reason, issues of power could not be dissociated from the ways in which we saw diversity being constructed, as well as the processes underlying its management. In the words of Lorbiecki and Jack:

> First, managing, or management, is presented as the privileged subject which sees diversity as an object to be managed. Distance is therefore created between "those who manage" and "those who are diverse", so that they are split into two distinct groups, with the properties of diversity being located solely amongst "the managed".
> (Lorbiecki & Jack, 2000: 23)

Our work involved precisely a critical exploration of the political, social and cultural conditions of diversity management. It resonated with the concerns of these two authors with issues of language and the politics of representation (Lorbiecki & Jack, 2000: 29). We thus explored issues of hegemony and hierarchy, and reflected on multiculturalism and interculturality as contested spaces where partial and fragmented representations were being negotiated. We summarise some of our concerns in the following paragraphs.

Social encounters – in what they display of action and representation – imply unconscious positioning configured according to worldviews and narratives about the world. Prejudices, stereotypes or simply common senses are situated in statements about culture, nationality or ethnicity, part of what one can call one's own 'culture' or 'cultural principles'. Such are the workings of *hegemony* and any study that calls itself critical must devote its time and effort to de-constructing those statements. In the activities devised for this module, individual values, attitudes and expectations were seen as being represented in the discursive configurations that sustained cultural, social and work organisations in which people and groups moved. This implied the construction of a critical awareness of the self and other, as well as of diversity and expectations towards diversity.

An understanding of the mechanisms of *hegemony* implies the identification of degrees of unspoken and unconscious tension or oppression that might lead to feelings of unease, which cannot always be made visible or voiced, even for the proponents of the oppressive act. Hence the search for tools that would help analyse who was defining what was relevant in multicultural interactions, under what circumstances and according to whose interests. Most of the time, clashes emerged precisely through different hegemonic discourses configuring not only broader aspects of social life, such as sexuality, gender, religion, ethical issues, but also aspects located at the micro level of social action, such as the use and recognition of particular social and language genres and styles, or the ways in which particular words or accents created social representations of individuals and their available resources, associated with a constant negotiation between identification and detachment, sameness and difference.

In organisational contexts, different roles display different scopes of action and validity assessments, usually organised in *hierarchical order*. Managing diversity also implied assessing these aspects as one finds them within the work, the institutional and the organisational cultures at play in particular encounters. Underlying issues of hierarchy and hegemony translate into situated dynamics of reproduction and resistance to what people perceive as already established *ways of doing* in particular local contexts, where formal hierarchies are already being informally configured – reproduced, but also eventually contested – in stable yet flexible communities of practice (cf. Wenger, 1998; Wenger *et al.*, 2001). One thus needs to make explicit the criteria that locate people and ways of doing in dominant or minority positions. In events recognised as multicultural encounters, how were hierarchies being reproduced as established ways of doing or how were they being resisted? How were particular attitudes being valued, silenced or ignored, both intentionally and unintentionally? And what were the processes that were constructing particular ways of doing as *efficient* or *appropriate* and for what particular interests?

Assuming instability in multicultural space

Conditions of interculturality necessarily imply positions of minority and exclusion. In spaces of multicultural intersubjectivity, culture risks concealing other aspects – of a historical, political, economical or another material nature – being negotiated in interaction. What we call *cultural* usually goes beyond our own partial definition of culture. The stance is thus one that implies heterogeneity, heterodoxy and multiculturalism right from the start, where stable meanings and fixed positions run the risk of being dissociated and destabilised. In a state of instability, feelings of unease and exclusion are indeed likely to prevail. *Spaces of multicultural intersubjectivity* are thus arenas where constant negotiation and reinvention of meanings takes place, making temporary sense of the hybridism and destabilisation involved. Acknowledging the workings of power and dominance implies assuming that any decision-making or problem-solving process necessarily involves the silencing of other solutions – which have not yet been allowed to be constructed through an act of naming (cf. Butler, 1997). As intercultural encounters imply intersubjective spaces of creativity as well as constraint, we must not lose sight of the idea that things can always be otherwise and can be interpreted from more than one place, prone to different historically and structurally motivated authorities. Such is the thinking involved in dyatopic hermeneutics. Dyatopics, i.e. the idea that cultural completeness is impossible and thus in need of being replaced by the careful exercise of comparison and confrontation with other coexisting (and conflicting) cultural versions (cf. Santos, 2004), opens up the possibility of acknowledging the existence of rival regimes of language use at play in the same space, fully located in different historical long-term duration processes and conflicting inventions of the future.[1]

Looking at theories of language, culture and social semiotics is helpful at this point. In the traditions of cultural and literary studies, social and cultural anthropological approaches to linguistics and the philosophy of language, any act of speech offers more than one point of view, precisely because of its polyphony. The semiotic configuration of language resources and structures can be said to enhance particular worldviews to the detriment of others. The ways we use language thus allow us to manipulate our own version of the world by highlighting some aspects of 'the reality' and silencing others. In fact, realities are created through representations, affected by and displayed in different media, configured by different materialities and orchestrated by different agents. The flexible and arbitrary nature of language can be used simultaneously for violent yet peaceful, conflicting yet consensual, among many other purposes. In fact, representations can never be seen in the abstract but always as happening in local sites of negotiation, tension and decision making.[2]

This assumes that there are no such things as neutral acts – acts of speech, acts of representation or any other. Claiming neutrality involves referring to the dominant discourses of neutrality available, for historical or ideological reasons, in our worlds. Arriving at a consensual view of things does not mean reaching a space of neutrality, but rather finding a space of partial agreement between the parties involved. It implies the dominance of one version to the detriment of a number of others, negotiated in order to move further towards some common aim, often leading to a different dimension of social action.

To reach a space of multicultural intersubjectivity thus implies embarking on intercultural encounters reflectively and critically. Likewise, the very process of gaining intercultural awareness needs to be deconstructed in this way, as it runs the risk of being located in motivations (such as 'making business more efficient' or 'improving global communication') associated with a new global order and a world of mobility permeated by inequality. Far from being neutral, the development of such a space is more about acknowledging multiplicity and taking sides for particular purposes, by making clear to whom they are going to bring benefit.

Critically Creative Mindset

Managing diversity has been defined as acquiring the necessary knowledge and dynamic skills to manage differences appropriately and effectively, while developing a creative mindset to be able to see things from different angles without rigid prejudgment (Ting-Toomey & Chung, 2004). This involves developing the kind of competent intercultural communication that 'emphasizes the importance of integrating the necessary intercultural knowledge, mindfulness, and interaction skills to manage identity-based issues adaptively and to achieve desired identity outcomes creatively' (Ting-Toomey, 2005: 228).

However, we still need to understand in what terms, and according to whose agenda, we are defining what counts as 'knowledge', 'desire' and 'interaction skill', as well as in what contexts they are being assessed as appropriate, efficient or as 'desired identity outcomes'. Such questions may push the concept of diversity a bit further, expanding it into one that involves a *critically creative mindset* that encourages us to see the issue of diversity from different angles and without rigid prejudgement.

In addition, and as mentioned above, any attempt to 'see' diversity is situated in a particular linguistic and social order, affecting individuals (at the intra and inter-individual levels) as well as groups (in-group and inter-group) and institutions. To decide on orientations for particular meanings and/or verbalise particular meanings implies silencing or discarding, for that moment, other ways of speaking or thinking. In intercultural training, one needs to find a position that will create awareness of such a fact. Managing diversity necessarily implies translating and mediating between the semiotic resources (i.e. 'languages') available for all actors involved in the configuration of a multicultural team.

Acknowledging miscommunication and partiality is crucial for the development of a critically creative mindset, since it is through miscommunication that the need for social and political critique emerges. Adding to an attitude of partiality and uncertainty, a critically creative mindset implies being aware of the historical, ideological, structural and organisational factors that may contribute to the construction of multi-layered intersubjective spaces, at the personal, intra- and inter-group, as well as institutional levels. The implications of this development thus include the following aspects: firstly, a critical awareness of how multicultural intersubjectivity is being forged by multiple and conflicting layers of meaning; secondly, a multicultural attitude that gives emphasis to partiality, uncertainty, exclusion or difference; and thirdly, an understanding of the interplay of the dynamics of power acting in the process of managing this diversity. As intercultural dynamics involves finding oneself in a place where nothing is central, a critically creative mindset means to embrace an attitude of marginality and exclusion. In the words of Evanoff:

> Not all individuals successfully make the transition to a multicultural perspective, of course. J. Bennett (1993) distinguishes between "constructive marginality", which achieves higher levels self-differentiation and integration [sic], and "encapsulated marginality", which results in psychological disintegration. Both the constructive and the encapsulated marginals have stepped outside of their original cultures into a cultural "void" (Durkheim's anomie), a place

beyond conventional social practices where no norms exist. The constructive marginal sees this emptiness as space for individual creativity; in the absence of clearly defined rules opportunities arise for creating new ways of doing things. ...Constructive marginals are in a good position to act as go-betweens in intercultural negotiations because they are capable not just of understanding the basic outlooks of two (or more) cultures but also of integrating perspectives which on the surface may seem "incommensurable". (Evanoff, 2006: 423)

To experience exclusion is thus crucial for a constructive understanding of the mixed feelings embodied in minority and uncomfortable positions. In a multicultural intersubjective space, all participants can be best seen as finding themselves in legitimate peripheral positions (Lave & Wenger, 1991), uncertain, not fully aware of the multiple authorities at play in that context. Spaces of multicultural intersubjectivity are prone to the emergence of alternative ways of gaining prestige and generating authority, in a dialogue between the formal and the informal agendas of institutional actors and the socio-historical lives (real and imagined) of the participants involved in a particular encounter. Such is the creation of a 'third space', as has been suggested by Gutierrez and colleagues in their work on learning and literacy in non-dominant communities in the USA, where they observed alternative spaces being created, contingent on participants' socio-historical lives that acted in resistance to the formal agendas of dominant educational institutions (Gutierrez et al., 1995). A critically creative mindset thus implies acknowledging these alternative authorities and managing them in a way that allows for transformation and empowerment on multiple levels of action.

What has been said above recognises that all spaces of interaction are inherently diverse, hybrid and multilayered, permeated by complex dynamics of creativity and constraint. To manage diversity, then, involves negotiating partial modes of understanding. This negotiation implies mechanisms of mediation that need to take into account the following basic aspects of intercultural encounters.

One, people never meet in a void. There are motivations, physical settings, group dynamics and roles involved in social encounters, partially represented in the minds of the participants in the interactions. Perceptions of these might clash because of different principles, values and assumptions that can be assessed *as if* they were *culture*.

Two, social interaction is constituted by a number of pre-established unwritten rules: not everything can be said, and what is being said is usually verbalised in particular modes and manners. What should be kept silent and what should be shared, either through words, gestures or body language, is usually also governed by rules grounded in cultural principles, motivations and values. Silences, for instance, can be valued or dismissed, depending on the grounds that rule silence in particular regimes of language use. One way of searching for a space of multicultural intersubjectivity is to search for what could be said and done but is not, or in what terms things could be done differently.

Three, people engage in partial modes of mutual agreement. Agreement is radically situated in particular configurations of space and time that constrain the scope of recognition of some, but not other, strategies as resources for further action.

To summarise, intercultural interaction is more susceptible to miscommunication than one would expect. One never knows exactly what is going on, thus sharing with others the mutual status of legitimate peripheral participants, not fully in control of the whole meaning implied by one's own actions. To be aware of this sense of *exclusion*, celebrate it and use it in positive terms in multicultural teams is a way of reaching the kind of critically creative mindset mentioned in this section, one that implies a sense of the unknown and the incomplete, both in others and in ourselves.

Negotiating Representations in Contexts of Intercultural Training

In this section, we discuss how we applied the two theoretical concepts described in the previous sections – that of a space of multicultural intersubjectivity and that of the development of a critically creative mindset – when thinking about diversity management as an act of negotiating representations in multicultural contexts. We will do so by referring back to the three aspects mentioned above as a means of mediating between a more theoretical approach to diversity management and a *modus operandi* in training. These were: firstly, developing a critical awareness of the construction of spaces of intersubjectivity created by multiple and conflicting layers of meaning; secondly, developing a multicultural attitude that gives emphasis to partiality, uncertainty, exclusion or difference; and thirdly, understanding the dynamics of power involved in the management of diversity. In the training activities, we explored these aspects at a personal, intra- and inter-group and institutional level. While we highlight one level or another, we acknowledge that they act simultaneously in intercultural encounters. At a first stage, our training activities focused on the development of a critical awareness of diversity and of the need for mediation and translation in the management of diversity. At a second stage, the activities concentrated on particular aspects of such awareness at the personal, the interactional and the institutional levels.

Towards critical awareness of diversity: Locating diversity at multiple levels

Deconstructing sameness and difference

We began by exploring how *sameness and difference* were being constructed in ongoing interaction. This implied exploring a complex interplay of identities and identifications. A number of aspects of the dynamics of sameness and difference were deconstructed at this first stage.

People's *expectations* of events, cultural backgrounds and participants' personalities – and false expectations of existing possibilities in particular cultures – were intrinsically linked to previous socialisations and to knowledges about the world as experienced in the past, as well as to the cultural values used to make sense of experience. By focusing on people's own perceptions of what different behaviours meant, we explored concrete ways in which diversity manifested itself in people's own experiences. We explored naturalised expectations (e.g. in relation to 'minor issues' such as eating habits) or more in-depth constructions of difference like ethnicity, class, religion or gender. Instances of diversity led to discussions about reasons for particular definitions of 'diversity', as well as ways in which assumptions and expectations about diversity could be affecting relations in the workplace and individual behaviour in working teams:

> *Discuss why these aspects are considered determining factors of diversity;*
> 1. *rank them according to order of importance in your opinion;*
> 2. *consider how they could affect relations in the workplace;*
> 3. *and provide suggestions for eliminating the possible conflicts they might lead to in the multicultural team.* (From activity 'Diversity Quiz')

At this training stage, it was important to understand in intuitive terms the ways in which *stereotypes and prejudices* were also ordinary tools used to make sense of the world and of one's own cultural sense of self. It was thus important to make explicit some of the mechanisms underlying the construction of stereotypes and prejudices, as well as to explain some of their motivations and origins. Stereotypes and prejudices not only mediated the assessment of behaviours and events where participants engaged, but they were also taken as particular personal and social types of generic representation of peoples, cultures, nations and other social categorisations (such as class, ethnicity, race, religion or gender). A critical reflection upon one's own/other cultures led to the recognition that there were more similar, rather than dissimilar behaviours across cultures, and to the adoption of an attitude of modesty towards one's insufficient knowledge about cultures and cultural backgrounds, be it one's own or others. The activities focused explicitly on particular vectors in the construction of difference, for instance, issues of gender and the relations between male and female colleagues in the workplace. In that particular activity ('Diversity Quiz'), by simulating a particular male behaviour in a multicultural team and exploring the ways in which this related or not to particular stereotypes of gender and national identities, issues such as implicit assumptions about gender and nationality, 'traditional' or 'modern' behaviour and ways of rationalising particular behaviours by males and females in the workplace were the *foci* of attention.

Any intercultural encounter implies a process of taking one's own fixed meanings, de-constructing them and creating things anew. This leads to a third aspect – that of the *ambiguity between the old and the new*. Dealing with the new and the different implies a reconfiguration of what was previously valued as positive, suddenly emerging as simply not fitting into the new situation. Known experience becomes surprisingly new. Accepting the unexpected, analysing it, incorporating it and making an attempt to explain it in multiple ways, implies involvement in a *learning process*. Some activities illustrated the existence of tensions located in people's own assumptions about, say, rules in the workplace, as well as the ways in which old assumptions contradicted one another in new situations. Underlying this tension between the old and the new were issues like ignoring or assuming and expanding on tensions, discussed with concrete examples.

The focus on the *politics of language, translation and cultural representations* was particularly strong in the debates about diversity and the management of diversity. Issues like linguistic representation, accents, linguistic ideologies and social representations related to particular language uses, as well as the politics involved in the definitions of dialects, regional or national languages as opposed to global languages such as English, and finally the use of linguae francae in multicultural contexts were present in many of the activities devised for this training

Diversity Management 179

module. This was related to the aim of deconstructing particular points of view in multicultural and multilingual interaction. It also aimed at de-naturalising associations between registers, dialects or languages and preconceived assumptions about their speakers, as well as reflecting on the associations between perceptions of language acquired at a local level, and their effect in organisational contexts situated on more global scales of transnational institutional life:

> *Do you think that the fact that she had that accent would make her speech less intelligible and, therefore, constitute a hindrance to that team's work? Should she be hired to work in a European institution?*
> *Do you agree or disagree?*
> *1. We often display prejudice against non-European performances of European languages.*
> *2. Linguistic performance of European languages must follow European standards.* (From activity 'Who's talking funny?')

Critical awareness of diversity and of management: Persons, groups and institutions

Training further applied these broader perceptions of diversity by locating them in personal, interactional as well as institutional levels.

The personal level of diversity was explored in activities where individual character, personality and values, as well as personal priorities, were assessed and debated. Training focused on assessments of personal priorities and their situated nature in biographical, historical and cultural configurations, as well as on the ways in which these could create conflicting perspectives of personal decisions, individual doings and mutual respect. This kind of debate privileged thinking about subjectivity and positioning, its complex multilayered nature and the corresponding conflicts and tensions, thus paving the way for issues involved in the construction of spaces of multicultural intersubjectivity that included critical awareness of the changing nature (over time and space) of both personal priorities and contexts of participation.

The meeting of subjectivities and differing priorities raises issues of actual management of diversity in group dynamics, starting at the personal and the interpersonal level. In various activities, aspects such as emotions, ways of relating to other people and ways of reading each others' dynamics were the *foci* of debate. Personal and emotional management of differences, socialisations into stereotypes and prejudices, as well as culturally centred behaviours were all seen to emerge in spaces of multicultural intersubjectivity, where diversity implies facing unexpected and unknown areas of the self. Again, this implied giving emphasis to the construction of a position of partial participation, apprenticeship and learning. It also raised issues on access and exclusion, dominant and subordinate positions, as well as discussions on ongoing definitions of dominant and minority groups:

> *What first conclusions can you reach regarding the behaviour of dominant and subordinate members in teams? What was the factor that led to the formation of a majority and a minority in this situation? What other attributes can, consciously or unconsciously, promote the formation of majority or minority groups in professional contexts? What makes a "majority"? Is it necessarily the number of people, or can there be other determining factors? Can a group carry a symbolic value, a hegemonic value that will put it in a majority position?* (From activity 'Outnumbered')

Group dynamics are thus quite important when it comes to managing diversity. The creation of rules of thumb in particular groups, the awareness of the sensibilities of different individuals involved in the groups and the extent to which they affect group interaction, are all important in the construction of shared contexts and resources. Looking for compromise, adopting different points of view and trying to effectively smooth out any possible friction between fellow workers is part of the role of a mediator – or a manager of diversity – within a group. Multicultural, as well as multidisciplinary, professional teams intersect different identities in multiple ways – culture, language, groups and solidarities, and institutional roles and profiles, all of them adding to the multilayered space of a multicultural team. For this reason, some activities focused on the need to orchestrate the multiplicity of legitimate discourses and authorities and to make choices, situated within the priorities of the group, the organisation and the institutions involved. This kind of debate led on to the institutional level and to the ways in which an institutional perspective is related to the process of managing diversity.

The introduction of an institutional level implied the awareness of further degrees of formality and constraint. Institutions involve public, formal and legitimised authorities and normativities that make it harder to resist, transform and mediate. Understanding these institutions implies understanding the historical reasons for their existence – for instance, how market-related practices or multinational business organisations are valued in particular contexts. As an example, values related to *efficiency, appropriateness* and *productivity* are situated in work orders that privilege particular versions of time management, working habits and rhythms to the detriment of others, considered less efficient and less productive, in unequal distribution. To keep to our example, different work methods might result in different forms of efficiency. While certain working genres and styles (e.g. the use of high degrees of formality and power distance) may be less efficient in some contexts, they will probably be useful or even necessary in others. The ability to assess these factors is an important asset when managing diversity and evaluating what styles are best suited to each context. Activities that focused on these aspects also allowed us to look at the extent to which institutions, and institutional ways of looking at correctness and efficiency, were affecting personal working styles. Issues of hierarchical distance, formality of informality, different perceptions of working times and rhythms, and spatial organisation were some of the aspects included in the training activities. They raised issues related to the different cultural – and language-related – ways of approaching work, organisations and institutions.

Exercising 'Diversity Management': The 'Cultural Layers' Activity

The selected activity, 'Cultural Layers', encapsulates most of the training aspects mentioned above. 'Cultural Layers' starts by analysing individual personalities and the assessment of individual values and priorities. It thus starts from the personal level of diversity and gradually expands its focus to an interpersonal and group level, which creates the space for critical reflection on the institutional and the historical nature of particular multicultural interactions and the management of diversity.

Cultural layers

Our personality is determined by numerous factors, which we can call cultural. Each individual values these factors in his/her own manner. So, for example, while family life is very important to some, it may not be valued as highly by others. In multicultural teams, this spectrum of influences is broadened, because the factors involved are even more varied.

Observe the following diagram. It represents three individuals working in a team and the cultural/environmental factors they consider more important, presented as layers. The layer closest to the individual is the one considered the most important.

Part 2: Intercultural Communication, Interaction, Management

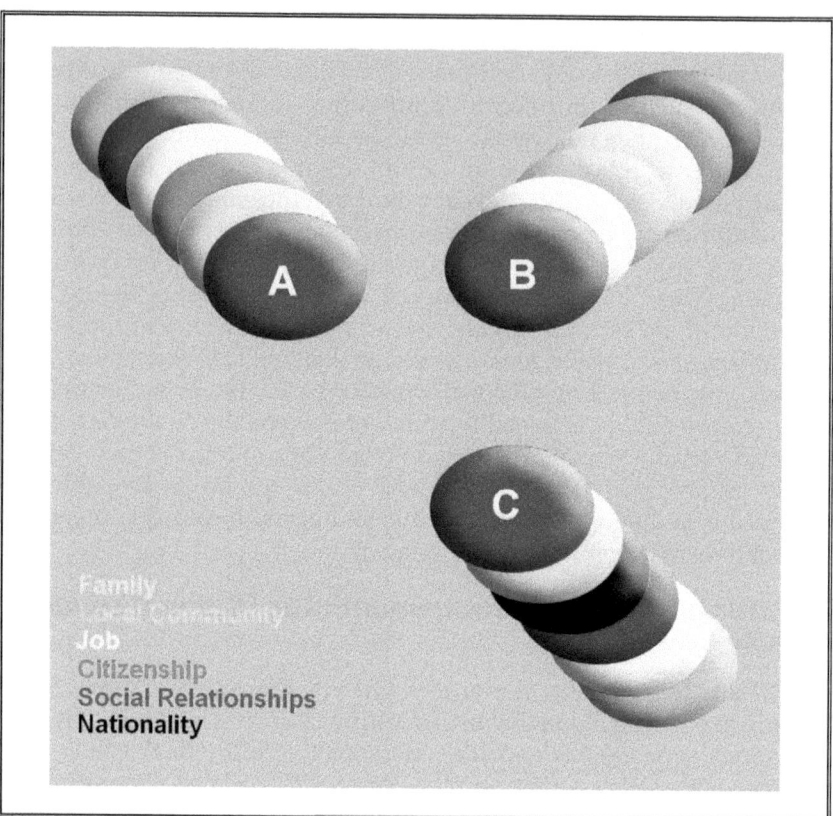

Guidelines for discussion

(1) (a) Comparing the personalities represented, can you imagine possible sources of conflict? To begin with, notice how A and C value family very much and consider their job of medium importance, while B prioritises the job and isn't much concerned about family life.
  (b) What conflicts do you think might result from this?
(2) What other important cultural influences can you think of? What other layers could you imagine in the diagram?
(3) Draw your own layer diagram, including any layers that you consider important.
  (a) In pairs or in small groups, compare your drawings and discuss whether you think there would be a conflict if you

were to work together. How could you deal with your differences in an effective way?
(b) Would your layer diagram look the same at all times? Would you have drawn your diagram in exactly the same way five years ago? Would you draw it differently at different times of the day?
(4) These different cultural values can cause conflicts in a monocultural team. In what ways do you think the situation would be different in a multicultural team? Would there be more layers to consider? Imagine the three people depicted in the diagram: first, assume they all come from your hometown. Then, imagine they come from three very different cultures – would you interpret their layer graphs in a different way?

Following the metaphor of the 'culture onion' (Utley, 2004: 33), the activity 'Cultural Layers' introduces the concept of layered personality. This encourages reflection on the various structural places of human socialisation and construction of cultural difference. It then guides trainees to engage in debates, not only about personal priorities, but also about the multiple socio-historical and institutional dimensions of such priorities. This leads them to reflect critically on the ways in which interests develop into conflicting or consensual knowledge shared by a particular group, and on the mechanisms that can help reach such consensual knowledge. The 'Cultural Layers' activity thus explores the aspects discussed in this chapter in greater depth, by making them visual and graspable on the one hand, but also by demonstrating their instability on the other. In a straightforward way, issues related to multicultural intersubjectivity gradually become a way of conceptualising the living, changing interactive space that requires constant adaptation and reframing from its participants, crucial in the construction of a critically creative mindset.

Managing diversity usually implies rationalising in terms of the broader discourses at play in the construction of the *intersubjective* space, usually described in terms of institutional, work or any kind of organisational systems of values at play in particular contexts, complying with interests located in institutional orders. Becoming aware of the counter-hegemonic and alternative versions of such rationalisations is the aim underlying the construction of *multicultural intersubjective* spaces and the development of a *critically creative mindset*. To analyse the actors involved in the processes of managing diversity is thus crucial. Who is managing diversity? At what level are we managing diversity? According to whose ideas and for what (whose) best interests?

Notes

1. For a sociology of absences and emergences, cf. Santos (2004). For an exploration of these ideas in socio-linguistic research in multilingual contexts, cf. Keating, (2010); in interculturality cf. Guilherme (2007).
2. For issues of dialogism and polyphony, cf. Bakhtin (1986). For an introduction to issues related to language, thought and culture, cf. the contested Sapir-Whorf hypothesis and work being developed by anthropological linguistics, Duranti (1997). For a systemic-functional approach to language, ideology and point of view, cf. Simpson, (1993). For a critical approach to language use and discourse, cf. Fairclough (2003). For work developed in cultural studies, cf. Hall (1997). For an up-to-date introduction to emerging debates in the philosophy of language, cf. Medina (2005).

References

Bakhtin, M. (1986) *Speech Genres and other Late Essays* (V.W.V. McGee, C. Emerson and M. Holquist, trans.). Austin, TX: University of Texas Press.

Bennett, M. (1993) Towards ethnorelativism: A development model of intercultural sensitivity. In R.M. Paige (ed.) *Education for the Intercultural Experience* (pp. 21–71). Yarmouth: Intercultural Press.

Butler, J. (1997) *Excitable Speech: A Politics of the Performative*. New York and London: Routledge.

Duranti, A. (1997) *Linguistic Anthropology*. London: Cambridge University Press.

Evanoff, R. (2006) Integration in intercultural ethics. *International Journal of Intercultural Relations* 30, 421–437.

Fairclough, N. (2003) *Analysing Discourse: Textual Analysis for Social Research*. London: Routledge.

Foucault, M. (1969/1972) *The Archaeology of Knowledge*. London: Routledge.

Gee, J.P., Hull, G. and Lankshear, C. (1996) *The New Work Order. Behind the Language of the New Capitalism*. Sidney: Allen & Unwin.

Guilherme, M. (2007) English as a global language and education for cosmopolitan citizenship. *Language and Intercultural Communication* 7 (1), 72–79.

Gutierrez, K., Rymes, B. and Larson, J. (1995) Script, counterscript and underlife in the classroom: James Brown versus Brown v. Board of Education. *Harvard Educational Review* 65 (3), 445–471.

Hall, S. (1997) *Representations*. Milton Keynes: Open University Press.

Keating, M.C. (2010) Changing participation in changing practice: Uses of language and literacy among Portuguese based migrant contexts. In M. Baynham, J. Collins and S. Slembrouck (eds) *Globalization and Language Contact: Spatiotemporal Scales, Migration Flows, and Communicative Practices*. London: Continuum.

Lave, J. and Wenger, E. (1991) *Situated Learning. Legitimate Peripheral Participation*. Cambridge: Cambridge University Press.

Lorbiecki, A. and Jack, G. (2000) Critical turns in the evolution of diversity management. *British Journal of Management* 11, 1–31.

Medina, J. (2005) *Language. Key Concepts in Philosophy*. London: Continuum.

Santos, B.S. (2004) A critique of lazy reason: Against the waste of experience. In I. Wallerstein (ed.) *The Modern World-System in the Longue Durée* (pp. 157–198). London: Paradigm.

Simpson, P. (1993) *Language, Ideology and Point of View*. London: Routledge.
Ting-Toomey, S. (2005) Identity negotiation theory: Crossing cultural boundaries. In W.B. Gudykunst (ed.) *Theorizing about Intercultural Communication* (pp. 211–233). Thousand Oaks, CA: Sage.
Ting-Toomey, S. and Chung, L. (2004) *Understanding Intercultural Communication*. London: Oxford University Press.
Utley, D. (2004) *Intercultural Resource Pack: Intercultural Communication Resources for Language Teachers*. London: Cambridge University Press.
Wenger, E. (1998) *Communities of Practice. Learning, Meaning and Identity*. Cambridge: Cambridge University Press.
Wenger, E., McDermott, R. and Snyder W. (2001) *Cultivating Communities of Practice: A Guide to Managing Knowledge*. Boston, MA: Harvard Business School Press.

Chapter 11
Working in Multicultural Teams

EVELYNE GLASER

Introduction

The challenges multicultural teams are facing in the contemporary work environment are a result of their inherent diversity that manifests itself in different communication and working styles, different ways of problem solving and different preferences concerning conflict resolution. In such a context, the team members' intercultural competence is a basic requirement to ensure successful cooperation. Due to inherent diversity in multicultural teams, it is necessary to support teams in their efforts to cooperate successfully. Both learning from experience and learning through reflection are conducive to better cooperation in multicultural teams and reduce the number of conflicts among team members. Following a discussion of some pertinent theoretical approaches to learning and teamwork, one of the team training activities developed by the ICOPROMO Project Team will be given closer consideration.

The Role of Teamwork in Organisations

Over the last two decades, we have witnessed a rapid increase of company mergers, acquisitions and the creation of geographically distributed business operations. This has had major repercussions on workforce diversity within organisations and has required employees to become physically and psychologically mobile. In an attempt to make the best possible use of experience and expertise and to tap the full potential of this diversity, more and more organisations – whether profit-oriented or not – have adopted the concept of teamwork. Multicultural teams are expected to cope better with the challenges of task diversity and complexity in the areas of problem solving, product development, production, marketing, customer services or administration (Marquardt & Horvath, 2001). However, human beings are not naturally born for teamwork (Dyer, 1977). Therefore, they must develop their team skills to be able to come to terms with modern working conditions. When teams are composed of members from different cultures, intercultural competence is a key requirement for all team members.

Within the framework of the ICOPROMO project, the section on *Working in Multicultural Teams* unites all the aspects dealt with in the other parts of the project. Ideally, in order to be able to work successfully in a multicultural team, the group members should reflect on their own self (*My Biography*); they should be objective and accurate observers (*Ethnography*); they should communicate effectively (*Intercultural Communication*) and interact successfully with people from other cultures (*Intercultural Interaction*); they should also be able come to terms with their emotions (*Emotional Management*) and deal with different issues of diversity (*Diversity Management*). Their goal should be to act in a socially responsible manner (*Social Responsibility*) in a world that still differentiates substantially between the materially privileged and those in need, between those who have a say and those who do not, and between those who have choices and those who do not.

Diversity in Teams

According to the heterogeneity model by McGrath *et al.* (1995), differences related to an individual's socialisation have a strong impact on team performance and group processes. Thus, culture-specific socialisation processes do not only foster an individual's skills and capabilities to perform certain tasks or to solve problems in a specific way, they also shape a person's attitudes, values, norms, behaviours and ways of thinking. In the course of our socialisation process, we learn to differentiate between 'sameness' and 'otherness' and, as a result, we also develop cognitive schemata that may give rise to stereotypes about those who do not belong to our in-group. Stereotypes are thus projections of our expectations related to behaviours or qualities that may be characteristic of our interaction partners who represent 'the other'.

Our own socialisation is therefore at the origin of the preferences we display in communication styles, working styles, problem-solving approaches, in short, in our behaviour. Hence, multicultural teams may comprise individuals who like to work by trial and error or members who prefer looking for the best solution before engaging in a specific task. They may be composed of individuals who tend to harmonise while others may be inclined to polarise; they may have members who are either conflict averse or ready to address controversial issues openly; they may be seeking equality among team members or accept a high degree of power distance; they may strive for continuity or for change; they may either have a strong preference for certainty and clarity or they may be open to face ambiguity. These are merely a few examples of the degree of diversity that can be inherent in a team. Literature often hails diversity as the key to creativity and to better team performance. However, there are countless examples of teams that have failed as a result of the differences between their members. To date, researchers are still debating whether cultural diversity in teams can actually enhance group effectiveness (e.g. Gebert, 2004; Thomas & Stumpf, 1999).

Notwithstanding existing or even future research results on the influence of diversity on the positive or negative performance of multicultural teams, it has become evident that multicultural teams need to go through a team learning process before they can function well because they can definitely not be effective from the first minute they are created. The team members have to spend a certain amount of time focusing on the development of a relationship and establishing the norms and regulations according to which they can work as a group. The greater their heterogeneity, the more time they will require for their 'forming', 'storming' and 'norming' stages, and the more they will be called upon to challenge their individual behaviours, communication styles and set principles (Tuckman, 1965).

Team Communication and Sub-groups

As research has shown, communication styles impact heavily on the problem-solving effectiveness of groups (Cooke & Szumal, 1994). Of the three general interaction styles – constructive, passive, aggressive – used in groups, constructive styles are conducive to team effectiveness, while passive styles undoubtedly hamper the success of a group. Aggressive styles generally have little impact on the quality of the solution, but meet with very low acceptance of the solution by the team members. Thus, communication clearly represents a key issue for multicultural teams. Raising awareness of and practising different communication styles should therefore be a core element of any kind of team training, in particular when team members from different cultures are involved.

Multicultural groups also need to become acutely aware of the dangers of 'faultlines', i.e. mental dividing lines that may open up with regard to geographical location, nationality, ethnicity or language, and which increase the likelihood that sub-groups will form within a team (Lau & Murnighan, 1998; Polzer et al., 2006). These 'faultlines' augment the probability for conflict and reduce the potential for trust in geographically dispersed teams. As DiStefano and Maznevski (2000) suggest, diverse teams should use sufficient time for the processes of cultural mapping, bridging and integrating. Doing this exclusively through the use of cognitive forms of learning may not always prove effective. Therefore, the ICOPROMO Project Team has attempted to create activities that also foster experiential learning (Kolb, 1984; Jarvis, 1987, 1995), as our emotions or spontaneous reactions and behaviours are not always 'logical' and can therefore not be reduced to cognitive processes.

Conflict in Teams

As a result of globalisation and improved information and communication technology, companies also increasingly rely on geographically dispersed or so-called virtual teams (Shokley-Zalaback, 2002) or on hybrid forms of teams consisting of small co-located sub-groups in different locations (Webster & Wong, 2008). While co-located teams work together face-to-face in the same location, Townsend et al. (1998: 17) define virtual teams as 'geographically and/or organizationally dispersed coworkers that are assembled using a combination of telecommunications and information technologies to accomplish an organizational task'. Only recently, the literature has also taken account of an increasing use of mixed forms of teams 'composed of a local subgroup as well as remote team members' (Webster & Wong, 2008: 42). These groups are referred to as semi-virtual or hybrid teams.

Hence, we define a group of people working together on a given task in the same location over a defined or undefined period of time as co-located teams. Co-located teams communicate face-to-face as well as using information technology. By contrast, a virtual team is a group of people whose members are dispersed across different geographical locations and who can only communicate via information technology. The third form, semi-virtual or hybrid teams, is composed of a group of members working in the same location and another or several other small groups working in other parts of the globe. The fact that these team members cannot meet face-to-face and are therefore restricted to the use of technology for communication makes them prone to task, affective and process conflict (Hinds & Bailey, 2003).

Task conflict results from the team members' disagreement on the content of their work. Affective conflict arises from emotional disagreements often related to anger, disappointment, trust erosion or outright hostility between team members. Finally, process conflict originates from disagreement over the approach to the task, the methods chosen and the group processes used. Given that virtual or semi-virtual teams face even more challenges than co-located multicultural teams, they require special attention and training.

As distance has a negative effect on shared context, familiarity and rapport building, the team members first and foremost need to learn how to question assumptions about their counterparts and they must reflect on the factors influencing communication, power, trust and relationship building. According to the literature (O'Reilly et al., 1997; Pelled et al., 1999), diversity increases the likelihood of task and affective conflict because it leads to different approaches to work prompted by different expectations, attitudes, beliefs and norms.

Although task conflict has been deemed to have a potentially positive effect on performance (Pelled et al., 1999) because it can help to avoid 'groupthink' (Janis, 1982), Lovelace et al. (2001) have shown that the benefits of task conflict only become apparent when open and collaborative communication prevails in the team. Otherwise, task conflict is likely to lead to affective or process conflict.

Affective conflict negatively impacts performance because much time and energy must be dedicated to conflict resolution. Even though virtual teams may find it easier to cope with emotional conflict because they can avoid 'contact' with the other team members, the effect on team performance remains detrimental due to negative attributions and overall loss of commitment to the task.

The success of conflict resolution depends heavily on the quality of the relationship that exists between team members. If team members feel that there exists a good relationship between them, their efforts towards resolving existing or emerging conflicts are greater than if no such relationship has been established. However, relationships are never stable nor are they immune to crises. Instead, they are 'organic, evolving, and dynamic, and do not automatically follow a linear path. They arise as we work and play together, with a spirit of inquiry about differences, especially those differences that threaten us or our ways of working' (Lebaron & Pillay, 2006: 6). As geographical distance makes it more difficult for team members to establish relationships, it is vital to provide them with training opportunities during which they become aware of the possible downsides of multicultural teamwork.

Learning Objectives

Despite the fact that it has met with some criticism, Kolb's (1984) experiential learning theory, based on the works of Dewey, Lewin, Piaget, James and Freire, remains a widely used theory of how managers learn from experience. Kolb argues that learning basically entails four abilities: the ability to experience, observe/reflect, conceptualise and to take action. He represents these four phases in his model of the learning cycle, which describes how the immediate concrete experiences serve as a basis for reflection and observation. The experience is then used for abstract conceptualisation and subsequently for active experimentation.

Even though Kolb (1984) argues that the learning cycle can begin at any stage, it is suggested that the learning process often begins with a person carrying out a particular action. She/he then sees the effect of the action. The second step is, therefore, to understand the effects in the particular situation. Hence, if the same action were taken in the same or similar circumstances, it would be possible to foresee its consequences. The third step would be to understand the general principle underlying a certain action. This principle (learning effect) would then be applied in upcoming similar situations. Therefore, it might make sense to depict experiential learning as a spiral rather than a circle, as the learner changes his/her behaviour because of previous experiences gained. Thus, when the action takes place under different circumstances, the learner is able to anticipate the possible effects of the action.

Jarvis (1987, 1995) developed the concept of experiential learning even further. His main criticism of Kolb's model was that Kolb did not take into account the different responses that could be generated by a specific learning situation. After testing Kolb's model extensively, he came up with a model that allowed for different routes, depending on individual learners. Some involved non-learning, some non-reflective learning and some reflective learning.

The principle of reflection or 'reflection in and on action' (Schön, 1983, 1987) is widely accepted in the context of learning. It also seems very appropriate for the development of intercultural competences. As Schön puts it,

> The practitioner allows himself to experience surprise, puzzlement, or confusion in a situation which he finds uncertain or unique. He reflects on the phenomenon before him, and on the prior understandings which have been implicit in his behaviour. He

carries out an experiment which serves to generate both a new understanding of the phenomenon and a change in the situation. (Schön, 1983: 68)

The main objectives of the training activities developed within the ICOPROMO project rely on the transformational model for the development of intercultural competence developed by the Project Team in a parallel project for the European Centre for Modern Languages (ECML: http://www.ecml.at/mtp2/Icopromo/html/Icopromo_E_Results.htm) (Glaser et al., 2007). According to this model (Figure 11.1), the 'new world order' impacts on the individuals and forces them to deal with different challenges. Depending on the individuals' personal dispositions, they have to develop their intercultural competence out of a need to cope with existing challenges. While going through this learning process, they are expected to become aware of 'the self and the other'; they hone their communication, sense-making, perspective-taking and relationship-building skills and accept to assume social responsibility. During this

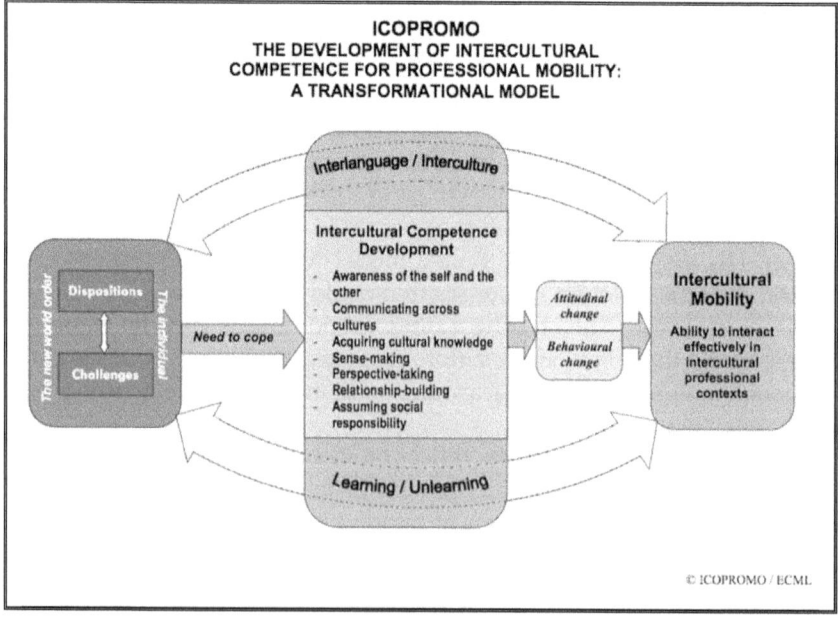

Figure 11.1 ICOPROMO – the development of intercultural competence: a transformational model (Glaser et al., 2007: 17)

reflective journey, they are encouraged to re-evaluate many of their attitudes and behaviours, thereby slowly becoming more culturally competent and able to move between cultures.

Thus, self-reflection, observation, critical analysis of problems, discussion with peers and action-taking are the main elements of the activities to facilitate working in multicultural teams developed within the framework of the ICOPROMO project.

ICOPROMO Activity *'Tension in Teams'*

The purpose of this activity is to make teams aware of the potential pitfalls faced by hybrid or semi-virtual multicultural teams, which can lead to serious conflict and eventually to unsatisfactory performance. The activity draws on an authentic collection of reflective essays written by students at an Austrian and a North American university drafted during their work on a semi-virtual multicultural team project. The students wrote the reflective essays at three different points in time during the project. These three subsequent stages allowed the trainees to reconstruct team processes and events. Due to restricted space, the current discussion renders only some extracts of the activity. The team at the core of this activity comprised of six members. On the US side there were three American students (Ashley, Jenny, John), on the Austrian side there was one Austrian (Anton), one Czech (Jiri) and one Spanish (Carmen) student. The team language was English, as it was the only language shared by all members.

The activity consists of three parts. In the first part, the participants read through extracts of the first set of reflective essays. The essays are authentic and have not been corrected or changed in any way except that they do not disclose the true identity of the authors, agents and the universities involved.

Activity *'Tension in Teams'* Part 1

Reflective Essays No. 1

Anton

My first impression of my team [in Austria] was quite good, as my teammates seemed to have a friendly and open attitude towards me. ...We got to know each other during class and also during our "social meeting" which was a good idea to organize. I think that we are able to do good work together because we already built up trust within our group.

One difficulty for our first assignment will be the Easter break in which my local team members travel back to their home countries, so communication will be as difficult as with our [US] members.

As my team members [in Austria] can communicate in English as well as in German, possible communication problems are not likely to arise.

John

Before this class I was already familiar and friends with Ashley. We are in the [same] program together and I am already aware of her capabilities. Jenny and I have placed our trust in Ashley as our team leader from our past positive experiences we have had with her.

I have worked in virtual teams before during my co-ops at [...] in London and New York City. The knowledge that I gained from working in virtual teams while on co-op is priceless and I hope that I am able to share some of my expertise with my teammates.

We have been briefed in previous classes of these cultural differences and both Ashley and I have experienced these rifts in cultural norms firsthand. If any problems arise due to cultural differences I believe that we will be able to immediately diffuse the situation.

Ashley

In the email, I briefly introduced myself, and encouraged the rest of the group members to reply introducing themselves, as well. The replies varied.

Within 24 hours, I received a reply from Anton, my teammate from Austria. ...I asked Carmen and Jiri if they received my email. They both said they did receive my email, and responded back. However, I did not receive their email. I am not sure what to expect from Carmen and Jiri, because I've not spoken with them.

Over a week later, I received an email from John. John is an ideal teammate; he is extremely knowledgeable about international affairs, and goes above and beyond in his school work.

After reading through these extracts, the participants are encouraged to discuss the following questions in small groups:
(1) What has happened so far?
(2) What is your impression of this team?
(3) Can you see any problems emerging in this team? What may cause these problems?
(4) If you were the designated team leader of this team, how would you proceed?
(5) Can you identify any differences in perceptions of individual team members and expectations? What may be the consequences for the team?

Although the two sub-groups work in two different geographic areas and work environments, they have not gone out of their way to map out the different circumstances to the other team members, which establishes an obvious 'faultline' from the very beginning. There is already a remarkable difference in the amount of trust extended to the co-located as opposed to the virtual team members concerning their abilities and expertise.

Activity 'Tension in Teams' Part 2

In a next step the participants read excerpts from the second set of reflective essays.

Reflective Essays No. 2

Anton

I have the feeling that our communication finally broke down. Not within our local group but with the Americans. We sent some work we had agreed on last week and I have not received any response from them. Maybe something went wrong with the e-mail transit. I am quite frustrated at the moment.

I would have expected the Americans to correct some of our mistakes. The grammatical and "using the wrong word" mistakes were still in the paper and I think that they have not even read our parts. Therefore we should improve our communication and ask them to read over our work again.

I wonder what the US group thinks about us, and why our communication is so slow. Maybe they have a lot of work at the moment.

Jiri

I also experienced some problems with my email address. I was very surprised when I received an email from Ashley who informed me, that she is still waiting for an answer (not only from me) and reactions to her proposal, though I sent it to her.

We also arranged our next telephone conference via Skype that was supposed to be held next Friday. ...But then problems started. The Americans didn't reply at all. They didn't send to us their Skype names and suggestions concerning our tasks. On Friday there was no phone conference, no discussion about our tasks. To be able to do the oral presentation of our project on Monday, we had to do a part of the task the Americans were supposed to do. Worst of all is that we didn't receive any email from our American team members for almost two weeks. I really wonder what happened.

Carmen

There is only one point that we, the Austrian team, have seen as a mistake: no one has read the complete text. The Americans have the responsibility to revise the English language aspects of the paper.

We have forgotten to talk about that in the videoconference, so we should say it by mail and we have to select very carefully which words we are going to use.

I would like to take more responsibility inside the team because I think that I can contribute profitably in it, but I have some limitations with the language. I feel sometimes that people don't understand the idea that I want to communicate. It is very frustrating for me. I can build a sentence, but the meaning that they understand is not the one that I want to communicate, so I have to give up with it.

John

... my first impressions and expectations had changed rather dramatically based on my experience thus far.

First, my team thought it would be a good idea to designate a team leader from both the University of A and from B. Both team leaders would be responsible for compiling the work from their domestic teammates and then communicate that material to the other team leader. We designated Ashley as our domestic team leader and she has done a good job with communicating with our Austrian counterparts, setting up team meetings, keeping everyone on task, and leading us towards a final product. However, after receiving a grade equivalent to a 'C' on the case study, it has come to my attention that this process is obviously not the best way to approach our virtual team cases. Jenny and I are going to have to take a more hands on approach and communicate with our Austrian counterparts as well. There needs to be more discussion between Ashley, Jenny, and I at home and with each individual in Austria in order for our team to arrive to the best possible solution for our final team project.

Also, I blame myself for the poor grade that our group received on the case study because I did not take the time to review the final product before we turned it in.

I initially believed that this classroom experience with virtual teams would help me fine tune my virtual team skills. So far this has not been the case because of my lack of involvement in communicating with my Austrian counterparts.

However, I have yet to establish friendships or personal trust with my Austrian teammates. I need to immediately change this so I can work more efficiently with them and leave them with a positive view of the University of A. Besides learning about virtual teams and completing work worthy of a good grade I still have hope that after this class has ended my three European teammates will spread the word about the talent, potential, and caliber of business students at the University of A.

Jenny

Wow, I'm shocked. I have many different expectations now than I had when the class first started.

It's really hard to communicate efficiently with everyone in a group from America; it's a million times harder to communicate with people from a country across the world with a six hour time difference.

For us American students, it's our last quarter and we have so many things that need to be done in order to graduate and I know that I'm guilty of not checking my emails and not responding as quickly as I can because I have so many other things going on with my capstone classes and working six days a week.

After the first few weeks, serious problems had arisen for the team, which resulted in process and affective conflict. As two of the US team members displayed a clear lack of involvement, there was hardly any exchange of relational information between the individual members. In addition, the time difference, different access to technology and numerous external commitments hampered the performance of the team.

At this stage, the participants are again encouraged to evaluate the situation by answering a series of questions in small groups:

(1) How would you evaluate the team and its work so far?
(2) Which areas can you identify where the team has already experienced problems? In your opinion, what are the main factors and reasons for this?
(3) Which critical incidents can you identify?
(4) What are the implications of all this for the team's performance?
(5) What are your suggestions for improving the situation of the team?

Activity 'Tension in Teams' Part 3

After discussing the issues above, the participants concentrate on the last set of reflective essays.

Reflective Essays No. 3

> *Anton*
>
> Ashley MSNed me and I could talk to her for quite a while (for the first time). This is very fortunate because my conversation with her unveiled some for me unbelievable things. As she is the only team member from America who answered our emails, I asked her what had happened to the other two members. She answered that they had absolutely nothing to do with our group project and had never sent her anything. For me, this explains a lot. Now I know why she is late with our work and she also apologized for this. I would have rather found out weeks ago than now that she is the only one doing something.
>
> My conversation with Ashley put new light on our problems. In my second personal reflection I wrote that the communication finally had broken down and now I know why. I will apologize to Ashley because I was quite unfriendly to her in one of my emails I sent her.
>
> I also realized that communication is the most important factor for a project with international virtual teams – when it works, you do well in your tasks and if not – you fail and you don't even know why.

John

All of this confusion could have been avoided if prior to setting the deadlines I would have informed all of my teammates that there was a very high possibility that my life was going to slide into complete chaos a few weeks before I left for New York City, that they should proceed on without me, and my assignments might be a few days late. I should have also taken on some non-crucial assignments so that the project could proceed and my work could just be added to the final product and would not serve as the backbone of the project.

One thing that I feel strongly about when it comes to the success of virtual teams is structure. Our team needed more structure to our work. We needed to set up a meeting time on instant messenger or Skype to discuss certain aspects of our project at least once a week. In a work setting this structure is established by the team leader. However, in our group we had two team leaders; one in Austria and one in the US. The lack of structure really hurt the efficiency with which our team worked.

Jenny

On top of the already difficult task of getting a group of people to have the same free time, add the extremely long distance and time difference into the mix and you get by far the hardest thing to ever successfully accomplish... a virtual team. I think that I would have definitely enjoyed the class more if I wasn't taking four others, if I didn't have two 30 page papers that were due by the end of the quarter, if I had the technology to better communicate with the people across the Atlantic and if I had more time to devote to the assignments that were due.

I think that the lack of face-to-face communication was detrimental to the project. We only had two videoconferences in ten weeks.

I also think that on my part of the group work anyways, I lacked the technology (i.e., Skype) to effectively communicate with the Austrian group members.

Also some of their emails were "gappy", meaning they didn't make sense and we had clearly not received a few of their emails either. To solve this problem we just again remained patient and I just let Ashley be the mail contact and communicator between all of us because her email was working the best. I don't know how the Austrian students felt about this but it seemed to start working better that way towards the end of the quarter.

There was a lot that everyone overlooked, i.e., cultural differences, language differences, time differences, differences in work ethics, schedule differences and expectation differences in general. I don't think that there is enough literature to fully prepare anyone and fill them in on the difficulties of working in a virtual team.

Ashley

As this project comes to an end, my impressions and thoughts of my team resemble a rollercoaster.

A few weeks into the quarter I realized that this group project may be similar to every other group project, with the typical "slackers" and the "over-achievers" and the constant tension between the two.

After confirming they would attend the meeting, neither Jenny nor John showed up for the meeting. At this point, I was annoyed with their work ethic and unreliable attitude of the US team members. ... I am conflict-avoidant: I spoke with Jenny and John on a few occasions, asking them to contribute more to the group, cite their sources, and attend scheduled meetings. However, I did not want to argue with my team.

Working virtually did not present as many obstacles as I originally thought. During the first few weeks, we had issues figuring out the time difference, using Skype, and communicating via MSN. However, in five weeks, I was able to communicate with the Austrians on a daily basis. We could ask and answer questions in a few hours, and even convey thoughts and ideas using Skype telephone. This class taught me that it is relatively easy to communicate globally. The language, distance and technological barriers are not as difficult as I once thought.

In small groups, the participants finally evaluate the team's performance by answering the following questions:

(1) What do you think of the different perceptions of individual team members regarding the overall teamwork?
(2) How do you evaluate the processes and interactions that took place in this team?

(3) What were the consequences?
(4) What were the different approaches employed by individual team members to enhance the situation? What do you think of them?
(5) What are your recommendations regarding possible strategies to avoid such situations?

In *Part 2* of the activity, the small groups fill in an evaluation form and judge the performance of the individual team members based on information obtained from the reflective essays. Finally, in *Part 3* the participants' attention focuses on the types of conflicts they could witness in the team interaction, namely, task conflict, affective conflict and process conflict. They try to find reasons for these conflicts. During the discussion it should become clear that geographical and emotional distance as well as the 'us against them' attitude represent major sources of conflict in teams. Teams must therefore develop clear process norms to avoid those pitfalls.

While proximity increases the amount of informal interaction and allows team members to learn about their concerns, personalities and preferred work processes, distance inhibits rapport building and the development of friendships or long-term relationships and trust. As a result, it tends to create in-groups and out-groups, reduces commitment towards the task and moderates the ability and willingness to deal with conflict successfully (Hinds & Bailey, 2003).

Conclusion

Working their way through the activities in the section on *Working in Multicultural Teams*, participants become increasingly aware of the dangers lurking behind teamwork across cultures. In order to avoid detrimental conflicts or the threat of in-group/out-group categorisation in multicultural teams, leadership and trust are two critical success factors. As Webster and Wong (2008) underline, team training must set in very early to ensure that the team members do not succumb to this categorisation. The activities developed within the ICOPROMO project offer a wide range of training opportunities for all types of teams at different stages of the team process.

As the infamous history of many teams has shown, it pays to take preventive measures and invest in training early on in a multicultural team's life cycle, instead of taking the likely risk that a team without any training is unable to cope with the numerous challenges involved in working across cultures.

References

Cooke, R.A. and Szumal, J.L. (1994) The impact of group interaction styles on problem-solving effectiveness. *Journal of Applied Behavioural Science* 30 (4), 415–437.

DiStefano, J.J. and Maznevski, M.L. (2000) Creating value with diverse teams in global management. *Organizational Dynamics* 29 (1), 45–63.

Dyer, W.G. (1977) *Team Building: Issues and Alternatives*. Reading, MA: Addison Wesley.

Gebert, D. (2004) Durch diversity zu mehr Teaminnovativität? *Die Betriebswirtschaft* 64 (4), 412–443.

Glaser, E., Guilherme, M., Méndez García, M.C. and Mughan, T. (2007) *ICOPROMO – Intercultural Competence for Professional Mobility*. Strasbourg/Graz: Council of Europe/European Centre for Modern Languages. On WWW at http://www.ecml.at/mtp2/Icopromo/html/Icopromo_E_Results.htm.

Hinds, P.J. and Bailey, D.E. (2003) Out of sight, out of sync: Understanding conflict in distributed teams. *Organization Science* 14 (6), 615–632.

Janis, I.L. (1982) *Groupthink: Psychological Studies of Policy Decisions and Fiascos*. Boston, MA: Houghton Mifflin.

Jarvis, P. (1987) *Adult Learning in the Social Context*. London: Croom Helm.

Jarvis, P. (1995) *Adult and Continuing Education. Theory and Practice*. London: Routledge.

Kolb, D.A. (1984) *Experiential Learning: Experience as the Source of Learning and Development*. Englewood Cliffs, NJ: Prentice-Hall.

Lau, D.C. and Murnighan, J.K. (1998) Demographic diversity and faultlines: The compositional dynamics of organizational groups. *Academy of Management Review* 23 (2), 325–340.

Lebaron, M. and Pillay, V. (2006) *Conflict across Cultures: A Unique Experience of Bridging Differences*. Boston, MA: Intercultural Press.

Lovelace, K., Shapiro, D.L. and Weingart, L.R. (2001) Maximizing cross-functional new product teams' innovativeness and constraint adherence: A conflict communications perspective. *Academy of Management Journal* 44, 779–783.

Marquardt, M.J. and Horvath, L. (2001) *Global Teams: How Top Multinationals Span Boundaries and Cultures with High-Speed Teamwork*. Palo Alto, CA: Davies-Black Publishing.

McGrath, J.E., Berdahl, J.L. and Arrow, H. (1995) Traits, expectations, culture and clout: The dynamics of diversity on work groups. In S.E. Jackson and M.N. Ruderman (eds) *Diversity in Work Teams. Research Paradigms for a Changing Workplace* (pp. 17–46). Washington, DC: American Psychological Association.

O'Reilly, C., Williams, K. and Barsade, S. (1998) Group demography and innovation. Does diversity help? In E. Mannis and M. Neale (Series eds) *Research in the Management of Groups and Teams Vol. 1, Composition* (D. H. Gruenfeld, Volume ed.), (pp. 183–207). Greenwich, CT: JAI Press.

Pelled, L.H., Eisenhardt, K.M. and Xin, K.R. (1999) Exploring the black box: An analysis of work group diversity conflict and performance. *Administrative Science Quarterly* 44, 1–28.

Polzer, J.T., Crisp, C.B., Jarvenpaa, S.L. and Kim, J.W. (2006) Extending the faultline model to geographically dispersed teams: How collocated subgroups can impair group functioning. *Academy of Management Journal* 49 (4), 679–692.

Schön, D.A. (1983) *The Reflective Practitioner – How Professionals Think in Action*. London: Temple Smith.

Schön, D. (1987) *Educating the Reflective Practitioner*. San Francisco, CA: Jossey-Bass.

Shokley-Zalaback, P. (2002) Protean places: Teams across time and space. *Journal of Applied Communication Research* 30 (3), 231–250.

Thomas, A. and Stumpf, S. (eds) (1999) Schwerpunktheft: Heterogenität in Gruppen. *Gruppendynamik* 30 (2), 111–205.

Townsend, A.M., DeMarie, S.M. and Hendrickson, A.R (1998) Virtual teams: Technology and the workplace of the future. *Academy of Management Executive* 12, 17–29.

Tuckman, B.W. (1965) Developmental sequence in small groups. *Psychological Bulletin* 63 (6), 384–398.

Webster, J. and Wong, W.K.P. (2008) Comparing traditional and virtual group forms: Identity, communication and trust in naturally occurring project teams. *The International Journal of Human Resource Management* 19 (1), 41–62.

Part 3
Voices from the 'Real' World

Chapter 12
Intercultural Relations at the Workplace[1]

GUENTHER ZOELS and THOMAS SILBERMAYR

Introduction

As soon as an individual interacts with others at the workplace, she/he is confronted with attitudes, values and beliefs diverging from their own. Taking intercultural aspects into account, this can lead to even more disagreements and difficulties arising from differing cultural backgrounds when managing work, also affecting business relations on a day-to-day basis.

For this project, interviews were conducted in order to find out how employees think and behave while working with colleagues from other cultures. The questionnaire itself focused especially on Austrian employees and their colleagues from the UK, the USA, France and China, who work in the field of plant engineering and construction. Since in the project business everything is mostly handled in teams, this seemed to be the perfect field for this kind of research as different cultures and countries from various positions in business, such as clients, suppliers, subcontractors, engineers etc., are confronted and have to work with each other.

In this chapter, typical situations and behaviors that the interviewees experienced are described in order to point out that there are differences when conducting business at an international level. Moreover, this chapter tries to give reasons why specific cultures behave in such a manner, also focusing on how their counterparts react and describing the conflict potential in such a given situation.

The Project Business

In the project business, regarding for example the engineering and construction field, the main objective is to engineer, organize and construct a plant for the customer, which meets his/her expectations. In order to conduct this project, the assigned company has to assemble a team that is in charge for the duration of the project, which is in charge of this project, consisting not only of people coming from different functions, where communication can already be limited, but in today's global business, also people from different cultures. This means that the team itself is not only confronted with language barriers, but also with the fact that some cultural characteristics are not understood and/or accepted, creating a potential conflict-laden work environment. The latter can, in particular, put additional stress on the team members, causing situations that can seriously threaten the efficiency and functionality of the project team, also endangering the project as a whole in the worst case scenario.

Experiences and their Consequences

Working with clients

Generally said, the customer is always right. This of course is true as a principle for each company that provides goods and services in order to have satisfied clients and a good reputation. But, in addition, culturally different aspects have to be considered when acting globally. As will be discussed later in this chapter, in Chinese culture it is important to respect the elderly and hierarchical orders. On the one hand, senior management, for example, is always given the most important seat at the table, making sure that it receives the best service available. On the other hand, when negotiating, non-Asian representatives can never be sure who really is going to be the decisive person. An Austrian colleague mentioned that at first he was astonished when the 'big boss' decided to take a nap during the meeting, which is perfectly normal for Chinese circumstances.

Moreover, an Ecuadorian employee mentioned that he found negotiating with South Korean representatives rather difficult for him. He explained that he felt that the South Korean clients assumed that the contract partner would know exactly what they expected without telling the partner what they wanted. Therefore, the counterpart had to ask questions about their expectations in the first place; otherwise, he would have had practically to read their minds.

In such situations, it is important to let the client go first, stating his/her expectations and suggestions, giving them the feeling that they are being heard and, consequently, the client will be more open to what the representative of the contracting company has to say. In addition, when working with foreign cultures it would be advisable to adapt to the cultural rules and norms of the client's home country, also preparing the representative for the cultural do's and dont's.

Negotiating with partners and suppliers

Taking a closer look at the relationship between the contractor and potential supplier, certain expectations and arrangements have to be negotiated and agreed on before the actual contract can be signed. This can be difficult if two parties with the same cultural background have to agree on the same expectations and processes of the project. Again taking cultural diversity into account, different countries have varying rituals of doing business.

In particular, Asian culture is characterized by traditions and patience when negotiating. For them it takes time to find an agreement and it is of great importance to give it the respect needed to demonstrate the significance of the deal. Furthermore, it is important to them to get to know the partners with whom they are going to discuss and seal the contract. As an Austrian employee stated: 'The Chinese do business because of two reasons: firstly of course because of the financial aspect, trying to get ahead of the game. The second reason for a Chinese company to conduct business is the person representing the company'. As a matter of fact, a Chinese company would make an agreement just because they have had a long-term business relation with a particular person. In that case, it doesn't matter which company this contact person represents. Thus, it is important to know that networking within the Asian culture, especially China, is common practice. It is crucial to be aware of the relational networking behind every partner, which is not easy to figure out especially for non-Asians. Building a relationship ('Guanxi') with a person would open up several opportunities since good relations create a good reputation among others, generating new contracts and business potentials. Of course, such a flourishing environment is accompanied by threats. Remember, there is no such thing as a free lunch: news of offending one business partner will travel fast, so that once positive business relations are affected by one single incident, this closes the door to the whole network. All of a sudden, these business partners will most probably refuse to cooperate with the 'culprit'.

A Chinese colleague also argued that one has to put great emphasis on choosing words diligently in order to create better relations. This might seem rather hard for some non-Asian cultures that are straightforward, bluntly saying what their objectives are. The Chinese like to circumscribe their expectations and requirements, almost creating a quiz for their negotiating partners, who are forced to ask a question back to solve the riddle, never exactly knowing where they are at. An Austrian colleague sarcastically compared the negotiating process with Chinese partners as, 'It is a long drawn-out chocking and suffocating with an assured consensus at the end of the procedure'.

On the other hand, the German culture in particular seems rude and aggressive, as a British employee mentioned. 'This can be rather complicated when such a culture is confronted with the exact opposite behavior, such as the Japanese culture, where individuals are very honorable and the attitude is highly anti-aggression'. People are more used to working things out in a smooth way, guiding the client through the process. It took him several years to learn that showing aggression in a business environment within the Germanic culture is a rather positive feature. Misunderstanding of this behavior can of course lead to several problems such as upsetting partners and clients, creating consequences such as loss of contracts and affecting relationships in a negative way especially when working with Asian cultures, which live by the principle of saving face.

A completely different picture is given when collaborating with Russians. An Austrian colleague pointed out that it is very hard and longsome to get to know Russian colleagues and business partners but, once established, the relationship endures. It is further very important when meeting colleagues and negotiating partners from Russia for the very first time not to be too friendly and open. This kind of behavior is seen in Russia as being fake and untrustworthy. This, the Austrian interviewee, found was very hard for cultures that are used to smiling at people, expressing their friendliness and using jokes as an icebreaker. Therefore, it is important to stay objective and rather emotionally cool when doing business until individuals have the opportunity to get to know each other. This type of behavior can be seen as showing respect to the partner by presenting oneself as serious and objective. Smiling and joking is therefore connected with having fun and taking things more lightly, which is not desired when conducting business.

Even though Germanic culture was described as aggressive and impatient within meetings, it is also said to be very organized, correct and reliable. These characteristics are mostly seen as very positive in the Asian world. In China, German companies have a good reputation for their accuracy and technology.

Unfortunately, such traits as being punctual and keeping up with the schedules also have their downfalls. This can be seen when negotiating with the Chinese or Russians. These cultures like to play with the time factor in order to achieve a better negotiation result: since Germanic cultures almost seem obsessed by their time schedule, Russians like to stretch negotiation meetings to the point where the partner starts to make tradeoffs just because he/she has another appointment or a plane to catch. When their counter partner decides to stay longer, they almost seem disappointed because they have lost their pressurizing medium 'time' for negotiation purposes, suddenly making topics accessible that they were unable to discuss before. In this way, a more flexible time schedule would help in order not to be outsmarted by the other side.

In general, it helps to be flexible and open-minded regarding the counterparty's culture. Being aware of these cultural traits makes it easier for individuals to understand the other person's behavior and maybe react with more sympathy, working around potential conflicts.

Working with colleagues

Intercultural working conditions in general

Even though it seems more likely that individuals from the same country have similar values and beliefs, it can be rather hard to ensure the same understandings and assumptions in order to work efficiently.

As mentioned earlier in this chapter, cultural differences are present. It is a matter of whether parties are aware of them in order to act in a more cooperative way.

A typical setting for intercultural misunderstandings may be a meeting: cultures differ in their presentation of issues, negotiating, time arriving as well as preparation. Starting with the German culture, the characteristics mentioned most frequently are correctness and punctuality, which are also expected from other parties. These are positive traits for Germanic conditions, but are seen as inflexible in more Southern cultures, as an Ecuadorian employee mentioned: 'Time schedule in Latin American business culture is more seen as a reference. Therefore, a meeting set up between 2 and 4 o'clock could start at 2 pm and could end at 4 in the afternoon. In that way people are more flexible'. Of course, this can create potential problems when meeting a culture such as the Germans. Therefore, when parties arrive late, this might give Germans the impression that they are not taking the meeting seriously enough. For them it is a matter of respect, whether the other party finds it worthy to show up on time. The same is held true for the situation when the other party is not prepared for the meeting. Since Germans and also Austrians are described as organized and punctual, always bearing their time schedule in mind, this might be an insult.

Austrian colleagues further stated that Italians are rather uncomplicated to work with at the beginning, signing framework contracts and general conditions in an unhesitant manner. On the other hand, problems arise later on, when they try to get rid of an unwanted regulation by arguing that agreements were not negotiated or certain parties didn't have the authority.

As mentioned above, just like their Latin American colleagues, Italians like to take deadlines as a reference, not so much as fixed appointments. As a matter of fact, Austrians therefore believe that Italians like to 'fiddle' a little with delivery times, postponing deadlines. This could be referred as the 'mañana philosophy'. This, of course, is in major contrast to the Germanic cultures, creating potential trouble spots.

Moreover, Austrian colleagues also stated that Italians like to talk a lot, sometimes even giving answers to questions that haven't been asked yet. For Italians, it might be common to talk about family and general topics next to the business issue. Since Germans and Austrians make a clear distinction between social life and business, this might create the impression that Italian co-workers are not prepared for the meeting and therefore don't take it seriously enough.

Another situation where cultures vary is admitting mistakes. Americans, for example, as an Austrian colleague stated, are almost harried when they are forced to ask another division outside the USA for help. He said that this became apparent when an American colleague justified himself by saying: 'Nevertheless we put the first man on the moon'.

In other cultures, such as the Chinese, companies set up regulations for enforcing exactness and preventing mistakes by punishing their employees for their bad working performance. This mostly includes deductions from the monthly salary for each mistake made, also negatively affecting the process of finding out which mistake happened, when and how. Finding and solving the mistake can therefore be time consuming, since people are then not willing to admit their mistakes and they do not help solve the problem. This can especially affect the information and working flow within a company in a way that obstructs efficient and effective working conditions.

Project teams

In the project business, it is common to work in teams. These teams not only consist of people from different areas and functions, but also from different cultures and countries.

When members of a specific business field or function talk with each other, certain vocabulary is created in order to make working more efficient. Therefore, an outsider might have a major problem understanding them. This is also true when various functions have to collaborate and way of thinking within a team. This does not only concern created vocabulary, but also general understandings and definitions. For example, a book-keeper will have a different understanding of costs than a person in the legal department or an engineer focusing on constructing a building.

Therefore, it is crucial for a team to find a common basis of understanding. If this is achieved, the team will start developing its own vocabulary and communication processes.

Intercultural Teamwork in General

Despite the fact that it is almost impossible to imagine in today's working environment not to be forced to build intercultural teams, is there a sense in working on an intercultural level? Are intercultural teams as efficient as homogenous cultural teams?

Problems

Intercultural aspects

As mentioned before, intercultural teams are confronted with a variety of challenges and difficulties, which makes working together more intense than in mono-cultural groups. The difference for intercultural groups is that because they have a different background regarding values and beliefs, each individual within the group has to justify their culture towards his/her team members. This can be very exhausting, because every time the group comes together, common values and beliefs as well as assumptions have to be discussed and adapted before actually being able to move on to the main issue. On the one hand, this can be a downside, but seen from the view of a mono-cultural team this can be positive, since the desired way of discussion in mono-cultural teams might not always be as it should be. For example, if a decision has to be made within a group, mono-cultural teams tend to handle it faster, since they don't have to discuss different aspects of cultural diversities. But, on the other hand, this particular point can be crucial since in intercultural teams various aspects have to be discussed, giving more opportunities to see the project as well as the decision from various angles.

Native speakers

When working and discussing within a group, a certain language, which is chosen at the very beginning of the group's existence, serves as the main communication language. As it is for international business today, English has become the most spoken language in business meetings.

English-speaking individuals have an advantage when discussing in these teams, as they have grown up with this language and can express their thoughts and feelings better than other team members. This does not only affect language barriers, but also the dynamics in the group. Whenever a team is set up, each member has a position within it; even if all team members might officially be equal, there will always be a team leader in some way. Therefore, English-speaking individuals unconsciously tend to take over and lead the discussions, having the power to form the direction of it in some way. Furthermore, other members get the feeling that they are being overruled and set back because native speakers have higher self-esteem to express their views because of this advantage, which others might lack. Therefore, it is advisable for native speakers, regardless of the language being used, to consciously keep this in mind As a result, it will be possible to have an even spread of opinions.

An example of this was also given by a British colleague who stated that he thought it was easier for him than for his Austrian colleagues to communicate with the management board just because he was able to use the impersonal English language. He had the feeling that his Austrian colleagues had to work with the German language and its barriers of formality, including addressing individuals as 'du/Sie'. Since he was speaking English with the management members it was usual to address them by their first name, giving him the possibility to build on a more personal relationship.

Moreover, it was stated by the interviewees that English-speaking individuals, especially North Americans as well as English and Irish, tend to assume that English is going to be spoken within meetings. Also, when moving to another country where English is not the official language, most of the time they will never learn the foreign language, since everybody around them adapts and speaks English to them anyway.

Conclusion

Taking a look at today's business, regardless of the field, globalization has made its way into the 21st century, putting companies and individuals into a new working environment, completely changing working habits and conditions. But just as companies have learned to compete and survive in a dynamic and rapidly changing environment, their employees have also adapted to the new conditions. Even though studies have shown that intercultural teams can work efficiently, the need for the development of new models and strategies has recently grown. It seems that the performance of these teams always gets stuck in the second quarter 'forming' of the 'team-clock' (Tuckman, 1965), never reaching the level of efficiency. Would it be wiser to keep the team's combination over a longer period of time? Should there be a development of international working regulations?

Regarding these questions and the situations described before, these cultural differences can't be neglected and there should be more emphasis on developing ways to make working in teams with different beliefs and values more efficient and effective.

Notes

1. This paper only reflects the authors' personal ideas and experiences. By no means may it be considered as an official statement of the Siemens Group.

References

Tuckman, B.W. (1965) Developmental sequence in small groups. *Psychological Bulletin* 63, 384–399.

Chapter 13
Sharing Reflections on Intercultural Learning

ISABEL FERREIRA MARTINS

Introduction

> As people charged with shaping learning, we have to hope that we are producing the biggest change with the least possible cost and effort and that time will show that we made a significant difference. (Rogers, 2001: 215)

These introductory notes are meant to contextualise my experience, as well as illustrate some of my views, which are necessarily related to it. My participation in the ICOPROMO project stems from my work on the development of the Entreculturas project in Portugal.

Launched in 1991, within the Ministry of Education, the Entreculturas project aimed to support the development of intercultural pedagogical practices in Portuguese state schools for dealing with the increasing social, cultural and ethnic diversity within the schools and to promote the inclusion of diversity.

Its incorporation, in January 2004, into the High Commission for Immigration and Intercultural Dialogue (ACIDI), as part of the public policy on immigrant integration, represented a turning point in its scope of action and a shift in the nature of the activities that had been developed until then, extended from an emphasis on schools to a focus on socio-political intervention. It meant the recognition of the need for an intercultural perspective in the daily working practices of public services, in general, and of other agents who interact with immigrants. Raising awareness of interculturality in the Portuguese 'host' society thus became a national goal and was perceived as an enormous challenge by the whole team involved.

I would like to stress that the ideas expressed here, though personally undersigned, are the result of ongoing collective and collaborative teamwork, developed over the years in search of the most suitable guiding principles to build up a coherent and comprehensive framework on which to ground our professional practice.

Hopefully, many readers will be able to relate to the views I express here. I hope that they may help illuminate the expression of our practice and develop in others the sense of belonging and identity of participating in a shared patrimony of experience.

Clarifying our Perspective

Meaning perspectives refer to the structure of assumptions within which new experience is assimilated and transformed by one's past experience. Perspectives provide "principles" for interpreting. (Mezirow, 1990: 2)

Over the years, as a result of the variety of situations that we came across in the Entreculturas project, we developed a framework for intercultural education and training.

The assumptions and principles implied in intercultural issues may be approached from different perspectives. From our particular perspective, intercultural education and training addresses, respects and challenges society as a whole. It is not a minorities', immigrants' or any specific group of professionals' problem. It concerns and is the responsibility of a wide range of stakeholders and professionals. 'It is a learning process for all, a capacity building process, rejecting all forms of discrimination, concerned with everyone's participation in a more open and plural society' (Nieto, 1999: 4). It emerges as a transversal answer to the complexity and diversity of modern society, to meet ongoing changes, mobility and a new political/geographical agenda.

According to Ouellet (1991), intercultural education is regarded as a learning process that includes:

- a better understanding of other cultures in modern society;
- better communication skills between people from different cultures;
- a more adequate attitude in the context of cultural diversity and understanding of psycho-social mechanisms that create racism;
- the ability to participate in social interaction, developing a sense of identity and common belonging to humanity.

This perspective enhances the importance of participation as a tool, comprehending knowledge, attitudes, values and skills. The development of a sound consciousness regarding the complex nature of cultural identities is also an intrinsic part of the intercultural learning process.

Developing an increased awareness of our own (multi)cultural identity is a key aspect of the intercultural learning process. To be able to deal with diversity and interact in a positive way within heterogeneous contexts requires specific capacities. These capacities are not innate, rather they have to be learned, within intentionally designed learning setups or training plans, as part of systematic socialisation processes, either in schools or in other non-formal contexts.

Regarding adults, or even young adults, these learning demands should be framed and embedded in contexts that are as close as possible to their real-life situations and in informal participatory settings (situatedness of experience).

In our experience, creating a reflective learning portfolio, for self- and meta-assessment of learned competences within the personal learning cycle, where the most significant life events are reported and justified, has proved to be an empowering element in the training process. What still remains to be learned and what has hindered any non-learning situations should also be documented. Developing a personal learning portfolio, supported within a tutoring process, has been shown to be a transformative experience that can significantly improve the trainees' learning competences.

Identifying Common Ground and the Boundaries of a Community of Practice

> Communities of Practice are groups of people who share an interest, a concern about a certain issue or a passion for a theme and therefore develop a specialized knowledge about it, interacting in a regular basis. They are made of people who engage in a collective process of learning in a shared domain of activity. (Wenger, 1998, adapt.)

Discovering the concept of community of practice (COP) represented a critical incident that allowed me to better understand the 'at home' feeling I had when working with certain expert groups and the difficulties I felt when facing some topics I was less at ease with.

This concept implies three dimensions: the domain – the common ground, research area, reason of being of the community (in our case, learning about interculturality); the practice – the methods, stories, cases, tools, documents, shared repertoire (practice is the shared history of that learning); and community building – relationship among members and a sense of belonging (common identity). Members build their community through mutual engagement. They interact with one another, establishing norms and relationships of mutuality that reflect these interactions and produce a shared repertoire of communal resources.

My immediate impression when I learnt about the ICOPROMO project was one of proximity with the underlying assumptions, objectives and expected outcomes. This comfortable feeling of belonging to that same COP and of sharing common concerns regarding intercultural education and training was decisive in my decision to take part in the project.

This cooperation essentially involved two stages: first, the evaluation of ICOPROMO training modules, which included participation in a transnational workshop in Lisbon; and later, the testing of some of the ICOPROMO activities during one of the seminars on training of trainers, as part of the Entreculturas project.

In fact, although through different paths, the ICOPROMO and Entreculturas projects have both been engaged in this common field of research of how to cope with diversity and foster democratic citizenship and social cohesion by developing better and more appropriate intercultural policies and practices.

Both projects have worked on the production and sustained implementation of challenging materials and training kits intended to question and improve the professional practices of teachers and other educational agents and social actors.

It is this engagement in the same learning and training community that legitimates, anchors, and nurtures our committed collaboration with the ICOPROMO project.

The Dissemination of the Training Modules

> Knowledge should be inclusive and provide people with a sense of social belonging... involving "higher-level basic skills" that is, cognitive and metacognitive skills... knowledge has metamorphosed from objective, codified knowledge, to subjective constructed knowledge... personally produced through social processes and culture. (Carneiro, 2001: 212)

The first remark I would like to make concerns the general framework adopted for the ICOPROMO modules, namely, their structure and components. In my view, all are important for the success and applicability of the modules: description, rationale, learning outcomes, competencies to be developed, expected duration, number of participants, materials required, debriefing, variations (whenever offered) are fundamental aspects that should be included in any activity designed for learning or training purposes. The omission of one of these categories can hinder the global understanding of all the issues involved in the situation, impoverishing the learning outcome.

The most critical aspect regarding the dissemination of the ICOPROMO project lies, in my opinion, in its dissemination within a training of trainers process, in particular regarding the grasping of the complexity of all the underlying assumptions (taken-for-granted beliefs) and the role and value of the modules as methodological tools to help create learning opportunities and promote self-reflection upon action.

As already mentioned, practitioners in the field of intercultural education and training require a set of competences, grounded on an epistemologically coherent approach within the theoretical framework of intercultural education and learning. However, as adults' trainers, they should be conscious of the mechanisms involved in adult learning processes to be able to build supportive motivational training/learning environments and monitor communicational strategies that are likely to arouse participants' interest, eliciting the views of everyone involved, without ever imposing convictions and ideas.

The following comments have been drawn from my reflections on the different possible dimensions and variables that should be taken into account and reflected in the scope of intercultural learning and the 'training of trainers' process, which personally I would prefer to call a trainers' development process.

These reflections, drawn from Entreculturas' experience, of designing and implementing training plans on intercultural learning, seem pertinent, as we notice a growing interest in the empirical 'making-of' process of developing intercultural education and training processes.

Intercultural learning should involve a perspective transformation, a paradigm change. This process can take place when reflecting upon practice through critical self-reflection, leading to a change of representations and to a more inclusive perspective by validating and embodying previous own experience in a new context (meaning negotiation).

The role of the training modules is to create contexts to promote the necessary interaction and stimulating environments that, hopefully, will trigger the motivation and energy for individuals to reflect on their own experiences, to unearth and question implicit assumptions. Our learning competence cannot be delegated to anyone else and what may facilitate learning for one person may not work at all for another! By offering different activities for each topic, trainers can select the most appropriate activities for each group of trainees.

About the training

Training typically involves instruction and practice aimed at reaching a particular level of competence or operative efficiency. As a result of training we are able to respond adequately and appropriately to some expected and typical situation. (Dearden, 1984; in Tight, 2002: 21)

The concept of training is generally applied to contexts where there is some specific skill to be mastered, where practice is required and little emphasis is placed on the underlying rationale. Here I would like to use a broader definition: training is always about learning, it means any intentionally designed initiative to produce learning, whatever the setting or level of the expected learning.

Training has generally been viewed as an empirical issue. However, emerging research on the specific adult learning epistemology and of the lifelong learning perspective has changed this perception.

There is now a greater investment in the search for the best methodologies and models to provide optimum conditions for adult learning, involving professionals from a variety of backgrounds.

We know that training efforts have the best chances for success when the trainees know about what is involved – supporting theories, implied attitudes and skills. Making explicit and systematising the competences that are expected to be developed in the 'learning how to learn' process (knowledge, attitudes, skills) is likely to facilitate trainees' awareness of what is involved in the learning cycle. One should always allow room for the evaluation of the training process, to reflect on the different steps of learning and the dimensions and proceedings involved, giving an opportunity for trainees to 'externalise and then internalise the learning about learning implications' (Smith, 1993) of the activity itself, as well as those implied in the running of the activity.

Training should always be designed to reflect, as closely as possible, the real-life conditions of what is being learned. It is important, however, to avoid the temptation of overloading an activity or any other type of training resource, always bearing in mind that (adult) learning generally involves some level of 'unlearning'.

To be aware of the 'conflictual' situations that learning may give rise to can help understand what is perceived as a 'resistance to learning', often translated into frustration or an aggressive attitude towards the trainer. Therefore, it is important that trainers are prepared to deal with it and are capable of creating an open environment that can foster behavioural change, 'dealing constructively with resistance, heightening the trainee's awareness of self as a learner and the sensitivity to learning itself. Trainees learn about learning as they become open to change in a climate of trust initiated by the trainer and then jointly maintained by both' (Smith, 1993: 141).

The importance and the role of experience as determinant factor in the training situation cannot be highlighted enough. 'The main distinctions between adult forms of learning and child education... lie in the extent to which the former involves negotiation, recognition of experience and a greater degree of partnership between learner and teacher, trainer, facilitator or whatever' (Tight, 2002: 29).

Adults bring their own experiences to training situations. In fact, it is the sum of all individuals' experiences that makes up one's uniqueness and forms the basis and the 'resource material to be worked upon' during the training situation. 'The best designed adult learning has to maximize the advantages of the experience adults bring with them to learning.... Failing to do so risks rejection of your message' (Rogers, 2001: 31).

The role of the trainer is to elicit each individual's experience through the proposed dynamics, thus helping achieve the expected results. Simulation and role-plays are useful tools for encouraging this motivation for learning. Nevertheless, if the situations included in the training activities are too complex or too detailed, they can in fact hinder the trainee's motivation, shifting the focus to trying to understand the proposed situation instead of performing required tasks.

Role-plays and simulations are useful and unique for modelling learning strategies; they can inspire attitude change or, at least, give participants an opportunity to 'experience' another person's world. They usually arouse powerful emotions in those who take part in them and they can be an effective and valuable method where the development of sensitivity and tolerance is involved, which is generally the case in the field of intercultural education and training.

Our experience has shown us that there is, however, no point in doing role-plays without a follow-up debriefing session. A debriefing period, where participants can evaluate, debate and rethink what happened in detail is an indispensable tool for the success of those methodologies.

Facilitating the learning process

Training does not necessarily require a teacher. The teacher's special contribution is to ensure that the learner makes the most effective use of intrinsic feed-back and to provide extrinsic feed-back until that stage has been reached. (Lovell, 1992: 39)

It is possible for a learner to train himself/herself once he/she is capable of self-evaluation, through modelling and positive reinforcement. This competence can be learned. Effective adult learning involves the integration of new learned material into a complex network of existing ideas and experiences.

Perhaps the most important contribution a teacher can make to the adult's learning... is to select, organise, present and translate new material in such a way that the learner can appreciate its relationship with what he already has. (Lovell, 1992: 54)

One of the qualities of a good learning facilitator (a trainer) is the ability to monitor each participant's preferences and learning strategies. What is certain, however, is that the most influencing factor in adult learning is what the learner has already integrated into his/her conceptual structure.

Our attitudes are rooted in our past experiences and therefore they have a significant impact on our responses and reactions, as well as on our perceptions and interpretations of reality.

Skills learnt in a specific context can be successfully transferred to a new and different context. One important role that the trainer should develop involves supporting and guiding trainees to assess their own performance, ensuring that practice is essential to the mastery of any skill. 'The skilled performer has sufficient spare capacity to correct problems before they develop. It is this ability to anticipate hazards that gives the appearance of being unhurried by comparison with the novice' (Lovell, 1992: 80).

Is it working? Every adult (trainer or trainee) wants to know the answer to this question, in any learning situation. The trainer must always provide learning feedback. This can be done in a variety of ways, more formally or informally, through praise and comments. Without feedback the learner is unlikely to improve. In our everyday day practice, we try to keep in mind that 'There is a simple rule about the optimum time to give feedback on learning: give it as soon as possible!' (Rogers, 2001: 39).

The decisive factor in any (adult) learning situation is the trainer. The biggest challenge any adult trainer has to face is being able to design activities that will give participants a good chance of getting it right the first time. One should keep in mind that successful responses are more likely to be repeated in the future than unsuccessful ones, so anything that can be done to prevent failure when dealing with adult learning is a positive step towards successful results. As adults, once we have made a mistake, it is much harder to unlearn it than it is for a child. 'Catch them doing something right!' is one of the good tips everyone involved in adult training should always be aware of.

Active listening skills, empathising with difference, accepting different perspectives and being able to deal with heterogeneous contexts are some examples of competences that trainers in the field of interculturality should have. Other important competences in this field include understanding and contextualising current thinking paradigms, being aware of our own and others' assumptions and perceptions. It is also important to be equipped with thinking tools that will help trainees approach diversity and proactively change, deconstruct and decode unexpected and contradictory information and thus favour an unprejudiced intercultural dialogue.

A list of general personal skills required for dealing with adult learning could encompass:

- Listening with respect, creating trust.
- Impartiality to facilitate discussion.
- Skills and tact to give helpful feedback – 'indirect' manner of teaching, using learners' ideas.
- Working in groups – ability to weld the group together and control it without dominating it.
- Spotting and resolving learners' problems, dealing with anxiety and stress.
- Sharing enthusiasm – keeping eye contact, varied voice inflexion.
- Ability to generate innovative ways of presenting ideas and skills.
- Clarity in simplifying complex matters, but without oversimplifying.
- Summarising and questioning.
- Being able to bear and handle silences.
- Willingness to change, resilience when facing stress.
- Warmth/presence, a natural authority and easiness. (adapted from Rogers, 2001)

The topics and the target groups

People must be aware that they are citizens of both a nation and the world. ...The knowledge that unity contains multiplicity and that multiplicity contains unity must be inculcated from the very first stages of education. If this is not done, those who focus on the unity of human race may forget diversity, while those who give pride of place to diversity are in danger of interpreting it simply as a catalogue of differences and may disregard human unit. (Morin, 2001: 205)

The primary target groups of the ICOPROMO training activities are undergraduate students, recent graduates, young professionals from various areas (within the scope of the Social Sciences), foreign language/culture educators and trainers and human resources managers. The secondary target groups include experienced professionals who have the need to structure and deepen their knowledge in this area by theorising and reflecting upon their previous experience and informal input; employers (big companies and European or other international organisations) and members of national or international non-governmental (or other) organisations, with multi-ethnic populations.

In my view, the modules could also be used with other professional groups, especially those involved in education and training that need to deal with diverse and heterogeneous populations in their daily lives. Extending these modules to other groups should, however, be done carefully, paying particular attention to the adaptation of the training situations to the specific professional contexts.

Regarding the topics selected for the modules, since there is a substantial overlap between some of them (working in multicultural teams, intercultural interaction and intercultural responsibility, for example) it may not always be easy to decide which topics to choose for each situation.

Exploiting this assumption of the overlapping nature of intercultural competences, the **intercultural competences** diagram (adapted from a model developed within ACIDI's Trainers' Network) shows an approach based on a knowledge, values/attitudes and skills taxonomy basis.

However, these cannot be seen as exclusive categories, they are interdependent and most of the examples listed in one field could also be included in another one, since these competences always presuppose a comprehensive 'know how', formalised knowledge and practical action.

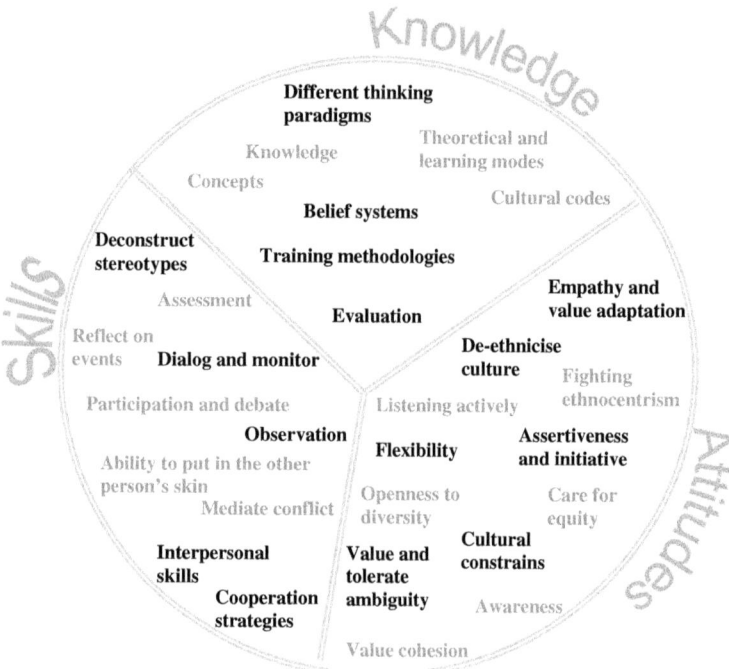

Intercultural Competences Diagram

Listing and classifying competences is a formal and stimulating exercise, but it cannot replace action and intervention. Its purpose is to support and bring clarity to practice.

Whatever the decision regarding the presentation of the ICOPROMO training modules, I think that the most important point is to ensure their development conditions, which means that the training may be integrated into broader intervention projects, to improve and deepen already ongoing work.

Final Reflections

Learning about interculturality can never be envisaged as a simple process. We have to assume that the complexity of the intercultural requires an integrated approach involving the three dimensions of particularisation, generalisation and singularisation, never in an *a priori* manner, but considering every situation in its actual context.

Below, I summarise a few reflections and remarks I gathered from my involvement with the ICOPROMO project:

(1) Pay attention to the conditions in which the training modules are disseminated – putting aside their unquestionable value, all modules can, if used inappropriately, inadvertently help disseminate cultural stereotypes and trigger counter effects, reinforcing prejudices and misconceptions.
(2) Organise the modules by expected competences rather than by topics – since most of the issues covered in each of the topics overlap. There is a risk of overemphasising the contents, in an essentialist manner, thereby undervaluing their true formative and reflective value. No classification or sequence will necessarily be consensual, but some different approaches can be considered.
(3) Enlarge or increase the diversity of the target groups addressed – the only constraint to the application of the various modules to a variety of contexts is that some of the modules' vignettes relate to very specific situations. In my opinion, this is a negative factor, since in the training situation an effort should be made to elicit the real experiences of every participant, regardless of their background or professional experience.
(4) The short duration of any training activity may be incompatible with the more ambitious development of learning or competences. Either the expected outcomes of each module can be 'downsized' to simple 'awareness raising' on that issue, or sets of modules can be structured into short training courses involving: in-service training, reflection upon action or any other learning methodologies.

Anything that can be done to deepen and develop the work of this project and the training products that result from it is worth the effort!

References

Banks, J. (1994) *An Introduction to Multicultural Education*. Needham Heights, MA: Allyn and Bacon.
Baumann, G. (1999) *The Multicultural Riddle – Rethinking National, Ethnic and Religious Identities*. New York: Routledge.
Carneiro, R. (2001) *Life Long Education for all a Curriculum for the 21st century*. In *Keys to the 21st Century* (pp. 210–212). Oxford and New York: Berghahn Books.
Dearden, R. (1984) Education and training. *Westminster Studies in Education 7*, 57–66.

Jarvis, P. (1995) *Adult and Continuing Education: Theory and Practice* (2nd edn). London: Routledge.
Katzenbach, J.R. and Smith, D.K. (2004) The discipline of teams. In *Harvard Business Review on Teams that Succeed* (pp. 1–26). Boston: Harvard Business School Press.
Lovell, R.B. (1992) *Adult Learning*. London: Routledge.
Mezirow, J. and Associates (1990) *Fostering Critical Reflection in Adulthood: A Guide to Transformative and Emancipatory Learning*. San Francisco, CA: Jossey-Bass.
Mezirow, J. and Associates (2000) *Learning as Transformation: Critical Perspectives on a Theory in Progress (Higher Education)*. San Francisco, CA: Jossey-Bass.
Morin, E. (2001) What future for the human society? In *Keys to the 21st Century* (pp. 202–205). Oxford and New York: Berghahn Books.
Nieto, S. (1999) *The Light in Their Eyes: Creating Multicultural Learning Communities*. New York: Teachers' College Press.
Ouellet, F. (2002) *Les défis du pluralisme en éducation: Essais sur la formation interculturelle*. Québec: Presses de l'Université Laval.
Perotti, A. (1997) *A Apologia do Intercultural*. Lisboa: Secretariado Entreculturas.
Rogers, J. (2001) *Adults Learning* (4th edn). Maidenhead: Open University Press.
Smith, R.M. (1993) *Learning How to Learn: Applied Theory for Adults*. Buckingham: Open University Press.
Tight, M. (2002) *Key Concepts in Adult Education and Training* (2nd edn). London: Routledge.
Wenger, E. (1998) *Communities of Practice – Learning, Meaning and Identity*. Cambridge: Cambridge University Press.

Chapter 14
Intercultural Education in International Management

ANNELI KANSANEN and LEENA VOHLONEN

Concordia res parvae crescunt, discordia maxumae dilabuntur.
(Sallustius)

Introduction

This chapter discusses the significance of professional mobility and its impact on personnel management. Special attention has been paid to the new challenges and competence requirements that increasing multiculturalism in the workplace has imposed on the management practices and human interaction of corporate leaders and experts. This chapter presents new areas of emphasis, new objectives and perspectives for management training, aiming to outline the limits and solutions in the practical implementation of such training. The views are based on the authors' many years of experience in the practice of continuing and supplementary training in Finland and their work as members of the ICOPROMO Advisory Team.

A good grasp of business operations and strong management skills are the basic requirements for an active organisation. Successful business is about people – things get done through personnel. Personnel are, no doubt, an organisation's most important and most expensive resource. It is through personnel that the business result is generated. Management is the activity that takes care of this resource.

Organisations are getting flatter and based increasingly on expertise and special competencies everywhere, and in every industry. The continuous pressure for change has an impact on management: work force is being imported from abroad, specialised experts are being sought through international networks, different organisational cultures blend in mergers, international corporations expand to all corners of the world – English often becomes the official language of the company. Free movement of labour in Europe invites people to look for work in other countries. Not everybody leaves their own country as a result of scarce employment opportunities – in particular, the young want work experience abroad.

The above-mentioned developments in international business inevitably have an impact on training needs. The greater the job-related responsibility and competence requirements, the greater the challenges to the education and training that lead to the position. The rapidly changing working environment also puts pressure on continuing and supplementary training. According to Nordisk Tänketank (Framtidens kompetenser, 2006), the most important challenges facing adult education include the following phenomena that have the greatest impact on management training:

- The globalised operational environment with rapidly moving and transforming markets, capital, information and people.
- Balance between global and local – location does matter, and community spirit is a great resource.
- Labour markets are becoming more and more complex.
- Human diversity is becoming more and more highlighted – the benefits from and the importance of multiculturalism, cultural sensitivity and communication skills.
- Individualism and cooperation – choice of group identity.

New Skills and Competencies for Managers

Management and leadership are inevitably international, whether they are concerned with managing oneself, managing things or managing people. In earlier times, it may have been enough that corporate managers became acquainted with the latest international trends, theories and experiences that were necessary and were implemented at a strategic level. Today, however, neither Finland nor any other European country is an isolated corner, but a part of the international operational environment.

The basic purpose of business operations requires the skill to make a profit within legal limits. In no industry can one find a manager who can do it alone, but in cooperation with the company's personnel. Motivated, pluralistic and multi-skilled personnel are the dream of every manager. In these times of crises and tougher competition in corporate life, this kind of team is in great demand (Gundling, 2003). The concept of a learning/developing/evolving organisation is coming up more and more clearly in management and organisational theories and is creating

Intercultural Education in International Management 231

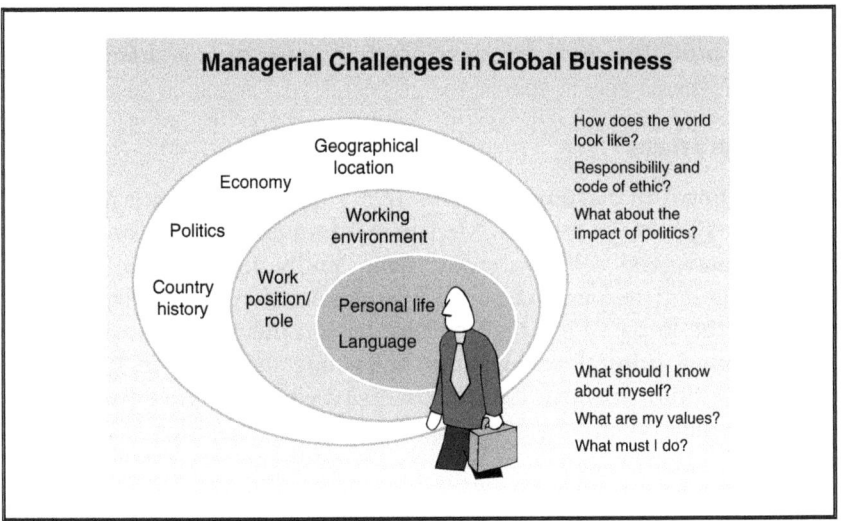

Figure 14.1 Effect of the challenging operational environment on international management

challenges as well as opportunities for management/leadership training. What are the challenges and opportunities it creates for management/ leadership training? (Figure 14.1)

The international aspect has brought a new focus for management training, developing the skills to manage the 'human resource'. The objectives are

- to develop the manager's self-awareness and understanding of his/ her own cultural background;
- to improve his/her skills to benefit from diversity;
- to manage the multicultural human resource.

In human interaction, people's talk, action or message do not live just in the speaker's own social reality, but they are and live in the relationships between people. People speak and use words to be understood. Subject matter and meanings are not only something that takes place inside one's head; it is action and interaction with other people and the environment (Kansanen, 2003). The kind of language the manager uses, what he/she says, does and thinks form the present management reality of the organisation. The manager's world view typically represents the culture where he/she was brought up and lives. In spite of individual differences, the world view of the surrounding society is more or less the same. Therefore, new knowledge, new skills and new attitudes must be developed in international management training.

Self-awareness

International management entails many qualities that are necessary in life management in general. Management training focuses on improving the managers' self-awareness, their ability to see themselves as individuals and as persons in their professional roles. Managers will recognise the impact their own culture has on their lives. Appreciation of one's own cultural background helps one to adopt an open and respectful attitude towards cultural diversity, whatever and wherever the encounter may be, in workplace discussions and meetings or customer contacts.

The international managers' self-awareness increases with exercises and reflection, which help them to analyse themselves as products of their own cultures: *Who am I? What am I like? What are the others like who come from different cultures? How will we build a community?* ICOPROMO activities, in particular those under Biography, Emotional Management and Multicultural Team Work, promote the kind of development discussed above (ICOPROMO).

Interaction

In cross-cultural situations, managers encounter values, attitudes and practices that are different from their own. Management training will enhance awareness of these differences and understanding of the reasons for these differences. At the same time, the training provides the participants with tools for coping in cross-cultural situations, acknowledging the difference without giving up one's own identity.

Because of the varying situations and practises of the working life, multiple communication skills and situational sensitivity are required of the management. These requirements are heightened by international activity with people working together in teams for various purposes (Hodgetts & Luthans, 2003). The challenges then are the different working practices held by the members of these multicultural teams. Outward procedures and actions can certainly be agreed on, but each individual's own interpretations of them are culture-bound and will always influence the practical implementation of the agreed course of action. Does a multicultural team have common working practices?

Diversity

Human diversity may sometimes seem strenuously challenging to an international manager. Different cultural backgrounds can, however, be an opportunity. Management training aims to highlight the opportunities and benefits inherent in a multicultural working environment.

However, the difficulty is to find ways to make the management see the potential benefits of diversity when practice seems to show that it only creates problems; to make the manager see diversity as an opportunity rather than a threat. And the question is always whether we can regard any manager as 'an international manager' unless he/she learns to tolerate, even foster, diversity. How can we encourage management to consider the potential benefits from diversity when diversity only seems to lead to problems? Can an international manager see diversity as an opportunity rather than a threat? Can we consider a manager international unless he/she develops his/her tolerance of diversity? (Trompenaars & Hampden-Turner, 2004).

Language and Communication Skills

As English has established its position as the modern lingua franca, we often imagine that knowing the language solves all communication problems. In some ways that is true, but, on the other hand, it also creates new challenges. Moreover, some even think that being able to speak English is not a foreign language skill at all – it's a basic requirement. International management training has a role in emphasising the importance of other language skills as well. A prerequisite for being an international manager is the ability to speak foreign languages. Understanding and speaking the employee's own language is always a sign of appreciation.

A common language is used in international companies and other contexts, a language that may not be the native language of any of the employees. In these circumstances, it can become very challenging to have in-depth discussions, for example, about strategic issues, goal-oriented annual review sessions or to solve inter-personal conflicts. Expressing one's thoughts and feelings is sometimes difficult even in one's own language, let alone a foreign one.

Emotion Management

The ability to control one's own behaviour and emotional intelligence are integral components of management/leadership skills. In international work situations, human processes are often extremely subtle. Human emotions are inevitably involved in all business operations. Emotions are equally important in advertising and selling as in financial and personnel management. The power of emotions is transferred into innovation, collaboration, assurance and persuasion. The passion to be good, be motivated to do one's best and to feel good about the work are factors that contribute to business success (Trompenaars & Hampden-Turner, 2004).

In an international environment, there may be more need for emotional intelligence than intelligence in the traditional sense. Management of emotions is challenging enough even without diverse cultural influences. Expressions of emotions are highly culture-bound. Therefore, everyday activities, such as encouraging people, voicing one's opinion, being annoyed or bored, etc., are expressed in ways that vary according to the person's cultural background. The significance of emotions in many situations in the working life is well demonstrated by the fact that many activities of the Emotional Management section are also adaptable to many other areas of development, e.g. Working in Multicultural Teams.

Teamwork

Working in multicultural projects and teams is a part of everyday management. Benefiting from the diversity among the team members and creating mutual understanding requires that the multicultural aspect be paid attention to in the team dynamics. The multicultural aspect brings new challenges into the processes of innovation, planning and decision making, of which the manager will have to become aware.

Project work, which is typical of international business and permanent team organisations in many industries, creates situations that require experts and specialists from different cultures to be in daily contact with each other (Hodgetts & Luthans, 2003). They are working in many different teams, as for instance daily self-managing teams, i.e. service teams; special project teams planning new systems; weekly department teams improving quality. It is necessary that the competency requirements of the team leaders, the marketing or product managers responsible for the efficiency of these kinds of teams include the multicultural component. International managers need fresh knowledge and skills in order to be able to benefit from the new opportunities presented by multicultural teams (Gundling, 2003).

Lifelong and Lifewide Learning

International business training focuses the managers' attitude towards an approach to management in general. Instead of being just adding on one's knowledge, management is continuous development and a willingness to learn. As a part of a working community, an international manager should have high moral standards and natural good breeding – and respect for the uniqueness of each and every human being. Internationally, there is now more and more open discussion and concern about the social responsibility, accountability and ethicality of companies and corporate management (Hodgetts & Luthans, 2003). The labour force is not just an anonymous mass of people. Workers/employees are thinking and feeling human beings and deserve to be treated with respect, regardless of cultural background. Employees are the greatest resource of corporations, and they should be well looked after. This way of thinking has not become sufficiently rooted in the economy, which is why continued efforts must be made to upgrade management thinking. The ICOPROMO subject areas Intercultural Responsibility and Ethnography are good examples of the kind of insight needed among international managers.

Practical Limitations and Solutions

Can the multicultural competencies of an international manager be developed, and if yes, how? Many people rely on literature. There is no harm in acquiring new knowledge. But is it possible to learn from books the experiential aspect so essential in education for internationalisation? Is getting own work experience the only way to develop as an international manager? The answers to both questions are yes and no. Some things need and can be learned from books and other people's experiences, but what can be learned from own experience is priceless. The developments in working tools and media have also introduced many innovative methods in which the learner's own activity and involvement are strongly integrated into the study process. Efficient utilisation of these new opportunities in management training is highly recommended.

The evaluation of all learning activities and other material, which was part of the ICOPROMO Project, emphasised the importance of activating and practical teaching methods in developing multicultural competencies. Evaluators suggested that the learning activities be built to simulate real-life work situations as closely as possible in order to allow the learners to draw on their own experience and to encourage reflection and action (Figure 14.2).

Learners are more willing to discuss and analyse issues, solve problems and situations, and to evaluate their own attitudes if the activities are based on real-life situations and phenomena. In most cases, continuing and supplementary training is targeted to people active in the working life. Experience has shown that in those circumstances there is no time or energy to study piles of course books or attend countless seminars.

The Finnish evaluation group viewed the activities produced by the ICOPROMO Project from a practical angle, on the basis of their own training experience (ICOPROMO, 2003–2006). Participants in intercultural training are often

- well-educated, usually managerial or expert level;
- from various cultural and language backgrounds;
- working in multicultural environments, various lines of business;
- working in different positions, being members of different kinds of teams;
- their work requires use of many languages: English, Swedish, Russian, Estonian, German, etc.

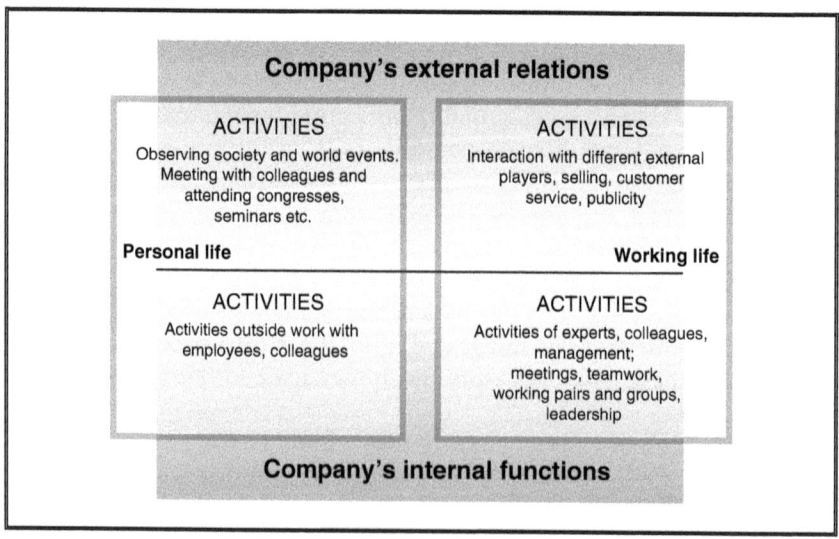

Figure 14.2 Dimensions of an international manager's interactive situations

The training process should provide tools for the course participants to develop their ability and skills to face diversity in different kinds of situations and different cultures, on the premises of their own personalities and cultural backgrounds. The ICOPROMO Project Group was multinational, and the activities reflect the authors' own backgrounds. This is an advantage in manager and expert training for multicultural competencies (ICOPROMO, 2003-2006).

Channels Available

It is quite rare that one will see a modern manager with a book in his/ her hand at airport departure halls or lounges – a laptop is more likely. Business life runs in real time, and daily communication takes place electronically on the web. The web is a channel independent of time and place, and the web is also the working environment of those being trained. The training has to take place where the course participants are situated. Web-based, virtual learning environments are available and suitable for busy business people travelling and working around the world. The new participatory economy forces companies to go increasingly virtual, both in the b-to-b and b-to-c sectors. This, in turn, increases the importance of this social medium. As an open and interactive learning medium, it lends itself perfectly for passing on both cognitive and implicit experiential knowledge (Kansanen, 2003). A virtual learning environment allows for new possibilities in most learning activities, e.g. any number of links to relevant sites can be provided, different kinds of surveys and value measurements could also be 'stored' on the web and course participants could compare their own profiles with those of others from different countries and different cultures.

Arousing Interest

In addition to the ubiquitous world – present everywhere – the challenges posed to training are related to content. How to arouse interest in issues that are part of an international manager's everyday life, but may seem trivial under all the pressures to be efficient and make profits? What makes the learning activities interesting and motivating? Obviously, the training must be structured in a very functional and practical way. The activities should be based on facts and reliable information, not fiction.

Experience has shown that some solutions work particularly well in practice and the best practices are social. Good examples are the genre-based social media, such as blogs, wikis and Facebook. An international manager's motivation to develop himself/herself comes from social activities. Many of the ICOPROMO activities are among those.

(1) The importance of giving interesting and descriptive names to the activities. The name itself contains a message and may invite the manager to try the activity. This seems to work particularly well in activities aiming for the participant's self-development and self-reflection. An example of this kind of activity is the activity called 'A new institution, a new group, a new me' (see Chapter 9). The activity 'secondary socialisation' is linked to the 'ingroup-outgroup' theory, which works extremely well in a social setting (ICOPROMO, 2003–2006).

(2) Combining different parts to make a whole may create added interest. Linking different factors and aspects of multiculturalism encourages course participants to find new perspectives to intercultural communication and interaction. Language is not a separate means of interaction, as is shown in the activity 'Language and culture and thought'. The relationship between language, culture, and thought has been a subject of discussion, even heated debate at times (ICOPROMO, 2003–2006).

(3) Relevance of the subtleties of human life. They are always interesting topics in training, and mastering them is thought to help in building trust. Anyone with practical experience knows that mere rational reasoning and facts are not sufficient in the working life – trust in people's action is necessary. Job responsibilities are made up of different kinds of processes in which each stage and task description is based on trust. In today's flat organisations and maximal efficiency, separate supervision is no longer needed. Quality outcome is based on a sense of responsibility and confidence in each individual's performance. Trust is an important basis for relationships in both mono-cultural and multicultural organisations. Only if people trust each other are they willing to share their experiences, ideas and beliefs. The concept of trust is difficult to grasp, and therefore it does not usually receive much attention in work. Human emotions are fascinating both for marketing communications professionals as well as financial specialists. The activity 'Why do I trust you' helps to demonstrate how to cope with and understand emotions in situations where complexity is added by the multicultural aspect. Different cultures base initial trust on different characteristics embodied by the trustee (ICOPROMO, 2003–2006).

(4) 'Bridging the gap'. A person becomes more receptive if the new phenomenon can be linked to something already familiar. Group dynamics is a familiar concept because it has been studied on professional and vocational courses since the 1960s. When flavoured by the multicultural ingredients, dynamics get a new, deeper meaning. In the activity 'Tensions in teams', the course participants explore their prior acquaintance with group dynamics in a different situation. Managers leading and working in a multicultural team have to cope with specific challenges not encountered in mono-cultural team settings. Understanding a team's development cycle and being able to interpret the different skills needed in order to succeed in each of these phases is vital. Additional challenges are posed by multicultural teams in the different phases (ICOPROMO, 2003–2006).

(5) Ethical questions as new objects of interest in business life. New phenomena and trends are always interesting in training contexts. The global economy has brought about new challenges that the course participants may not have even been prepared to think about earlier (ICOPROMO; Intercultural responsibility). Global movements have forced companies to take an interest in phenomena that have generated development needs for those working in international environments. Ethical issues and accountability cannot be avoided in international operations (Hodgetts & Luthans, 2003).

(6) Case study as a basis. A traditional and always effective method is to build a case study based on a real-life situation. Company-specific training is particularly interested in analysing cases based on the real problems of a real company. The ICOPROMO activity 'BMW-Rover Case Study' (see Chapter 6) offers an excellent opportunity to find parallels with one's own activity (ICOPROMO, 2003–2006).

(7) The basic elements of human behaviour, such as emotions, responsibility, trust, common goals and tolerance of differences have a great impact in multicultural contexts. In the ever-changing operational environment, international managers need to improve their personal and professional competencies in order to integrate multicultural teams and professional mobility. Functional solutions can be built to support the development process.

The ICOPROMO Project outcome is a good example. We must remember that one of the challenges to the production of management development solutions is the narrow cultural perspective. Training solutions are often too culture-bound. A new way to produce multicultural management training is through a multicultural planning team. In this respect, the ICOPROMO model is highly recommendable. There is increasing need for solutions that bring members of different cultures, different disciplines and different working contexts together in an international team.

References

Framtidens kompetenser (2006) On WWW at http://www.nordvux.net/down load/2623/ntt_rapport.pdf.
Gundling, E. (2003) *Working GlobeSmart*. Palo Alto, CA: Davis-Black Publishing.
Hodgetts, R.M. and Luthans, F. (2003) *International Management – Culture, Strategy and Behaviour*. New York: McGraw-Hill.
ICOPROMO (2003–2006) ICOPROMO: Intercultural Competence for Professional Mobility. Leonardo da Vinci Project 2003–2006. Unpublished manuscript.
Kansanen, A. (2003) *Kokous- ja neuvottelutaito*. Porvoo, Finland: WSOY.
Trompenaars, F. and Hampden-Turner, C. (2004) *Managing People*. West Sussex: Capstone.

Conclusion: Intercultural Competence for Professional Mobility

MANUELA GUILHERME, EVELYNE GLASER and
MARÍA DEL CARMEN MÉNDEZ GARCÍA

This book was intended to provide both theoretical reflections on and practical examples of various aspects involved in what we call 'Intercultural Competence for Professional Mobility'. Within this umbrella theme, competence was understood as a broad concept that encompassed the *doing* as well as the *being*, both accomplished through the dynamics of dialogue, collaboration and exchange in workgroups. The notion of mobility, as used by the authors in this book, also goes beyond physical and territorial displacement and career progression. Mobility is therefore viewed as a change that is both intrinsic and extrinsic to the individual, which may nonetheless result from, and in, physical movement and career change or re-assignment. With this book, we attempted to target both trainers and trainees in the field, as well as in-service professionals and undergraduate and graduate students with a clear interest in the matter and who want to work in fields where intercultural competencies are required. Scholarly speaking, we were determined to break ground in scientific fields that have developed separately, as far as intercultural research is concerned, i.e. the field of Education, focusing more on citizenship issues and critical discourse analysis, and the field of Business training, centred on the practicalities of communication and generally restricted to the immediate interests of those involved in a negotiation. We also sought support from other disciplinary and interdisciplinary work, such as that produced in the field of teamwork and intercultural communication in Management and Communication Studies, respectively, as well as in Foreign Language Education. Taking this as our starting point, we then expanded our work into the eight core themes presented above, where we explored aspects of intercultural communication and interaction already singled out by previous work and also highlighted some new elements that we believed were worth exploring and offered the potential for further research.

In our opinion, one of the most noteworthy achievements of this book is the way it combines the work and perspectives of academics in the field, who themselves have different viewpoints and come from different departments and national contexts, with the standpoints and experience of professionals, either in private international companies or in the national public sector, who need and have managed to develop intercultural competence in the course of their everyday routines. We also attempted to maintain a balance and directly tie in the theoretical input with practical illustrations in each topic, so that our readers and users can relate their own experience and knowledge to the contents of each topic, can more clearly implement our suggestions and be better informed so as to take our proposals a step further.

This book is inspired by ethnic, cultural and linguistic difference and its aim is to identify efficient and productive ways to manage this difference in the context of multicultural teamwork. The book offers a kaleidoscopic approach to the gamut of experiences, patterns, rationales, interdisciplinary concepts and notions that permeate every chapter, underpinning both the theorisation of each aspect highlighted and the construction of practical activities for the intercultural training of active and prospective workers in multicultural and global settings and organisations. Our work intends to act both as a source of enrichment and as a challenge for the multicultural and intercultural team worker. Communication among people from different social, ethnic or linguistic backgrounds has become a common feature in modern societies and, as a result, diversity has become all the more evident in human communication. Therefore, the success of intercultural interactions greatly depends on the understanding of the processes that uphold each specific act of communication. The inherent difficulty of teamwork is contemplated in an intercultural setting where further diversity can both hold the key to creativity and success or can hamper progress and lead to failure. Diversity, which becomes apparent in communication styles or learning styles and goals, may give rise to conflict. The examples of activities provided in each of the chapters aim to illustrate the all-important subtleties of the motives that make up the invisible web that structures intercultural communication. Intercultural competence seems to be closely related to the development of competencies that allow the individual to foresee and see through this invisible web.

In sum, the need for cultural reflection and the building of intercultural competence are increasingly pervasive in our daily professional and private lives, as we are more and more likely to interact and cooperate with people from very different cultural backgrounds. This being said, no one can fruitfully be exempted from dealing with issues related to cultural diversity. In professional life, the workplace is no longer confined to one location. Employees and managers need to display a great deal of mental and physical flexibility to meet the requirements of the career challenges of today. This is especially true for teamwork in all its forms, which is co-located, virtual or semi-virtual and has become prevalent in modern day organisations. Team members typically come from different cultures, speak different languages, have undergone different forms of socialisation and therefore subscribe to different values, norms and beliefs. Establishing common ground with others and developing the necessary empathy and degree of intercultural awareness, while constantly challenging one's own perspectives, has therefore become almost a daily obligation for all those involved in the work process. Modern societies face issues of migration and integration, but have often failed to find ways of dealing with these challenges responsibly.

Therefore, it has become a necessity for all those involved in the world of work to display sensitivity and competence across cultural contexts. To achieve this, individuals must be supported in their intercultural learning process. This means that, for instance, in the field of education, curricula need to be adapted accordingly, and in the workplace, facilities need to be created to enhance this learning process, as it does not happen accidentally. If left to themselves, without any guidance, individuals are in fact prone to increase culture-related prejudices and stereotypes in their contacts with other cultures rather than alleviating or eliminating them. In order to create meaning out of cultural differences, intervention through training and support is needed for individuals who enter into contact with 'otherness'.

Language clearly plays an important role in the process of developing intercultural competence. Through the study of a foreign language, it becomes easier to enter the cognitive concepts of another culture. However, language learning alone is not sufficient to grasp the complexity of another culture and to finally achieve intercultural competence. It must be complemented and supported by training situations that allow an individual to gradually develop a different worldview and to embrace diversity. In addition, it must be pointed out that becoming interculturally competent is a process of changing one's mindset, which requires an initial readiness on the part of the individual. It is also misleading to believe that it is an abstract state that can be achieved incrementally. Instead, we must recognise that – unlike reaching the top of a mountain – it is a goal that can probably never be fully achieved. It is a process of continuous transformation that, ideally, never ends.

Through the funding of projects such as the ICOPROMO, which is the basis of this book, or the INCA Project also mentioned in one of the chapters, the European Commission's Leonardo da Vinci Programme has supported our efforts to foster intercultural competence in higher education and the professional world. The practical instruments designed in the course of these projects are suggestions of tools that hope to enhance the proactive development of a more intercultural mindset. What the instruments produced under the auspices of the ICOPROMO Project have in common is that they underline the authors' belief that intercultural competence cannot be achieved through, on the one hand, cognitive processes alone or, on the other hand, simply through the mechanisation of skills. We believe that, to change individual attitudes, it is necessary to work on various aspects and dimensions, such as those we focused on in our eight axes. We must plumb the depths of our own perceptions, values and beliefs, in order to become critical of ourselves and our own culture, as well as critically aware of the workings of the intercultural exchange and, finally, creative enough to develop new solutions and original hypotheses.

Through our collaboration on this project, we have managed to pinpoint eight axes. We recommend these as the main themes for professional development and scientific research on intercultural cooperation. Although they may overlap, we also believe that they constitute possible units of a 'third space', which may provide us with fertile ground for examination and practice. Some of them provide a more general look at intercultural group work, such as Working in Multicultural Teams, Diversity Management and Intercultural Interaction. However, most of them focus on specific aspects of the same process, for example Biography, Communicative Interaction, Ethnography, Emotional Management and Intercultural Responsibility. Our approach to these topics nevertheless reveals a coherent and consistent convergence on power issues, the dynamics of intercultural group work, cultural wealth and exchange, experiential learning, personal feelings and group cohesion, and evident and imperceptible responses. Although each chapter attempts to shed light on one particular issue or aspect of the dynamics of intercultural working and considers the requirements of the field identified, they all share a common understanding of the notion of intercultural competence in general as a comprehensive notion that encompasses both a number of capabilities to deal with and make the most of ethnic, cultural and linguistic diversity, and the development of individual and collective identities in the process of intercultural dynamics. With this book, we aim to offer some reflections on previous intercultural experiences and situations as well as to provide some plausible intercultural conditions for the purpose of professional development and character building. It also promotes the examination of emotional unfolding without hindering ethical scrutiny or the analysis of communication strategies. It suggests applying principles of ethnographic observation to intercultural working while looking into the functioning of power negotiations in multicultural group or team work. Each axis focuses on one particular element of the intercultural dynamics of multicultural working without losing sight of the various overlapping aspects.

With this book, we have therefore aimed to provide readers with a variety of approaches to the issues that may arise in a multicultural workforce. None of the contributions can claim to be all-encompassing or exhaustive. Each contribution cannot but act as a catalyst for reflection. It is up to the readers to pick and choose their individual strategy to cope with these issues in their own environment. If any of the ideas and approaches presented in this book prove to be viable ways for coping with interculturality in the workplace, and inspire further experiments and challenges to do so, the authors will consider they have, for the time being, fulfilled their purpose.

For Product Safety Concerns and Information please contact our EU Authorised Representative:

Easy Access System Europe

Mustamäe tee 50

10621 Tallinn

Estonia

gpsr.requests@easproject.com

www.ingramcontent.com/pod-product-compliance
Ingram Content Group UK Ltd.
Pitfield, Milton Keynes, MK11 3LW, UK
UKHW022217250326
4937IPUK00005B/35